UNDERSTANDING JEWISH THEOLOGY
Classical Issues and Modern Perspectives

UNDERSTANDING JEWISH THEOLOGY
Classical Issues and Modern Perspectives

Edited by
Jacob Neusner

Classics in Judaic Studies
Global Publications, Binghamton University
2001

Cover artwork entitled "Panorama" by Suzanne R. Neusner.

Library of Congress-in-Publication Data:

Jacob Neusner, *Understanding Jewish Theology: Classical Issues and Modern Perspectives*

1. Judaism   2. Jewish Theology

ISBN 1-586840-90-8

Published and Distributed by:
Classics in Judaic Studies
Global Publications, Binghamton University
State University of New York at Binghamton
Binghamton, New York, USA 13902-6000
Phone: (607) 777-4495 or 777-6104; Fax: (607) 777-6132
Email: pmorewed@binghamton.edu
http://ssips.binghamton.edu

CLASSICS IN JUDAIC STUDIES

Publisher: Global Publications, State University of New York at Binghamton
Address: LNG 99, SUNY-Binghamton, Binghamton, New York 13902-6000

Editor-in-Chief
Jacob Neusner, *Bard College*

Editorial Committee
Alan J. Avery-Peck, *College of the Holy Cross*
Bruce D. Chilton, *Bard College*
William Scott Green, *University of Rochester*
James F. Strange, *University of South Florida*

Table of Contents

Acknowledgements

The editor is indebted to the following for permission to reprint excerpts from copyrighted material:

Farrar Straus and Giroux for Abraham Joshua Heschel, *Man is Not Alone,* © 1951 by Abraham Joshua Heschel, and *God in Search of Man,* © 1955 by Abraham Joshua Heschel.

Jakob J. Petuchowski, American Jewish Congress, Basic Books Inc., Publishers, N.Y., for Jakob J. Petuchowski, "Not by Bread Alone," from *Heirs of the Pharisees,* by Jakob J. Petcuhowksi, © 1970 by Basic Books, Inc., Publishers, N.Y. (First published in *Judaism* VII, 3, summer, 1958, pp. 229-234, © 1958 by American Jewish Congress).

American Jewish Congress, Schocken Books, Inc., and Gersham G. Scholem, for Gershom G. Scholem, "Tradition and Commentary as Religious Categories in Judaism," *Judaism* XV, 1, winter, 1996, pp. 23-39, and Gershom G. Scholem, *The Messianic Idea in Judaism,* © 1971 by Schocken Books Inc., pp. 282-304.

Abraham Joshua Heschel for Abraham Joshua Heschel, *The Earth Is the Lord's,* pp. 39-55, © 1950 by Henry Schumann, Inc.

Behrman House, Inc. for Solomon Schecter, *Some Aspects of Rabbinic Theology,* © 1936 by Behrman House Inc.

Arthur Hertzburg and American Jewish Congress for Arthur Hertzberg, "Judaism and the Land of Israel," *Judaism* XIX, 4, fall, 1970, © 1970 by American Jewish Congress.

Abraham Joshua Heschel and Charles Scribner's Sons for "The Meaning of Observance," from *Man's Quest for God,* by Abraham Joshua Heschel, © 1954 by Abraham Joshua Heschel. Reprinted by permission of Charles Scribner's Sons.

David S. Shapiro, Rabbinical Council of America, and Walter S. Wurzburger, editor, *Tradition,* for David S. Shapiro, "The Ideological Foundations of the Halakhah," *Tradition* IX, Nos. 1-2, 1967, pp. 100-122, © 1967 by Rabbinical Council of America.

Jewish Publication Society of America for Moses Hayyim Luzzatto, Mesillat Yesharim, © 1966 by Jewish Publication Society of America.

Isadore Twersky and American Jewish Congress for Isadore Twersky, "The Shulhan Aruk: Enduring Code of Jewish Law," *Judaism* XVI, 2, 1967, pp. 141-158, © 1967 by American Jewish Congress.

For
Margalit Leah Berakhah

INTRODUCTION TO THE 2001 EDITION

This anthology sets forth the principal category-formations of the theology of Judaism and how those category-formations — God, Torah, Israel — have developed in modern times. The essays collected here have stood the test of time. After more than a quarter of a century, a new generation continues to find enlightenment in these authoritative statements. None is dated, all remain reliable accounts of their respective subjects.

The one question left open requires consideration here. It is, how the category-formations of Judaism in its formative, and authoritative writings — the Rabbinic documents of the Oral Torah of the first six centuries of the Common Era — form a working system, not merely a static structure. And that requires us to look at the classical, normative formulation of matters in the authoritative documents that define the theology and law of Judaism. Here then is an account of the mythic monotheism of the Written Torah, as mediated by the Oral Torah. These are the writings that altogether define the normative system of Judaism. They show us the dynamics of a set of ideas that account for all that happens, and can happen, in the world under the aspect of the Torah.

I

Judaism — everyone concurs — sets forth the theology of ethical monotheism. What does that mean?

A religion of numerous gods finds many solutions to one problem, a religion of only one God presents one to many. Life is seldom fair. Rules rarely work. To explain the reason why, polytheisms adduce multiple causes of chaos, a god per anomaly. Diverse gods do various things, so, it stands to reason, ordinarily outcomes conflict. Monotheism by nature explains many things in a single way. One God rules. Life is meant to be fair, and just rules are supposed to describe what is ordinary, all in the name of that one and only God. So in monotheism a simple logic governs to limit ways of making sense of things. But that logic contains its own dialectics. If one true God has done everything, then, since he is God all-powerful and omniscient, all things are credited to, and blamed on, him. In that case he can be either good or bad, just or unjust — but not both.

Responding to the generative dialectics of monotheism, the Oral Torah — the Oral [part of] the Torah revealed by God to Moses at Sinai, to adhere to the language of the documents examined here — systematically reveals the justice of the one and only God of all creation. God is not only God but also good. Appealing to the facts of Scripture, the Written part of the Torah, in the documents of the Oral part of the Torah, the sages ("our sages of blessed memory") in the first six centuries of the Common Era constructed a coherent theology, a cogent structure and logical system, to expose the justice of God. Here in detail I show how and with what result. I identify the *logos* of God — the theology seen whole in the Torah, Written and Oral, as set forth by sages in its originally-oral, memorized component.

The theology of the Oral Torah conveys the picture of world order based on God's justice and equity. The categorical structure of the Oral Torah encompasses the components, God and man; the Torah; Israel and the nations. The working-system of the Oral Torah finds its dynamic in the struggle between God's plan for creation —to create a perfect world of justice — and man's will. That dialectics embodies in a single paradigm the events contained in the sequences, rebellion, sin, punishment, repentance, and atonement; exile and return; or the disruption of world order and the restoration of world order. None of these categories and propositions is new; anyone familiar with the principal components of the faith and piety of Judaism, the Written Torah, the Oral Torah, and the liturgy of home and synagogue, will find them paramount. It is not in identifying but in forming them into a logos — a sustained, rigorous, coherent argument, that can be set forth in narrative-sequential form — that I make my contribution, hence the title of this book.

II

Let me set forth a somewhat more elaborate synopsis of the same story in these few, still-simple propositions, by which I mean to define the four principles of the theology of the Oral Torah:

1. God formed creation in accord with a plan, which the Torah reveals. World order can be shown by the facts of nature and society set forth in that plan to conform to a pattern of reason based upon justice. Those who possess the Torah — Israel — know God and those who do not — the gentiles — reject him in favor of idols. What happens to each of the two sectors of humanity, respectively, responds to their relationship with God. Israel in the present age is subordinate to the nations, because God has designated the gentiles as the medium for penalizing Israel's rebellion, meaning through Israel's subordination and exile to provoke Israel to repent. Private life as much as the public order conforms to the principle that God rules justly in a creation of perfection and stasis.

2. The perfection of creation, realized in the rule of exact justice, is signified by the timelessness of the world of human affairs, their conformity to a few enduring paradigms that transcend change (theology of history). No present, past, or future marks time, but only the recapitulation of those patterns. Perfection is further embodied in the unchanging relationships of the social commonwealth (theology of political economy), which assure that scarce resources, once allocated, remain in stasis. A further indication of perfection lies in the complementarity of the components of creation, on the one side, and, finally, the correspondence between God and man, in God's image (theological anthropology), on the other.

3. Israel's condition, public and personal, marks flaws in creation. What disrupts perfection is the sole power capable of standing on its own against God's power, and that is man's will. What man controls and God cannot coerce is

man's capacity to form intention and therefore choose either arrogantly to defy, or humbly to love, God. Because man defies God, the sin that results from man's rebellion flaws creation and disrupts world order (theological theodicy). The paradigm of the rebellion of Adam in Eden governs, the act of arrogant rebellion leading to exile from Eden thus accounting for the condition of humanity. But, as in the original transaction of alienation and consequent exile, God retains the power to encourage repentance through punishing man's arrogance. In mercy, moreover, God exercises the power to respond to repentance with forgiveness, that is, a change of attitude evoking a counterpart change. Since, commanding his own will, man also has the power to initiate the process of reconciliation with God, through repentance, an act of humility, man may restore the perfection of that order that through arrogance he has marred.

    4. God ultimately will restore that perfection that embodied his plan for creation. In the work of restoration death that comes about by reason of sin will die, the dead will be raised and judged for their deeds in this life, and most of them, having been justified, will go on to eternal life in the world to come. In the paradigm of man restored to Eden is realized in Israel's return to the Land of Israel. In that world or age to come, however, that sector of humanity that through the Torah knows God will encompass all of humanity. Idolaters will perish, and humanity that comprises Israel at the end will know the one, true God and spend eternity in his light.

Now, recorded in this way, the story told by the Oral Torah proves remarkably familiar, with its stress on God's justice (to which his mercy is integral), man's correspondence with God in his possession of the power of will, man's sin and God's response.

    If we translate into the narrative of Israel, from the beginning to the calamity of the destruction of the (first) Temple, what is set forth in both abstract and concrete ways in the Oral Torah, we turn out to state a reprise of the Authorized History laid out in Genesis through Kings and amplified by the principal prophets. Furthermore, the liturgy of synagogue and home recapitulates characteristic modes of thought of the Oral Torah and reworks its distinctive constructions of exemplary figures, events, and conceptions. In defining the religion that the world calls "Judaism" and that calls itself "the Torah," sages have maintained from the very beginning in saying they possessed the Torah revealed by God to Moses at Mount Sinai ("Moses received Torah at Sinai and handed it on to Joshua, Joshua to elders, and elders to prophets, and prophets handed it on to the men of the great assembly"). By situating the theology of the Oral Torah as the pivot between the Written Torah and the liturgy and piety of the faith, the sages register that claim.

III

How have the sages set forth their conception of an integrated theological system and structure? It is by reading Scripture as a philosopher reads nature: as source of facts to be generalized into abstract, governing principles of a harmonious and proportionate character.

Imagine Eden as a philosopher would: a world of pure reason, where all things serve their assigned purpose and stand in proper rank. Form a mental image of a world where all things cohere to a single inner logic and so are to be explained in an orderly way. Contemplate a social order in which whatever happens is for good and sufficient cause. Conceive of a kingdom so governed by a moral calculus, that an ethical physics describes actuality: each action produces an equal and opposite reaction, a perfect match, a mirror of the deed in the responsive deed. And try to picture a world of peace, in which nothing happens to change the perfect, the acutely just balance of matters.

Contemplate in mind that here, in this perfect world of universal mind and self-evident rationality, is a steady-state world: do this and that will happen, do not do this and that will not happen — measure for measure in all matters. The rational intellect encompasses all, which is why everything is subject to such an exact, reasonable accounting of force and reaction thereto. Among the principles of intellect that inhere in this Eden the most important, the innate sense of justice, ultimately prevails. Fairness and equity rule, and that explains why with thought everything certainly makes sense. Then the task of intellect will be to uncover and reveal how all things are to be justified, meaning, shown to be just to begin with.

Consider how, in this social cosmos conceived by men of reason who take up the task of justification, principles of order describe the final outcome of all transactions, all relationships. Well-ordered nature finds its match in well-construed society of humanity. And at the third dimension of existence, the anthropological, in addition to the natural and the historical, the very traits of man himself correspond to those of nature. The same rule that governs the tree governs me, the orderly mind maintains.

Change then defies imagining. In place comes the realization, in full maturity, of what one already is. The *telos,* the ultimate end and goal, of all things, present at the outset, explains and governs what happens, but nothing happens to violate that rational rule. The acorn grown up has not changed but has only realized its end. Teleology then takes the place of history as a mode of organizing existence. In such a world the future is present even now, the oak in the acorn. Inertia and stasis characterize the teleological universe, in accord with the rules that dictate cause and effect. Proportion and balance, complementarity and commensurability — these traits of the well-ordered world everywhere characterize the men and nations, their relationships, and the destiny meted out to each and to all by the purposeful intellect that has made things just so, that philosophers name in diverse ways but most commonly, God.

That is why, in this imaginary world that philosophers alone can conceive (with God in their image, after their likeness), in such a purposeful realm rationality yields compelling explanations for all things, a single integral rationality or *logos* commands. Before the cosmic intellect that has conceived all things in a single reasonable, purposeful way there are no mysteries, neither about the past and what lies hidden, nor about the present and what comes into view, nor even about what lies over the distant horizon of the future. Since rules govern, reason suffices to explain the past, understand the present, and dictate what is going to come about in the future.

Not only public history but private life conforms to the same reasonable laws: do this and that will happen. The well-examined life of persons and their destiny recapitulate those rules of reason, so that, purposeful and properly ranked, private lives embody — and even match item for item — the principles of public order. All things come under the one orderly law of reason, for every thing its place, for every person a calling, for every event a purpose. And that is why those who master the givens of reality and reflect reasonably about them make sense of all being, all doing.

Then in mind — to continue for just a bit longer this exercise in imagining a society situated in utopian eternity — address the question of history, the disruptions of events, and readers will understand how reason masters, how logic controls even the chaos of man's remarkable doings, the ones that destroy perfection. In line with the inner logic of the whole, time and change do not — or at least ought not — mar this Eden, where perfection consists in stability in proper balance and proportion. And when change (not just fulfillment of innate *telos*) marks time, change is a problem that requires explanation. And time is subject to the requirement of accountability: how come? If rationality consists in the meting out of measure for measure, so that good is responded to with good, and evil with evil, then that of which history consists — what is remarkable by reason of its sheer illogic — finds no place but must be explained (away). For in this domain of contemplation of what is, or can be made, perfect, men know the rules and how they work and are applied. Consequently, through knowing the regularities of eternity that supersede the random moments of time, the past yields its secrets of how things really work. The present rehearses the rules in the here and the now. The future promises only more of that same regularity and certainty. The categories, past, present, and future lose all currency.

So events take place, but history does not happen. Events now stand not for that which disrupts, but that which embodies rules or that actualizes potentials, much as the well-conceived experiment in the laboratory allows the testing of hypotheses. And the same rules govern nations and families, social entities measured in multiples or even the individual in his or her person and life. Public affairs and private ones match in conforming to the governance of order, purpose, reason. These virtues of the well-constructed intellect not only account for history and the course of nations in the unfolding of time but also prevail in the streets and marketplaces and households. There fairness and a balanced exchange in the marketplace of small affairs match in structure and proportion the workings of applied reason and practical logic in the relations of men and nations. In this philosophers' Eden, all things bear reasoned explanation, and there are no mysteries. Here then we discern the remarkable, hopeful vision, the fantasy-world of intellectuals who conceive that ideas make all the difference and minds command and reason governs.

Now, if readers can imagine such a world perfected by the tastes and aspirations of the rational mind, then readers can enter into the world portrayed by the documents of the Oral Torah. These are the writings of "our sages of blessed memory" who set forth the authoritative statement of Rabbinic Judaism in its formative age, the first six centuries of the Common Era. The writings, read all together and all at once as a single coherent statement, portray the reason why things are now as they are. And they show the logic of that reason, revealing its integrity in the working of justice throughout. As sages portray the Written part of the Torah and set forth the Oral part, the Torah lays heavy emphasis upon the perfection of the timeless, flawless creation that God forms and governs in accord with wholly rational and accessible rules. If everything fits together and works coherently, it is because, as philosophers maintain in their realm of reflection, a single, unitary logic ("logos"), the logic of monotheism comprised by the one just, therefore reasonable and benevolent, God, prevails.

IV

But for sages there was this difference: while philosophers uncovered the order of nature, employing mathematics abstractly to describe, and natural history comprehensively to organize, and reason to analyze, the facts of the world, it was into the facts of Scripture that sages pursued their comparable analysis. For all that I have asked as a supererogatory act of imagination — a world of pure reason, everything in place and in rank, all things serving an assigned purpose — encompasses the cosmic conception of sages as much as philosophers. To show exactly what it means to treat Scripture as a source of irreducible and irrefutable facts, a single example suffices. Various figures in the written Torah commence the classification of virtue or vice that they embody:

> Esther Rabbah VIII:i.1:
> 1. A. R. Berekhiah commenced by citing the verse, "'Who has wrought and done it? He who called the generations from the beginning' (Is. 41:4):

Here is sages' counterpart to a theory of teleology:

> B. "From the beginning of the creation of the world, the Holy One blessed be he designated for every one what was suitable.
> C. "Adam was first of all creatures,
> D. "Cain was first of murderers,
> E. "Abel was first of all victims,
> F. "Noah the first of all those who would be saved from disaster,

Now, as always, we turn from humanity to the part of humanity identified with the Torah:

> G. "Abraham was the first of all the circumcised,

H. "Isaac the first of all those who were bound for sacrifice,

I. "Jacob the first of all those who were without blemish,

J. "Judah the first of the tribes,

K. "Joseph the first of the pious,

L. "Aaron the first of the priests,

M. "Moses the first of the prophets,

N. "Joshua the first of the conquerors,

O. "Othniel the first of those who divide the spoils,

P. "Samuel the first of those who anoint,

Q. "Saul the first of those who are anointed,

R. "David the first of the singers,

S. "Solomon the first of the builders,

From Israel, we proceed to the gentiles, as is commonly the case in antonymic discourse, once this comes to mind, then the opposite, enters:

T. "Nebuchadnezzar the first of the destroyers,

U. "Ahasuerus the first of those who sell [people at a price],

V. "Haman the first of those who buy [people at a price]."

To formulate a theory of the purpose or goal, sages frame matters in the language of origination, that is, they name the acorn out of which the oak will grow. The question of origins — and even exact definition — of various virtues and vices is answered by appeal to the starting point, Scripture, the sole source of pertinent facts; the sequence of the advent of its exemplary figures then accounts for where and when the various categories originate. But I see no scriptural sequence, rather, sages' characteristic: humanity in general, Israel in particular, and then the antonym for Israel, the gentiles, Israel's enemies. Scripture then provides data for sages, as much as nature and history do for philosophers. The entire classification-system of virtue or vice then emerges in the narrative of Scripture, when the data of the narrative are properly systematized.

What we see is a single, seamless story — and not a very complicated one at that. In these accounts so far as is possible in their own words I tell the story of how sages portrayed the story of the world from start to finish: the rules that account for reality. And that story will strike the reader as remarkably familiar, its cogency sustained by its very commonplace quality: here is the story that we in the West who practice both Judaism and Christianity have been telling ourselves for so long as we have possessed Scripture. And, further, those who practice Judaism will find themselves entirely at home, because in the prayers recited three times a day, they encounter the same tale that the sages of the Oral Torah tell. That is because sages read Scripture — the facts it supplied or oral tradition contributed — as philosophers read nature. They thought philosophically about Scripture. The logic that they uncovered imparted that rationality and coherence to the theological convictions they set forth, to the system they devised to account for the unity of being, the conformity of all reality to the few simple rules of reason that God embodied in his works of creation.

V

To make this point more concrete: as philosophers sought to generalize out of the facts of nature, so sages brought system and order to the facts of Scripture, drawing conclusions, setting forth hypotheses, amassing data to them. Analytical principles comparable to those of natural history, specifically, guided them in their reading of the facts that Scripture provided. These involved, in particular, the classification and hierarchization of data in a taxonomical process of comparison and contrast: like followed like rules, unlike, opposite rules. And the rules that classify also hierarchize, e.g., what is classified as sanctified or as unclean will then possess the traits that signify sanctification or uncleanness, and these traits will also order themselves, this time at levels of intensity, for example (a case comes in a moment). The classification of matters and their hierarchization — the quest for generalizations, governing rules or principles — therefore prior to the identification of verses of Scripture that validate said classification.

What is primary is the governing conception of a prevailing logic, a governing reason articulated endlessly out of a few simple propositions of order and coherence. Throughout, a highly articulated system of classification is at work, one that rests on a deep theoretical foundation. The basic method involves a search for abstraction out of concrete data. A variety of cases deriving from Scripture is subjected to generalization, and the whole is then set forth in the form of a generalization sustained by numerous probative cases. The generalization, moreover, is itself elaborated. Cases that validate the generalization are selected not at random but by appeal to common taxonomic traits, and then the generalization not only derives from the cases but from a very specific aspect thereof. These cases are all characterized by sudden and supernatural intervention in a crisis, such as the situation under discussion now requires. Or a set of kindred propositions is established through a sequence of cases; no effort is made to order the cases in a compelling sequence. It is adequate to state the generalization and then adduce probative cases out of Scripture.

That carries us to the move from structure to system. That is because the whole represents the systematization of Scripture's evidence on a given topic, and it is the systematization of the data that yields a generalization. Let me give a single example, in the framework of *Halakhic* discourse, that is, the formulation of norms of behavior, of how facts of Scripture (and in some details, what is set forth as oral tradition of Sinai) are dealt with, the way in which sages conduct their inquiry. In the present case sages wish to prove that hierarchization governs the social order, with the several castes related to one another in descending order:

> Mishnah-tractate Horayot 3:5, and Tosefta-tractate Horayot 2:8:
>
> A. A priest takes precedence over a Levite, a Levite over an Israelite, an Israelite over a mamzer [a person whose parents may not legally ever marry, e.g., brother and sister], a mamzer

over a Netin [a descendant of the cast of Temple servants], a
Netin over a proselyte, a proselyte over a freed slave.
B. Under what circumstances?
C. When all of them are equivalent.

The initial hierarchization having been established out of self-evident
facts, the variable is introduced involving the Torah, so making the
point that the Torah violates natural hierarchies in favor of God's
choice:

> D. But if the mamzer was a disciple of a sage and a high priest
> was an am haares [in context: ignorant of the Torah], the
> mamzer who is a disciple of a sage takes precedence over a
> high priest who is an am haares [M. Hor. 3:8].

We now turn to the complementary compilation of laws, the Tosefta,
which contains citations and glosses of the Mishnah's rules as well as
free-standing statements:

> E. A sage takes precedence over a king; a king takes
> precedence over a high priest; a high priest takes precedence
> over a prophet; a prophet takes precedence over a priest
> anointed for war; a priest anointed for war takes precedence
> over the head of a priestly watch; the head of a priestly watch
> takes precedence over the head of a household [of priests];
> the head of a household of priests takes precedence over the
> superintendent of the cashiers; the superintendent of the
> cashiers takes precedence over the Temple treasurer; the
> Temple treasurer takes precedence over an ordinary priest; an
> ordinary [T. Hor. 2:10F-H].
> F. A priest takes precedence over a Levite; a Levite takes
> precedence over an Israelite; an Israelite takes precedence
> over a mamzer; a mamzer takes precedence over a Netin; a
> Netin takes precedence over a proselyte; a proselyte takes
> precedence over a freed slave. Under what circumstances?
> When all of them are equivalent. But if the mamzer was a
> disciple of a sage, and a high priest was an ignoramus, the

mamzer who is the disciple of a sage takes precedence over a
high priest who is an ignoramus.

Matters having been set forth, the Tosefta makes its comment, and it
is a harsh one:

> G. A sage takes precedence over a king.
> H. [For] if a sage dies, we have none who is like him.
> I. [If] a king dies, any Israelite is suitable to mount the throne
> [T. 2:8].

From sages, the Tosefta's formulation turns to the hierarchy of holy
classes in Israel: priests, prophets, messianic priests (anointed
ones):

> J. [A high priest anointed with oil takes precedence over one
> dedicated through many garments.]
> K. A prophet takes precedence over the high priest anointed
> for battle,
> L. and the high priest anointed for battle takes precedence
> over the prefect,
> M. and the prefect takes precedence over the head of the
> weekly course [of the priests, who take care of the cult in a
> given week],
> N. and the head of the priestly course takes precedence over
> the superintendent of the cashiers,
> O. and the superintendent of the cashiers takes precedence
> over the treasurer.
> P. And the treasurer takes precedence over an ordinary priest.
> Q. And an ordinary priest takes precedence over a Levite [T.
> Hor. 2:10A-I].

In a well-ordered system, the same principles that govern classes of
persons must pertain to classes of objects, that is, the comparison
and contrast of the indicative traits. The principle of hierarchization
applies to matters of sanctification of objects in place of persons, now

a synagogue, an ark, wrappings for a scroll of the Torah, and so on upward or downward, as the passage may require:

> Mishnah-tractate Megillah 3:1:
> A. Townsfolk who sold (1) a street of a town buy with its proceeds a synagogue.
> B. [If they sold] (2) a synagogue, they buy an ark.
> C. [If they sold] (3) an ark, they buy wrappings.
> D. [If they sold] (4) wrappings, they buy scrolls [of the prophets or writings].
> E. [If they sold] (5) scrolls, they buy a Torah scroll.

What goes up must come down, and a trait of legal formulation proves blatant, which is, the acutely formal ordering of thought into word-patterns; this is a way in which how things are said conveys the same message as what is said:

> F. But if they sold (5) a Torah scroll, they should not buy scrolls.
> G. [If they sold] (4) scrolls, they should not buy wrappings.
> H. [If they sold] (3) wrappings, they should not buy an ark.
> I. [If they sold] (2) an ark, they should not buy a synagogue.
> J. [If they sold] (1) a synagogue, they should not buy a street.
> K. And so with the surplus [of the proceeds of any of] these.

By listing in sequence the lesser to the greater, then the greater, to the lesser, levels of sanctification — the categories being givens (synagogue, art, scrolls) — beyond the specific rule that is set forth, the principle is established that matters of sanctification are subject to the rules of hierarchization. Sages rarely find it necessary to spell out the generalization that their array of particulars yields. It is self-evident, and even my supplying ordinals is superfluous.

From what is concrete we turn to abstraction, here involving matters of status. The case is important to show how a single mode of thought, a cogent approach to organizing the data of the everyday world as much as of the Heavens, pertains throughout. Not only so, but, so far as possible, the work of bringing order out of the chaos of facts requires an effort to cover sets of data. These sets, e.g., of opposites, may be shown to match or to contrast. The more sets of data one can assemble in a single system, the more one achieves in showing the inner logic and integrity of all creation in all its category-formations. Here we have a protracted example of how sages match opposites, organizing data in two distinct groups, each group governed by its own indicative traits, and then showing how the two groups form a single coherent complement or match. When, later on, we consider the theological exercises of complementarity and correspondence, which define the modes of thought of the Oral Torah when the work of explaining man and defining God comes to hand, we find in play exactly the same large principles. That accounts for the exemplary quality of the rather odd composition of law that we now consider.

Here hierarchization organizes the data of both sanctification and uncleanness in a single structure, even though there is no necessary correspondence of the details of the one to those of the other. The points of differentiation, both as to sanctification and as to uncleanness, however, are the same, arrayed in sets of opposites, a most successful exercise in comparison and contrast to show complementarity and correspondence:

Mishnah-tractate Kelim 1:5, 6-8
1:5 A. Ten levels of uncleanness pertain to man:
B. (1) He whose atonement [sacrifice] is incomplete [solely in respect to the purificatory sacrifice] is prohibited in regard to Holy Thing(s) but permitted in regard to heave offering and in regard to tithe.
C. (2) He [who] [became unclean so as] to be a tebul-yom [who awaits sunset to complete his purification] is prohibited

in regard to Holy Thing(s) and in regard to heave offering but permitted in regard to tithe.

D. (3) He [who] [became unclean so as] to be one who had suffered a pollution is prohibited in regard to all three.

Sages derive all of the governing facts from Scripture, as commentaries to the passage show. The first triplet matches the character of uncleanness that disqualifies a man from eating food in a given level of sanctification with the level of sanctification imputed to foods that have been subject to a given set of rules. Now we proceed to more severe levels of uncleanness and the effect of that uncleanness upon objects, not foods. Here the governing laws are located in Leviticus Chapter 15:

E. (4) He [who] [became unclean so as] to be one who has intercourse with a menstruating woman conveys uncleanness to what lies [far] beneath him [in like degree as he conveys uncleanness to a spread that lies] above [it and directly underneath him].

F. (5) [If] he [became unclean so as] to be a Zab who has suffered two appearances [of flux], he renders the couch and the chair [on which he sits or lies] unclean and needs bathing in running water but is free of the offering.

G. (6) He [who] saw three [appearances of flux] is liable for the offering,

We proceed, at a still more virulent level of cultic contamination, to the uncleanness described in Leviticus Chapters 13 and 14:

H. (7) He [who] [became unclean so as] to be a leper that is shut up [for examination to see whether signs of uncleanness will appear] conveys uncleanness through coming [into a house] but is exempt from loosening [the hair], and tearing [the clothes], and from shaving, and from the bird [offering].

I. (8) And if he was certified [as a leper], he is liable for all of them.

Now comes the most virulent source of uncleanness of all, the corpse:

> J. (9) [If] a limb on which there is not an appropriate amount of flesh separated from him, it renders unclean through contact and through carrying but does not render unclean in the tent.
> K. (10) And if there is on it [the limb) an appropriate amount of flesh, it renders unclean through contact and through carrying and through the tent.
> L. The measure of flesh that is appropriate is sufficient to bring about healing.

The point subject to dispute is a minor detail; the formulation in anonymous terms signals that the law that is set forth is normative:

> M. R. Judah says, "If there is in one place enough [flesh] to surround the member with [the thickness of] the thread of the woof, there is sufficient to bring about healing."

Having descended to the lowest layers of uncleanness, we move upward from the initial to the highest levels of sanctification, which is the antonym of uncleanness so far as sages are concerned:

> 1:6 A. There are ten [degrees of] holiness(es):
> B. (1) The land of Israel is holier than all lands.
> C. And what is its holiness? For they bring from it the omer, and the first fruits, and the Two Loaves, which they do not bring (thus) from all lands.

What sanctifies the Land, in this construction, is what originates from the Land for use on the Temple altar. Next comes a level of sanctification indicated not by what is done but by who or what is excluded:

> 1:7 A. (2) The cities surrounded by a wall are more holy than it [the land].

B. For they send from them the lepers, and they carry around in their midst a corpse so long as they like. [But once] it has gone forth, they do not bring it back.

Our next level of sanctification is marked by what may be done within the designated area:

1:8 A. (3) Within the wall [of Jerusalem] is more holy than they
B. For they eat there lesser sanctities and second tithe.

Here we see the diversity of signifiers, since what marks the next area as more holy is, once more, who may not be permitted to enter the area, and that criterion governs to the end:

C. (4) The Temple mount is more holy than it.
D. For Zabim, and Zabot, menstruating women, and those that have given birth do not enter there.
E. (5) The rampart is more holy than it.
F For gentiles and he who is made unclean by a corpse do not enter there.
G. (6) The court of women is more holy than it.
H. For a tebul-yom does not enter there, but they are not liable on its account for a sin offering.
I. (7) The court of Israel is more holy than it.
J. For one who [yet] lacks atonement [offerings made in the completion of his purification rite] does not enter there, and they are liable on its account for a sin-offering.
K. (8) The court of the priests is more holy than it.
L. For Israelite(s) do not enter there except in the time of their [cultic] requirements: for laying on of hands, for slaughtering, and for waving.
1:9 A. (9) [The area] between the porch and the altar is more holy than it.
B. For those [priests] who are blemished or whose hair is unloosed do not enter there.
C. (10) The sanctuary is more holy than it.
D. For [a priest] whose hands and feet are not washed does not enter there.

E. (11) The Holy of Holies is more holy than they.

F. For only the high priest on the Day of Atonement at the time of the service enters there.

The pattern for sanctification is clear: a set of available facts — most of them explicit in Scripture, some of them derived by processes of reasoning from Scripture's facts — is organized and laid out in the established pattern of ascension to ever higher levels; but the facts are available, not established through any program of investigation. The single standard pertains: relationship to the same locus of sanctification. If, now, we match the two sets of data, we find that the correspondence is formal, not substantive, but, nonetheless, the effect of the comparison and contrast is clear, transcending the somewhat incongruous details.

VI

So far our consideration of sages' modes of thought has attended to material culture. What about the abstractions of thought? Hierarchization governs intellectual matters as well. The rules of argument turn out to follow the same principles of organization as the rules of cultic uncleanness. Only the details, the operative criteria, differ as the requirements of the case dictate. We clearly differentiate among types of data, posing what is relevant to the issue and dismissing what is not, so Meir. Sages maintain that whatever is in the Torah falls into a single classification. Nonetheless, we do give priority to what is relevant, to what is a precedent, to law over exegesis, exegesis over a tale, an argument a fortiori over an analogy, and so on, the whole properly hierarchized:

Tosefta-tractate Sanhedrin 7:7

I. "And in the case in which there is one who asks to the point and another who asks not to the point, they answer the question of the one who asks to the point, and the one who asked not to the point has to state, 'I asked a question not to the point,'" the words of R. Meir.

J. And sages say, "He does not have to do so.

K. "For the entire Torah is deemed a single matter."

Now a sequence of indicators of hierarchy drawn from logical argument is set forth:

L. [If there is] something relevant, and something not relevant, they attend to what is relevant;

M. a precedent and what is not a precedent — they attend to what is a precedent;

N. a law and an exegesis — they attend to the law;

0. an exegesis of Scripture and a tale — they attend to the exegesis of Scripture;

P. an exegesis and an argument a fortiori — they attend to the argument a fortiori;

Q. an argument a fortiori and an analogy — they attend to the argument a fortiori;

From the character of the argument, we turn to the standing of the participant in the debate:

R. a sage and a disciple — they attend to the sage;

S. a disciple and a common person — they attend to the disciple;

T. if both were sages, both disciples, both ordinary folk, both laws, both questions, both answers, both precedents —

U. the speaker has the right from that point [to make his own choices].

The method is consistent throughout. We begin with the premise that species of the same genus are subject to a process of classification, meaning, hierarchization, and then accomplish the work by a systematic ordering of the data by appeal to the pertinent traits of taxonomy and hierarchization. Time and again the process of taxonomy and hierarchization takes over a genus of data and accomplishes both speciation and hierarchization. What forms data into a single class, e.g., relationship to what is holy or status as to uncleanness, also speciates the data of that class (alike in some ways, different in others), and at the same time hierarchizes.

At the same time hierarchization within one system may be shown to conflict with hierarchization within another, the latter then disrupting the results of the former. The hierarchization is accomplished by appeal to causation; that which causes but is uncaused takes priority over that which is caused, and the rest follows. A further demonstration derives from the character of penalties, the more severe marking the more consequential deed. In both cases we assess the relative standing of causation, at both the opening and the concluding phases of a sequence of actions (causation, penalties for action or inaction). Hierarchization is accomplished by applying a single, established criterion to two or more classes that are to be ordered; then the result of hierarchization will be subject to exegesis to yield a generalization. Reasoning by a process of comparison and contrast between two distinct classes of being shows how the two correspond, and the evidence is drawn from nature and analyzed through a process of pure reason: likeness and unlikeness. Abundant details are carefully matched throughout, and the proposition is demonstrated beyond any reasonable doubt.

The upshot is that Scripture's facts are organized and sorted out in such a way as to present a generalization,. Generalizations are to be formulated through that same process of collecting kindred facts and identifying the implication that all of them bear in common. But Scripture may also be asked to provide illustrative cases for principles that are formulated autonomously, as the result of analytical reasoning distinct from the sorting out of Scriptural precedents. Then Scripture is asked only to define in concrete terms what has been said abstractly. Successive propositions organize and rationalize a vast body of data, all of the facts pointing to the conclusions that are proposed as generalizations. The proof then lies once more in the regularity and order of the data that are collected. The balance and coherence of the opposed laws yield the besought generalizations. The method in no particular will have appeared alien to elementary students of natural history or simple logic in the schools of certain ancient philosophical traditions.

So sages set forth the rational version of the myths of Scripture: creation and its flaws, Eden and the loss of Eden. But their logic, involving as it did the insistence on perfect and unchanging world, sought out what complements and completes an account, modes of thought that will occupy us later on. Thus, they taught how, also, Eden is to be recovered. Adam and his counterpart, Israel, in the cosmic drama acted out every day, here and now, in the humble details of Israel's ordinary life embodied the simple story of the world: unflawed creation, spoiled by man's act of will, restored by Israel's act of repentance. The rationality of an orderly and balanced world set forth in the Oral Torah comes to full realization in the match of Eden and the Land of Israel, Adam and Israel, the paradise and paradise lost, with one difference. Adam had no Torah, Israel does. Adam could not regain Eden. But Israel can and will regain the Land. Sages' teleology imposed itself on eschatology, so forming a theory of last things corresponding to first things, in a theology of restoration.

Private life conformed; it too revealed that same flawless character that the world does — when reason takes over, and exception is explained (away). Exchanges of goods — scarce resources — likewise aimed at a perfect balance. Time, for sages, stood still, history bore no meaning, all things could be shown to exemplify rules and embody regularities. Scripture then conveyed lessons of not history and its admonitions but logic — the logic of creation and its inner tension — and its inexorable result.

VII

Here, we confront the actualization in mythic language of the philosophers' Eden, set forth in abstract terms. Sages in these proportionate, balanced and measured components revealed a world of rules and exposed a realm of justice and therefore rational explanation. It was the kingdom of Heaven, so sages called it, meaning the kingdom of God. For that Eden in the abstraction of natural history that was invented by philosophy corresponds to the conception of the world and its perfection set forth by the theology of the sages. They accordingly conceived of a philosophical Eden out of Scripture's account — its authorized history of the world from Eden to the return to Zion. What the observed facts of nature taught philosophers, the revealed facts of Scripture taught our sages of blessed memory. Therein theology differs from philosophy — but, in the Oral Torah in particular, the difference is there and there alone and no where else.

Working with the facts provided by Scripture and their own observations of nature, they cobbled together an account of the world, embedded in the written part of the Torah itself, that realized the philosophers' ideal of a world of reason and order, balance, and proportion, equity and reliability. Others emerged from Scripture with quite different visions of the world from Eden onward, different perspectives on different realities. Those who framed the Authoritative History from Genesis through Kings certainly thought in a different way from sages, in a historical way. And others, who found in Scripture the secret of events to come, not to restore Eden but to transform creation altogether, took yet a third way, the apocalyptic one. We need not catalogue all of the diverse hermeneutics that Scripture was found by various groups to sustain or even require. Among the heirs of Scripture in late antiquity, sages alone approached Scripture as an exercise in rationality and emerged from Scripture with a world that followed accessible rules and realized a universal logic.

A single statement in detail of that view in general suffices to call attention to the regularities and order, the correspondences, that sages found linked nature and man in a perfect match. Stated very simply, to sages man and nature correspond. God created the same matching traits in nature and in man:

Abot deR. Natan XXXI:III.1

A. R. Yosé the Galilean says, "Whatever the Holy One, blessed be he, created on earth, he created also in man. To what may the matter be compared? To someone who took a piece of wood and wanted to make many forms on it but had no room to make them, so he was distressed. But someone who draws forms on the earth can go on drawing and can spread them out as far as he likes.

B. "But the Holy One, blessed be he, may his great name be blessed for ever and ever, in his wisdom and understanding created the whole of the world, created the heaven and the earth, above and below, and created in man whatever he created in his world.

C. "In the world he created forests, and in man he created forests: the hairs on his head.

D. "In the world he created wild beasts and in man he created wild beasts: lice.

E. "In the world he created channels and in man he created channels: his ears.

F "In the world he created wind and in man he created wind: his breath.

G. "In the world he created the sun and in man he created the sun: his forehead.

H. "Stagnant waters in the world, stagnant waters in man: his nose, [namely, rheum].

I. "Salt water in the world, salt water in man: his urine.

J. "Streams in the world, streams in man: man's tears.

K. "Walls in the world, walls in man: his lips.

L. "Doors in the world, doors in man, his teeth.

M. "Firmaments in the world, firmaments in man, his tongue.

N. "Fresh water in the world, fresh water in man: his spit.

O. "Stars in the world, stars in the man: his cheeks.

P. "Towers in the world, towers in man: his neck.

Q. " masts in the world, masts in man: his arms.

R. "Pins in the world, pins in man: his fingers.

S. "A King in the world, a king in man: his head.

T. "Grape clusters in the world, grape clusters in man: his breasts.

U. "Counselors in the world, counselors in man: his kidneys.

V. "Millstones in the world, millstones in man: his intestines [which grind up food].

W. "mashing mills in the world, and mashing mills in man: the
spleen.

X. "Pits in the world, a pit in man: the belly button.

Y. "Flowing streams in the world and a flowing stream in man:
his blood.

Z. "Trees in the world and trees in man: his bones.

AA. "Hills in the world and hills in man: his buttocks.

BB. " pestle and mortar in the world and pestle and mortar in
man: the joints.

CC. "Horses in the world and horses in man: the legs.

DD. "The angel of death in the world and the angel of death in
man: his heels.

EE. "Mountains and valleys in the world and mountains and
valleys in man: when he is standing, he is like a mountain,
when he is lying down, he is like a valley.

FF. "Thus you have learned that whatever the Holy One,
blessed be he, created on earth, he created also in man."

Shorn of theological and mythic language, the statement says no less
than natural philosophy does in its insistence upon the teleology of
nature, its hierarchical order. As philosophers follow a procedure of
comparison and contrast, resting on the systematic sifting of the data
of nature, so too do sages. But here, nature and Scripture (without
differentiation as to source or effect of derivation from nature rather
than from Scripture) yield correspondences that are deemed
concrete and exact. We begin with a proposition clarified by a
parable, and then proceed systematically through the parts of nature
and their counterparts in the body of man.

So each group working with its chosen source of facts,
philosophers and sages pursue the same issues in much the same
way. Intellectuals to their core, confident of the capacity to
contemplate, to conceive in mind for speculative analysis a real world
that corresponds to the world realized alone in mind, both
philosophers and sages insist upon the primacy of reason. Logic
ruled. It was logic that they had the capacity to discern. All things can
be made to make sense. Proper analysis transforms the apparent
chaos of nature's data into the compelling order of purposeful system

and structure: streams in the world, streams in mind, a world of complement and balance. A vast and ordered universe yields its secrets to those who discern regularity in close reading of actualities. Then, in place of mysteries come reliable knowledge, facts that yield the laws of life. So both philosophers and sages can have set forth a single conception of the world.

VIII

But when they answered the question, Whence the knowledge of the rules of the ordered society, the world of balance and proportion in all things and of equitable exchange? sages took their leave of philosophers. Instead of reading nature, they read the Torah. In place of searching for regularities of nature, they found patterns in the Torah. Instead of an abstract, natural teleology, to be defined through systematic work of hierarchical classification, comparison and contrast, they invoked the will of God. This will they showed to be dependable, regulated by rules man can discern, wholly rational, entirely just. Then, instead of an inquiry into natural history, guided by considerations of hierarchy, order, and ultimate purpose, sages contemplated the condition of Israel, explaining how those same principles of intent and order governed, the same modes of rational explanation functioned, the same media of reasoned thought in the form of applied reason and practical logic guided thought. That is what distinguished sages from philosophers and turned them into theologians: the privileged source of truth that the Torah constituted.

How, in concrete terms, did theology take its leave from philosophy? It was through the appeal to revealed facts of the Torah in place of the discovered facts of nature. Further, sages' aesthetics required the recasting of those truths from the abstract language of generalization into the concrete myth form of a massive narrative, regularized and ordered into governing rules. Take, for example, the heart of the system of the dual Torah, the conviction of God's rule of a world of order that is to be explained by appeal to the principles of justice. Then events serve as the source of moral truth. Destiny is dictated by God, and God's hegemony realizes a morality defined by justice. So justice, not chance, governs Israel, specifically, God's plan. For God has a purpose in what he does with Israel. This point is set forth by reference to exemplary actions, a narrative of what counts. So God sent Israel down into Egypt so that he would have occasion to perform miracles, so that the whole world would know that He is God and there is no other:

> Sifré to Deuteronomy CCCVI:XXX.2ff.
>
> 2.A. "And how on the basis of Scripture do you say that our ancestors went down to Egypt only so that the Holy One, blessed be He, might do wonders and acts of might, and so that his great name might be sanctified in the world?
>
> B. "As it is said, 'And it came to pass in the course of that long time that the king of Egypt died...and God heard their groaning, and God remembered his covenant' (Ex. 2:23-24).
>
> C. "And it is said, 'For the name of the Lord I proclaim; give glory to our God.'

The purposeful character of God's actions now is spelled out in further cases:

> 3.A. "And how on the basis of Scripture do we know that the Omnipresent brought punishments and the ten plagues on Pharaoh and on the Egyptians only so that his great name might be sanctified in the world?
>
> B. "For to begin with it is said, 'Who is the Lord, that I should listen to his voice?' (Ex. 5:2).
>
> C. "But in the end: 'The Lord is righteous, and I and my people are wicked' (Ex. 9:27).

We move from the punishment of Egypt to the miracles done for Israel, also purposefully:

> 4.A. "And how on the basis of Scripture do we know that the Omnipresent did wonders and acts of might at the sea and at

the Jordan and at the Arnon streams only so that his great
name might be sanctified in the world?

B. "As it is said, 'And it came to pass, when all the kings of the
Amorites that were beyond the Jordan westward, and all the
kings of the Canaanites [that were by the sea, heard how the
Lord has dried up the waters of the Jordan from before the
children of Israel until they had passed over, their heart
melted]' (Josh. 5:1).

C. "And so Rahab says to the messengers of Joshua, 'For we
have heard how the Lord dried up the water of the Red Sea
before you' (Josh. 2:10).

D. "Scripture says, 'For the name of the Lord I proclaim; give
glory to our God.'

Not only miracles, but suffering and martyrdom serve God's purpose:

5.A. "And how on the basis of Scripture do we know that
Daniel went down into the lions' den only so that the Holy
One, blessed be He, might have occasion to do wonders and
acts of might, and so that his great name might be sanctified in
the world?

B. "As it is said, 'For the name of the Lord I proclaim; give
glory to our God.'

C. "And Scripture says, 'I make a decree, that in all the
dominions of my kingdom men tremble and fear before the
God of Daniel...' (Dan. 6:27-28).

6.A. "And how on the basis of Scripture do you maintain that
Hananiah, Mishael, and Azariah went into the fiery oven only
so that the Holy One, blessed be He, might have occasion to do
for them wonders and acts of might, and so that his great
name might be sanctified in the world?

B. "As it is said, 'It seems good to me to declare the signs and
wonders that God Most High has done for me...how great are
his signs, and how mighty are his wonders, his kingdom is an
everlasting kingdom' (Dan. 3:32-33).

What is important here is two traits of mind. First, theological truth is
discovered in revealed Scripture. But then, second, the facts that are
adduced are ordered into generalizations that are subject to the tests

of verification or falsification: philosophical modes of thought applied to the data of theology: the search for the logic of God. What philosophers of Judaism accomplished in medieval times, joining Torah to reason, sages accomplished in the very process of formulating the Torah, oral and written, for the ages.

IX

Now, as a matter of fact, sages also differed from their philosophical continuators in the Middle Ages. They adapted philosophical modes of thought to their own purpose and dispensed with philosophical doctrines as irrelevant to that purpose. In according privilege to revealed truth set forth by God's revelation in Scripture, they transcended philosophy. If philosophy found in nature, through the rules of natural history, the logic of the world, sages studied the origins of nature in the Torah, the account of the program and plan of the Creator of that creation that natural history ordered. So sages sought the logic of God's mind, to which, through the whole Torah, oral and written, and its account of creation, they possessed sole access. They spoke in particular of revealed truth, rather than talking in general terms (in abstract symbols, for instance) of truth set forth in nature. Accordingly, they pursued a theological program — the logic of God — rather than the philosophical program that addressed the world of universal wisdom. The question of whether theology is philosophy's method applied to God's concerns, or philosophy is theology in a secular mode, need not detain us.

It follows that when we imagine the world as philosophers conceive it, we find entry into the world as our sages of blessed memory imagine it to work. But if the method is the same, the message that emerges proves mighty-different. That is because the Torah for sages takes the place of nature for philosophy. Its narratives, transformed into exemplary cases, replace social thought about mankind in general. Sages' appeal to these examples make unnecessary historical inquiry, based on sustained narrative, into what men have done. Sages find a better way to identify the rules that the results yield, whether then, whether now; to them history is monumentally irrelevant.

Sages accordingly find in the Torah the account of the balanced and orderly world that God has made. That then serves as counterpart to philosophers' reasoned picture of man's domain and its laws, nature's realm and its regularities. Corresponding to the book of nature that contains the lessons of physics, biology or astronomy that philosophers consult to find the laws of the tangible world for this Eden's philosophers is the Torah. There, and not in nature, concurring with philosophers about teleology's and intentionality's yielding a rational and ordered universe, sages find the record of God's purpose, God's intent in creating the world:

> Genesis Rabbah I:I.2
>
> A. In the beginning God created" (Gen. l:l):
>
> B. The word ["in the beginning"] means "workman."
>
> C. [In the cited verse] the Torah speaks, "I was the work-plan of the Holy One, blessed be he."
>
> D. In the accepted practice of the world, when a mortal king builds a palace, he does not build it out of his own head, but he follows a work-plan.
>
> E. And [the one who supplies] the work-plan does not build out of his own head, but he has designs and diagrams, so as to know how to situate the rooms and the doorways.
>
> F. Thus the Holy One, blessed be he, consulted the Torah when he created the world.
>
> G. So the Torah stated, "By means of 'the beginning' [that is to say, the Torah] did God create..." (Gen. 1:1).
>
> H. And the word for "beginning" refers only to the Torah, as Scripture says, "The Lord made me as the beginning of his way" (Prov. 8:22).

In the Torah God wrote out the record of his plans and acts. Read rightly, the laws of the Torah yield law for the wise who can discern regularity and perceive purpose. The facts of nature take second place to the facts of the Torah; there is found the encompassing

account of the realm of perfection that Eden promised and that the
Torah's social entity, Israel both man and nation — Israelite man,
the kingdom of priests and holy nation of Israel — realize.

Here therefore is where philosophers and sages part
company, for philosophers turn to the natural world, sages to the
Torah, for the facts that, for both parties, will yield reliable
knowledge concerning the regularities and rationality of the orderly
world awaiting explanation. In the Oral Torah the facts of nature are
subordinated to the facts of the Torah. Facts that derive from other
sources, for example, those of nature not set forth in Scripture, or
those of history and politics not deriving from the Torah but the ken
of Israel, appear only very rarely in the discourse of the Oral Torah.
When they do, moreover, they turn out to replicate facts of nature,
history, or politics that Scripture has already designated as
noteworthy. The counterpart of nature for philosophy's natural
history, Scripture provides nearly all of the remarkable facts that
demand attention. The Torah's are the data demand and yield
regularization, comparison and contrast. The Torah's are the facts
that may contradict a hypothesis or demonstrate it, but it is rare that
facts deriving from any other source prove a point and, once a
hypothesis resting on the Torah's facts is set forth, facts deriving from
some other source *never* come under consideration at all, except,
perhaps, to form exceptions that can be explained by appeal to the
rule established in the Torah's facts. To prove a point, it suffices to
set forth three or more cases from the Torah; these establish a
pattern, and the pattern is its own proof.

The world we contemplate encompasses happenings but not
history in the conventional sense. The Torah sets forth narrative, but
considerations of time and change do not pertain. That is because, as
I emphasize, the narrative yields cases that produce generalizations,
examples of how things are in general. The narrative yields those
rules of the social order that correspond to the laws of physics,
biology, or astronomy. Events properly ordered — compared and
contrasted and shown to conform to rules — match the regular

movement of the stars or the balance and proportion of the imaginary atom. The same calculus, the counterpart-mathematics — these pertain to the affairs of the natural world and those of the world of man portrayed by nature and the Torah, respectively. That is why time and change represent flaws in Eden, where stasis attests to perfection: all things in place and order, why change anything? Then, if considerations of temporal order do not apply to the Torah's account of affairs, we have to reconstruct in accord with the rules of natural history the record of human events set forth in the Torah.

X

How are we to envision this multi-layered reality and account for the unity and harmony of things — the cosmic logic of it all? Let us conceive of the description of creation to correspond to the problem of cartographic representation of complex data in different layers. Here is what we may call the geography of creation as sages' cartography portrayed it. First, contemplate the Torah as a thin translucent overlay over everyday reality, a set of sheets all together joined, with each imposing its lines of structure joined with the lines of the others upon the ordinary and imparting proportionate shape to the workaday world. Seen through the mediating colors and light of these translucent sheets, the ordinary world conforms to the Artist's vision of harmonious Eden, man and nature living in perfect peace.

But how are we to conceive in our mind's eye the colors that lend nuance to the ordinary world? To follow that vision we must discern in these sets of translucent sheets the characteristics of each one, not only the joined traits of them all, all together and all at once. For each sheet in visual-outline form contains a portrait of a given moment or event in the Torah: Israel at the sea, Israel at Sinai, Israel in the Land and at the Temple, Israel leaving for exile, Israel returning to the Land — these events are all reproduced in visual tableaux. So too are Abraham at Moriah, Isaac blessing Jacob, Jacob wrestling with the angel, Jacob at the well, Jacob and Laban, Joseph in Pharaoh's court, Moses at Sinai, Moses at the rock — great moments, each individually outlined in a few deft strokes. Now, the sheets being separate and translucent, they may be combined and recombined to make designs, to yield patterns, of a different order. Then today's drawing, Israel today, contemplating its condition in exile, at the base, is given structure and balance when the light-bearing sheet is placed on top: Israel going into exile, Israel returning from exile. So too the sheet portraying Jacob wrestling w.th the angel or Abraham at Moriah may overlay the sheet that conveys the lines of Israel's struggle to endure until redemption.

All of the sheets together then contain and portray whatever happens that matters, whoever makes a difference, in the Scriptural record. Seen all together, the whole set yields a picture of everything, all together, all at once, in a single moment of perfect revelation, that the Torah wishes to portray. For these pages, like the translucent maps in the old geography books, which are formed by differentiated pages and colors, all of them distinct in their own right, but the entire set visible all together and all at once, form a map. But this map portrays severally by pages and then jointly when bound together not ranges of mountains and valleys along with places of human settlement, sites of battles and the locations of industry, mining, and agriculture. Rather, this imaginary map formed by the differentiated layers of the Torah holds together events of time and space, transactions of massive weight in the course of the life of Israel and the nations, happenings in the private life of those persons of enduring memory within Israel that carry consequence, embodying the rules that apply.

Our translucent pages work best — but not only — in sets of two, producing an interesting complication of color. These sets form binary opposites in the principles of balance, complementarity, proportion and commensurability that define perfection. Contemplate these pairs in their mixtures of colors: yellow and red, together producing orange; yellow and blue together yielding green, for instance, and so throughout. Envision then translucent sheets, the yellow, Eden, the blue, its match and counterpart in time, the Land of

Israel, and the green, the world to come. Or see with the mind's eye these translucent sheets: the yellow, Israel, the red, the nations, the orange, judgment — and so throughout. The variegated colors of reality all break down into the simple components of which they are comprised; the components of world order and of social order and of historical order all prove susceptible to analysis and division, then also to synthesis and union.

XI

Then what of events and persons? In the kingdom governed by orderly rules formed into balanced opposites, consequential events find their match, persons their counterpart. These prove few and seldom show movement. Eden matched by Land of Israel yields a predictable match: Adam's fall from Eden and Israel's expulsion from the Land of Israel. Yet another page may be superimposed on the page of Adam and Israel, Eden and the Land. Eden's counterpart in time locates itself in the Temple of Jerusalem, in which case Adam's=Israel's counterpart can only be God, who leaves the Temple when Israel leaves Jerusalem. Even God, capable of anything, subjects himself to the analogies of the mortal king, matching in mourning the motifs of ordinary lamentation:

Pesiqta deRab Kahana XV:III
1. A. Bar Qappara opened discourse by citing the following verse: "In that day the Lord God of hosts called to weeping and mourning, to baldness and girding with sackcloth; [and behold, joy and gladness, slaying oxen and killing sheep, eating meat and drinking wine. 'Let us eat and drink for tomorrow we die.' The Lord of hosts has revealed himself in my ears: 'Surely this iniquity will not be forgiven you until you die,' says the Lord of hosts] " (Is. 15:12-14)
B. "Said the Holy One, blessed be He, to the ministering angels, 'When a mortal king mourns, what does he do?'
C. "They said to him, 'He puts sack over his door.'

D. "He said to them, 'I too shall do that. 'I will clothe the heavens with blackness [and make sackcloth for their covering]'" (Is. 50:3).'

This composition compares common practice among royalty with verses of Scripture that describe God's state of mind and action. The demonstration is detailed and systematic, and the explanation, in context, compelling. The match of king to The King of the world once more rests on the fundamental conviction of a perfect match, a world we can understand by appeal to governing rules and illuminating analogies.

Two other realms of meaning — other sets of translucent sheets — produce participants of consequence, whose activities require rational explanation by appeal to the principles of balance, complement, and order. These are the people, Israel, and the individual Israelite. The people, Israel, find their counterpart in their progenitors, Abraham, Isaac, and Jacob (rarely: their wives as well). What happens in the life of the people recapitulates what happens in the life of the patriarchs that produced the people. Or Israel matches Adam, as we noticed: the expulsion from the Land is weighed in the balance against the expulsion from Eden. The individual Israelite finds his place within Israel, events of his life their counterpart in what happens to the whole of Israel ("all Israel"). Just as rules of justice and equity govern the whole of Israel, so inexorable justice, meting out true equity for merit, true penalty for sin, rules the life of the individual. This complementary pattern finds its weightiest moment in the match of individual death and resurrection, on the one side, and Israel's exile and ultimate return to the Land, on the second, and God's abandoning of the Temple but restoration of, and return to, the Temple, on the third — and there are no other dimensions.

So in the particular realm formed by Israel we see the working out of those general rules of order and balance that describe the philosophers' Eden. And just as philosophers proposed to show the purpose and order of nature, so sages pronounced the shape and structure of the future — because in the timeless world of the permanent present sages contemplated, what was, is, and will be is wholly on record in the Torah, properly understood. The future matches and balances the past, and that is why, time and again, sages speak confidently about what is going to happen. Take the case of the match of beginning and ending, Adam and Israel, Eden, and the Land. Creation comes to its natural conclusion with Israel in the Land, the drama of Eden having come to resolution, through the Torah, in the perfection of Adam in Israel. Just as Adam lost Eden, so Israel lost the Land, but creation will come to rest and balance when Israel recovers Eden.

The system invokes the Torah as its dynamic, around which clusters of other key-categories or concepts finds their position: Eden-Sinai-Land, Adam-Israel-Land — these define the anticipation that sages precipitate: a fully systemic construction. So too, the future in a different perspective: if part of a prophecy is fulfilled, the rest of the prophecy will be realized in due course, a perfectly reasonable and proportionate conception. So too the players in the cosmic drama, Israel and the nations, must not lose their sense of proportion; each has his assigned role, including the dimensions of his part. Along these same lines, a simple logic prevails in the conception of Israel's past, present and future in this logical sequence of action, reaction, resolution: sin, punishment, comfort. That hermeneutics of philosophical perfection produces the exegesis of diverse texts to make the point, with every thing with which the Israelites sinned, they were smitten, and with that same thing they will be comforted.

The analytical inquiry in fact promises to demonstrate a proposition, not merely investigate data that yield one, as in our time we should understand the work. For the generative question that governs throughout, what is going to happen to Israel, and what is Israel supposed to do? derives not from the data, nor even from the problem of ordering the data, nor yet from the proposition that the work in the end yields. It derives rather from the system that calls attention to these data rather than some other, because these data will yield exactly what the system to begin with knows to be true. And that is, that Israel recapitulates the life and teachings of the patriarchs. More to the point, what the patriarchs did governs what Israel now endures. That matters because of what must come: prediction, or, in my language, explanation and anticipation. The system that works out its intellectual disciplines in the identification of what requires analysis and in conducting analysis through a labor of comparison and contrast and generalization therefrom means to set forth the principles that govern what happens to Israel in the future.

XII

This encompassing, enormous but simple theological system, bearing its own principles of reason and order, animates discourse, start to finish. The sage responsible for a cogent statement did not pretend to approach the data in a spirit of mere curiosity; not a philosopher seeking the order of this, the natural world, he was a theologian, intending to set forth the logic of matters having to do with God's actions and intentions in this world, with Israel. The data that he examined presented facts supplied by God in the Torah, and the task he took for himself was to turn those facts into useful knowledge of God's plans and program for Israel in the world. The sage drew upon a model of explanation that itself emerged from an established system, a construction of ideas that formed a given, that sustained all further thought and animated it. Then he knew exactly what he was going to find, which is what he set out to demonstrate.

Now we turn to blunt answers to fundamental questions of systemic description, analysis, and interpretation: if this is what we know, what else do we know? I deal with three questions that require specific answers.

[1]   What is at stake? It is an explanation of Israel's present condition, and — I cannot overstress — still more urgent,

the identification of the operative reasons that will lead to viable hypotheses concerning Israel's future prospects. Here the systemic subtext shapes articulated thought: the present properly analyzed and explained contains within itself the entire past, the whole future, all together, all at once. We turn to Abram because we wish out of the past to know the future and because we take as fact that Israel's future recapitulates the past of Abram. God has laid out matters from beginning to end; Scripture not only records the past but provides the key, through patterns we can identify in the present, to the future. The premise of analysis then is, when we understand the facts in hand, we also can learn the rules. So in a world created in accord with the requirements of exact balance, proportion, correspondence, complementarity and commensurability. There are no mysteries, only facts not yet noticed, analyses not yet undertaken, propositions not yet proved.

[2]   How to explain the present? The sages' method of explanation will identify the rational principle that is involved. Scripture's facts do not suffice: the patriarchs asked. Reason is demanded: why did they value these experiences? Then rationality is established by appeal not to the given of Scripture but to the conviction that the familiar traits of perfection characterize creation and the Creator. That is to say, the conceptions that in general the paramount method of Classical philosophy in its account of nature — teleology joined to order — govern here as well. That is why applied reason and practical logic and not the given and revealed of Scripture alone everywhere sustain thought. Sages do not paraphrase or recapitulate Scripture and its narrative, they transform Scripture into facts to be analyzed and reconstructed. The results yield the self-evidently valid doctrines. These prove to be few but paramount: the perfection of creation, the centrality of the Torah as a source of established facts, the subservience of God — therefore creation and history — to the same reason that animates the mind of man. All things are subject to the rules of logic and order that man's own mind obeys, and explanation in the end must derive from the sources

of nature and its laws and the Torah and its regularities, each recapitulating the mind and will of the loving and merciful and reasonable God, in whose image, after whose likeness, man is made.

[3]   What of the future? Sages compared themselves to prophets and insisted that their knowledge of the Torah provided a key to the future. Knowing why noteworthy things take place provided them with that key. For a model of anticipation will extrapolate from the results of analysis and explanation those governing rules of an orderly world that define a useful hypothesis concerning the future. Having identified regularities and defined descriptive laws, then accounted for those rules by spelling out the systemic reasons behind them, sages had every reason to peer over the beckoning horizon. For their basic conviction affirmed the order and regularity of creation, its perfection. If, therefore, they knew the rules and how they worked (including remissions of the rules), sages insisted they could predict how the future would take shape as well.

Given what we know about past and present and the signals of Providence that explain the condition of the world, what shall we anticipate for time to come? Like the prophets before them but thinking along quite other lines to reach comparable conclusions, sages spoke with certainty, therefore, about what Israel may expect in the future. But there was this difference. Prophets invoked God's explicit statements about the future. Sages' message, by contrast, took shape as a result of the analytical soundings sages made and explained, the data they formed into rules, the rules the logic of which they set forth by way of explanation. Theirs was the way of the natural historian and the philosopher. But for them the path carried them into Scripture, not nature, and into the logic of God's plan for the world, not the *telos* of nature's impersonal perfection.

XIII

That explains why what sages produced in the manner of philosophers is not philosophy but theology. Philosophy discovered the rules of the natural world, theology, those of the realm of the supernatural; the same principles of reasoned inquiry into factual regularities and rational explanations based on those descriptive laws of how things are governed both inquiries. Analyzing nature and Scripture, respectively, philosophy and theology worked in the same way and produced matching results. Because the world is the way we conceive God made it — that is, perfect, therefore, orderly and purposeful for philosophy, rational and ultimately benevolent for sages' reading of the way the Torah defines it — we can identify anomalies and conduct analyses, explain the results with rational explanations, and extrapolate from the order of the present the shape and structure of the future.

That systematic exegesis of the world in accord with the hermeneutics of the Torah defines the theology of the Oral Torah: its focus and the source of its coherence and cogency. Had The Philosopher, Aristotle, read the Written Torah and chosen the media of law, myth and exegesis for his discourse, his lectures would have recapitulated the results set forth by the sages. May we claim that the documents of the Oral Torah are what he would have written? Working with the particular facts ordered by sages, he would have done something quite akin in method and in modes of thought and points of insistence, if not in form let alone in particular doctrine.

But there is this caveat. Had Aristotle compared the Written Torah's theory of Eden and the Land, Adam and Israel, with the everyday world's actualities — whether his own student's conquest of Jerusalem or scattered Israel's inconsequentiality among the nations — he would have recognized the incongruity of the result. Then he will have abandoned the task of the mythic re-presentation of nature through Scripture, of theological instead of philosophical discourse. Nature sustained Aristotle's philosophy. Israel's actualities contradicted sages' theology. For the world realized by natural Israel, whether in Aristotle's time, in the fourth century B.C.E., or in the time of our sages of blessed memory, the first six centuries C.E., testified to the absurdity of the vision of rationality and order, within the framework of God's logic, that the Torah portrayed. In no way did the natural world of Israel in actual history ever validate sages' account of the theological world of mythic, holy Israel. Instead of an imaginary world of balance, match, complementarity, and proportion, Israel lived in a real world of disproportion, where the wicked prospered and the righteous suffered.

Absurdity piled onto absurdity into the ultimate climax of space and time, the Temple mount ploughed over, the only offerings these days the flesh and blood of the Israelite martyrs themselves. That is the everyday world confronted by the second century sages who produced the Mishnah and its concomitant traditions. A competing, repressed minority competing with Israel over the true message of the shared Scriptures, the Christians two hundred years later found themselves rulers of the world-empire, Rome. That is the (to them) utter absurdity faced by the fourth and fifth century sages who produced the Talmud of the Land of Israel, Genesis Rabbah, and Leviticus Rabbah, among other foundation-documents of Rabbinic Judaism. The world they confronted in no way validated their fiercely-held convictions about the ultimate rationality of all things. If everything is subject to a reasonable explanation by appeal to regularities that wisdom may discern, then why are things the way they are?

How then did sages construct this fantasy-world of theirs, so vastly unlike the everyday world in which they lived out the life of Israel in a politics of triviality amid kingdoms and empires not called "Israel," one empire, Iran, pagan and, heirs of Ahasuerus, by no means benign, the other, now-Christian Rome, laying claim to the same noble lineage, but now as Israel after the spirit on the authority of not the Torah of Sinai, written and oral, but the Bible, Old and New Testaments alike? Specifically, what convictions, resting on what evidence, led them to the conclusions that, in their comprehensive account of theology, they set forth?

The answer is clear from what has already been said: Scripture, the written Torah, set forth a corpus of unassailable and generative facts, out of which all else was to be, and was, discovered and reconstructed (or, in more descriptive language, fabricated). So to understand the theology of the Oral Torah, we must take as our starting point that theology's sources of the conviction of the orderly character of all being. We commence with the starting point of all else: the rule of justice, therefore also of law, that governs all else.

PREFACE

This reader serves a particular purpose in a specific context. It is intended to spell out the character and distinctive structures of the theology of classical Judaism and to show what happens to these structures in contemporary responses to the modern situation of Israel, the Jewish people.

To be sure, many people suppose that "Judaism has no dogmas" or that "Judaism is a religion without theology." The dogma of dogma-less Judaism ignores the simple fact that the Judaic tradition teaches many truths of a particularly, wholly theological character, beginning with the statement that God is one, the Torah was given by God and contains the exhaustive and eternal statement of his will, and Israel is the people called by God to his service. These constitute not this-worldly assertions about historical and sociological "facts," but religious views upon, and interpretations of, the facts and meanings of the life of the Jewish people. And since these views come to us in abstract and sophisticated formulations and phrased in philosophically rigorous arguments, they are to be understood as theological.

Some argue that while in the history of Judaism, various statements of a theological nature have been laid down, still "Judaism has no theology." By this they mean that the varieties of belief and interpretation over the ages pose an obstacle to the formulation of one, specific Judaic theology. But every formulation of Judaic theology, whether in the rational, or the mystical, or the legal modes of expression, addresses itself to at least three central issues: the nature of God, the character of Torah, and the meaning of the life and history of Israel, the Jewish people. That is why I call these categories "structures"—the building-blocks of all Judaic thinking. They are everywhere central in the theological undertakings of diverse thinkers. Moreover, the design and layout of these structures exhibit variation in detail, but remarkable consistency in general modes of articulation. God always is one, and the meaning of unity must be explained. God furthermore relates to man, and the character and quality of that relationship has to be contemplated. Torah always involves three elements: revelation,

1

study, and fulfillment. No serious religious thinker in Judaism therefore will ignore the problem of defining revelation, the necessity of
explaining the centrality of the study of Torah, and the social and cultural effects of Israel's devotion to the way of Torah. "Israel" and its
election, its central role in the revelation of God's will and the ultimate
redemption of mankind—these issues too are never going to be absent
from theological reflection, whatever its particular mode or style.

That is why I claim we may indeed undertake a survey of the
theology of Judaism, examine the articulation of its classical issues in
contemporary language, and ask about the affects of the modern
situation of the Jewish people upon the fundamental theological
structures of the classical tradition.

I have chosen to do so through the writings of living theologians
and other Jewish thinkers (not all of the men we shall listen to want to
be called theologians), because their modes of thought and expression
speak to and are congruent with our situation. They speak in our language and to us. But what they have to say derives from the classical
literature of Judaism and conforms to its main assertions.

At the same time, I have made no effort to delineate the special
theological traits of several movements in modern Judaism, for example, to spell out Reform Jewish views of God, or the Reconstructionist interpretation of the meaning of Israel's election, or Orthodox
Jewish theology of Torah. These important and distinctive expressions
within contemporary Judaic theology deserve treatment in a different
setting. No movement in modern Judaism stands by itself in the consideration of classical Judaic theology. All expressions of modern
Judaism confront the issues raised in part III of this reader: the meaning of God after the Holocaust, the modulations of the way in which
Torah is studied and of the contents of Torah, the modern changes in
the condition of Israel, the Jewish people. My claim therefore is that it
is possible to describe "Judaism" through the writings of great theologians and to do so in terms of the central categories of thought and
analysis revealed in their work.

Obviously, a theological description omits reference to what people
actually believe and do. For that purpose a different approach is called
for, the one called history of religions. The historian of religions will
ask about the mind and imagination of the entire community, not merely
of the religious elite constituted by theologians. In the introduction I distinguish the approach of the theologian from that of the historian of
religions. My *Way of Torah: An Introduction to Judaism* (Belmont,
1970, 1973²: Dickenson Publishing Company) and *Guideposts on the*

Way of Torah (Belmont, 1974: Dickenson) attempt to describe, from the perspectives of history of religions, the main outlines of the Judaic religious experience. In like manner, my *American Judaism: Adventure in Modernity* (Engelwood Cliffs, 1972: Prentice Hall) takes up several categories in the analysis of history of religions—the foci of holiness within the Judaic tradition—and discusses them through extended quotations of other writers, as well as through my own comments. These foci of holiness—holy people, holy faith, holy man, holy land, holy way of living—are described and illustrated through the data of the Judaic experience in America. The description tends toward a certain irony. In my discourse I speak through the voices of others, who serve as reliable witnesses to the state of the tradition and the condition of Israel in America. But concerning each main idea I thereby say precisely what I have to say. Here by contrast I make no effort to shape the words of others into a single, coherent statement of my own. I identify with the writings before us. But that is not the same thing as attempting to speak through them, as in *American Judaism*.

I undertake this work because of my responsibilities as a teacher and entirely in the interest of my students, young scholars in the study of religions. Brown University brings together young men and women worthy of my best efforts—and of abilities better than mine—and capable of participating in the academic analysis of the Judaic religious tradition within the study of religions. Our students are our glory. Without them we cannot be teachers, our scholarly efforts bear no meaning. This is a work provoked and given meaning by my undergraduate students.

A bibliography for the study of Jewish theology is provided by Professors Fritz A. Rothschild and Seymour Siegel in "Modern Jewish Thought", *The Study of Judaism: Bibliographic Essays* (N.Y., 1972: Ktav Publishing House, Inc., for Anti-Defamation League of B'nai B'rith) pp. 113-184. Because of the excellence of this bibliography the editor did not regard further bibliographical suggestions as necessary.

This book was in press when our first daughter, our fourth child, was born. On the date of her birth, it is dedicated to Margalit Leah Berakhah. May her generation not need books about Judaism, may they *be* those books.

Providence, Rhode Island   Jacob Neusner

10 February 1973
9 Adar I 5733

INTRODUCTION

The religious experience of Judaism comprehends both the perceptions of ordinary folk and the teachings of the creative elite—prophets, rabbis, philosophers, mystics, scholars, lawyers, and sages. To find out about the ordinary Jew one turns to the prayers he recites, the festivals he celebrates, the various ritual and mythic testimonies to the Jews' shared religious imagination. But these do not constitute the whole of the Judaic tradition, only part of it. The other part comprises the way in which theological thinkers interpret religious experiences, make sense of them. How do they produce an account of the central issues of the Judaic religious life, make them accessible to reason and constitutive of a formidable intellectual tradition? The power of Judaism is to be laid open to the experience of the student not only through examination of the liturgy and piety of the ordinary people, but also through the analysis of the central issues in Judaic theology. There we are able to see the theologians at work, to examine their modes of thought and procedures of argument, to see how they appeal to sacred Scriptures and mediate the claims of law, revelation, and tradition to their own time.

My purpose as anthologist is to present Judaism through the minds of some of its thinkers, particularly of the twentieth century. I have asked, What are the dominant theological foci of Judaic thinking? How have the central issues of Judaic religious life elicited from contemporary masters a coherent and cogent statement? In introducing each selection I have tried to raise and answer two questions. First, what is the issue addressed by the writer before us? Second, why is his thought important, even suggestive beyond itself? What is to be learned in context about the Judaic religious experience as a whole from the explanation of the part of it in hand?

I believe Judaism is best characterized as "the way of Torah," because the whole of its history is contained within the symbol, "Torah," the issue of the revelation at Sinai, and the way the contents of Torah have been elaborated and interpreted since then. In *The Way of Torah: An Introduction to Judaism* and *Guideposts on the Way of Torah* my

purpose is to introduce the student to the Judaic tradition viewed from
the perspective of the historian of religions. My claim is that one may
understand that tradition only by taking into account the religious life
and imagination of the *entire* community, not only of its virtuosi. Therefore I concentrate on the liturgy and piety, or spirituality, of the synagogue, which everywhere in classical settings serves to express the Jew's
view of himself and the world, of man and God, of man and man, of
man and himself, and of the relationships between the private person and
the community as a whole.

The central problem facing the historian of religions is, How are
we to make sense of the facts of Jewish life fairly widely known in the
West? The Jews you are likely to know are not apt to exemplify the
classic religious tradition of Judaism. Some of them are not likely to
know much about that tradition. How is a student of religions to describe "Judaism" and to define it, therefore, if he cannot ask what "the
Jews" believe, why they believe it. The answer therefore has to comprehend two parts.

First is the nature of the classical tradition. Second come the
modern expressions and formulations of that tradition, alongside the
innovations within its modes and symbols but outside of its historical
framework, produced in the encounter with modernity. Finally one
asks, In what way do modern Jews—or the vast majority of them—
constitute a religious group at all? How are we able to speak of
Judaism as a living religion? My claim, at the end, is that the Jews do
constitute a religious group, because the central elements of the classical
mythic structure of Judaism persist and continue to shape their imagination about, and perception of, reality.

What does it mean to be a Jew? In part you have to consider
the afore-mentioned views of reality, the mythic elements formative of
the Judaic interpretation of the experience of man with God. But in
part you have to take seriously the data of modernity, the evidence of
continuity and change, within the classical mythic structure, located in
the experience of the modern world.

It goes without saying that the word "myth" is used not to mean
something false, a fairy tale, but the view, in the words of Fred Streng,
"That the essential structure of reality manifests itself in particular
moments that are remembered and repeated from generation to generation," preserved in myths which "reveal the truth of life." The
Judaic mythic structure, present in virtually every ceremony and rite,
liturgy, festival and celebration, formative of the Jewish imagination
and understanding of the world and of history, centers upon the

themes of creation, revelation, and redemption, the creation of the world by one God, the revelation of the Torah at Sinai, the redemption of Israel in the end of time.

Judaic thought, however, exhibits the capacity to transcend and transform the mythic perception of the world, to treat abstractly and with intellectual rigor and sophistication the primary and fundamental elements of the classical myth of Judaism. Creation therefore becomes the occasion for reflection on the nature of the one God. Revelation focuses upon the Torah, the five books of Moses revealed at Sinai, later on understood as the corpus of religious truth as a whole. Redemption centers upon the history and meaning of the life of the Jewish people, "Israel." The mythic structure thus evokes its counterpart in the structure of religious ideas systematically elaborated, that is, of theology, represented by the concepts of God, Torah, and Israel.

Just as from the perspective of history of religions I attempt to describe the mythic structure of classical Judaism, so here, through the writings of theologians, I try to spell out the substance of the theological structure of classical Judaism. To be sure, for the most part I select living writers, because they are concerned with expressing the classical theological ideas to contemporary people. But my view is that what these writers have to say is an accurate representation of the classical viewpoints of Judaic theology. Their basic ideas, while phrased in contemporary language, would be immediately comprehensible to the great philosophers, theologians, and rabbis in the history of Judaism. That the contemporary theologians draw upon the classical literature in an entirely authentic spirit will be immediately evident.

From the viewpoint of history of religions "Torah" is a way of living. The components of that way of living expressive of the classical mythic structure consist in the prayers said daily and on the Sabbath, the description of rites of passage, and the religious values and modes of life and religious perceptions of the rabbi, and philosopher, and the ordinary man. But there is another, important side of "Torah as a way of living." It is represented by people able to show the way of Torah to the community as a whole. Their teachings take the form of legal instructions, to be sure, about matters not ordinarily regarded as subject to law or legislation at all. The law, or *halakhah*—the way things are to be done —constitutes the authentic description of Torah as a way of living. But while paying attention to the meaning of specific Jewish observances, I stress what presently is virtually unperceived by uninformed people, gentile and Jew alike: the *halakhah* cannot be divorced from the theological convictions of Judaism. On the contrary, the *halakhah* stands as the true realization, the effective concretization in everyday actions, of those very theological convictions.

That is why the *halakhah* constitutes the sole authentic, truly normative mode of practical discourse in Judaism. There is no other way. The Judaic tradition holds that a person is not what he says or what he thinks, but what he *does*. The *halakhah* explains what the Jew is to do. Out of its rules and regulations of action therefore emerges a picture of what the Jew is supposed to *be*. The *halakhah*, of course, comprehends important ethical questions, and in my account of the Torah as a way of living, I include ethical literature. These two—law and ethics—constitute the theologically decisive statement of Torah as a way of living.

Finally, we turn to the modulations and revisions of the classical theological categories in the modern age. Just the historian of religion will explain the elements of continuity and those of change in the mythic structure of classical Judaism, so the theologian will propose to illustrate the corresponding elements of continuity and change in the theological structure of the ancient tradition.

These too are set forth within the categories of God, Torah, and Israel. What happens to ideas about God in modern Judaic theology? What are the central issues facing those who reflect upon the meaning of God and his works?

Obviously, the two great issues are, first the very formulation of a modern theological system, and second, the problem of theodicy posed so tragically by the experience of the Holocaust. These predominate in modern Judaic religious discourse, and so here too are predominant.

What of Torah—the tradition of learning, of study and interpretation, of the holy books? What has happened in modern times to the concept of Torah as revelation and as study? How have the old subjects of Torah been studied in new ways, and new subjects been made into "Torah"?

Last, what has happened to the idea of "Israel" as the holy community? What is the nature of the Jewish people today, and what constitutes the basis of its unity as a single community among mankind? What, in summary, are the religious issues facing the Jewish people out of its modern experience?

At the end comes a statement of religious affirmation made in full awareness of the primary challenge of modernity, which is secularity.

This reader reflects a mirror-image of the approach of history of religions to the description of Judaism. The latter asks about the community as a whole. Here we want to know about the leaders of the community, the guides, those who set the religious norms and establish the theological values of the Jewish people as a whole. The historian of religions asks about what *everybody* was apt to know and do and believe. Now we want to know about the creative minority and about the ideas that make sense of the knowledge, deeds, and beliefs of the ordinary people. It is only when the approaches of history of religions and of theology stand together and complement each other that a fairly balanced description of the primary traits of the Judaic religious tradition, past and present, is to be attained.

Obviously, I have had to select a few essays out of many possibilities. In the extended bibliography in *The Way of Torah* are found numerous suggestions of books and articles, readily available in English, for further study. Since my purpose is clear, the grounds for inclusion and exclusion will be equally evident, even though alternative selections for nearly every purpose are available. I have tried to choose authentic and well-informed, responsible accounts. But in each case I choose writings to which I myself am committed. The commitment does not necessarily include complete agreement or belief. It is to the accuracy and Judaic authenticity of the author. The several voices to which we are about to listen speak for me, and I say so without apology. In the introductions to the individual papers I shall explain what I mean to have them say, the questions they answer.

PART I

THE THEOLOGICAL STRUCTURE
OF CLASSICAL JUDAISM

In *The Way of Torah* we observe that the recitation of the *Shema*
—"Hear O Israel, the Lord our God, the Lord is one"—contains the
proclamation of the entire Judaic creed. The *Shema* celebrates God as
creator of the world, revealer of the Torah, and redeemer of Israel.

These three elements—creation, revelation, and redemption—
produce in theological discourse three corresponding categories. The
first is the concept of one God. The second is the belief in the Torah as
the divine revelation—and not in the Torah given at Sinai alone, but in
all the later insights into, and interpretations of, that Torah. The third
is the conviction that the religious community constitutes a holy people,
Israel.

We now consider the exposition and explanation of these three
theological categories.

First, what is the meaning of the belief in one God? What is the
relationship between God and man?

Second, how is modern man to understand the conception of
revelation? What is the relationship between the revealed Torah and
the attempts over the centuries to explain and enhance the original
revelation through the writing of commentaries? How is the possibility
of new and creative effort to be preserved in the face of the original
and comprehensive revelation?

What did "study of Torah" as a religious ideal mean in the life of
the Jewish people? How did it shape and affect the everyday activities
of the Jews?

Third, how does classical Judaism view the Jewish people, Israel,
and understand its election? And, to introduce an essential corollary,
what is the historical religious relationship between the Jewish people
and the land of Israel, the holy people and the holy land?

The answers to these questions do not constitute the whole of
classical Judaic theology, but they address its fundamental and predominant concerns.

MONOTHEISM

The *Shema* asserts that God is one. The unity of God implies several things. First, God is unique. None other is like him. Second, God is one alone, there are no others. Third, God is the ultimate; all being, all life, begins with him. There is no reality beyond him, no power above him, no other source of vitality.

These are the primary assertions of classical Judaic theology. They stand at the beginning. For Judaism, starting with the Hebrew Scriptures, God is transcendent, above nature. He is not immanent or part of nature. He is not subject to the laws of nature. He makes those laws. He is not affected by the deeds and doings of men. He decrees those deeds, determines the history of men and nations. Whatever happens reveals part of the divine decree or plan for the world.

Abraham Joshua Heschel, until his death in December, 1972, professor at the Jewish Theological Seminary, points out that monotheism cannot be taken for granted. The appeal of the contrary view—that there are many gods, that these gods are part of, and express aspects within, nature—is considerable. But the concept of unity is compelling. Man seeks integration, wholeness, completeness—and these lead to the preference for unity over diffusion, coherence over disorder.

We address to him these questions: What are the dimensions of the concept of unity? Is the idea static and one-dimensional, or does unity represent a supple idea with many sides, many potentialities?

Whence comes the vision of unity, the ideal of ultimate unification with God? How does biblical literature express this idea?

Is unity primarily a negation of the multiplicity of Gods? Does it contain only a denial, or an affirmation?

In what ways does the oneness of God express the uniqueness of God? If one means "only," then what reality is there beyond God?

What place is there for evil in the world made by one God? If God is the ground of all being, then where is God?

13

I

ONE GOD

Abraham Joshua Heschel

(From *Man Is Not Alone. A Philosophy of Religion*, by Abraham Joshua Heschel. N.Y., 1951: Farrar, Straus, and Young, Inc., pp. 111-123.)

THE ATTRACTION OF PLURALISM

It is strange that modern students of religion fail to realize the constant necessity for the protest against polytheism. The idea of unity is not only one upon which the ultimate justification of philosophical, ethical and religious universalism depends, but also one which is still beyond the grasp of most people. Monotheism, to this day, is at variance with vulgar thinking; it is something against which popular instinct continues to rebel. Polytheism seems to be more compatible with emotional moods and imagination than uncompromising monotheism, and great poets have often felt drawn to pagan gods. The world over, polytheism exercises an almost hypnotic appeal, stirring up powerful, latent yearnings for pagan forms; for it is obviously easier to an average mind to worship under polytheistic than under monotheistic thought.

Yet, while popular and even poetic imagination is fascinated by a vision of ultimate pluralism, metaphysical thought as well as scientific reflection is drawn to the concept of unity.

UNITY AS A GOAL

It is impossible to ignore the patent fact that unity is that which the uninterrupted advance of knowledge and experience leads us to, whether or not we are consciously striving for it. In our own age we have been forced into the realization that, in terms of human relations, there will be either one world or no world. But political and moral unity as a goal presupposes unity as a source; the brotherhood of men would be an empty dream without the fatherhood of God.

14

Eternity is another word for unity. In it, past and future are not apart; here is everywhere, and now goes on forever. The opposite of eternity is diffusion not time. Eternity does not begin when time is at its end. Time is eternity broken in space, like a ray of light refracted in the water.

The vision of the unbroken ray above the water, the craving for unity and coherence, is the predominant feature of a mature mind. All science, all philosophy, all art are a search after it. But unity is a task, not a condition. The world lies in strife, in discord, in divergence. Unity is beyond, not within, reality. We all crave it. We are all animated by a passionate will to endure; and to endure means to be *one*.

The world is *not* one with God, and this is why His power does not surge unhampered throughout all stages of being. Creature is detached from the Creator, and the universe is in a state of spiritual disorder. Yet God has not withdrawn entirely from this world. The spirit of this unity hovers over the face of all plurality, and the major trend of all our thinking and striving is its mighty intimation. The goal of all efforts is to bring about the restitution of the unity of God and world. The restoration of that unity is a constant process and its accomplishment will be the essence of Messianic redemption.

NO DENIAL OF PLURALITY

Xenophones, looking at the universe, said: "All is one." Parmenides, in taking the one seriously, was bound to deny the reality of everything else. Moses, however, did not say: "All is one," but: "God is One." Within the world there is the stubborn fact of plurality, divergence and conflict: "See, I have set before thee this day life and good, death and evil" (Deuteronomy 30:15). But God is the origin of all:

I am the Lord, and there is none else;
Beside Me there is no God . . .
I am the Lord, and there is none else;
I form the light, and create darkness;
I make peace, and create evil;
I am the Lord, that doeth all these things.

(Isaiah 45:5-7)

WHITHER SHALL I GO . . .

The vision of the One, upon which we stake our effort and our ultimate hope, is not to be found in contemplations about nature or

history. It is a vision of Him who transcends the scenes of both, subdued yet present everywhere, giving us the power to aid in bringing
about ultimate unification.

Whither shall I go from Thy spirit?
Or whither shall I flee from Thy presence?
If I ascend up into heaven, Thou art there;
If I make my bed in the netherworld, behold, Thou
    art there . . .
And if I say: Surely the darkness shall envelope me,
And the Light about me shall be night,
Even the darkness is not too dark for Thee . . .

                                        (Psalms 139:8-12)

Mythopoeic thought is drawn to the beauty of the sparkling
waves, their relentless surge and tantalizing rhythm. Abiding in the
fragment, it accepts the instrumental as the final, it has an image, an
expression that corresponds to its experience. In contrast, he who
takes the ineffable seriously is not infatuated with the fraction. To his
mind there is no power in the world which could bear the air of
divinity.

Nothing we can count, divide or surpass—a fraction or plurality—
can be taken as the ultimate. Beyond two is one. Plurality is incompatible with the sense of the ineffable. You cannot ask in regard to the
divine: Which one? There is only one synonym for God: One.

To the speculative mind the oneness of God is an idea inferred
from the idea of the ultimate perfection of God; to the sense of the
ineffable the oneness of God is self-evident.

HEAR, O ISRAEL

Nothing in Jewish life is more hallowed than the saying of the
Shema: "Hear, O Israel, the Lord is our God, the Lord is One." All over
the world "the people acclaim His Oneness evening and morning, twice
every day, and with tender affection recite the *Shema*" (*Kedusha* of
Musaf on the Sabbath). The voice that calls: "Hear, He is One," is
recalled, revived. It is the climax of devotion at the close of the Day of
Atonement. It is the last word to come from the lips of the dying Jew
and from the lips of those who are present at that moment.

Yet ask an average Jew what the adjective "one" means, and he
will tell you its negative meaning—it denies the existence of many
deities. But is such a negation worth the price of martyrdom which Israel
was so often willing to pay for it? Is there no positive content in it to

justify the unsurpassed dignity which the idea of One God has attained in Jewish history? Furthermore, doubts have been raised whether the term "one" is at all meaningful when applied to God. For how can we designate Him by a number? A number is one of a series of symbols used in arranging quantities, in order to set them in a relation to one another. Since God is not in time or space, not a part of a series, "the term 'one' is just as inapplicable to God as the term 'many'; for both unity and plurality are categories of quantity, and are, therefore, as inapplicable to God as crooked and straight in reference to sweetness, or salted and insipid in reference to a voice" (Maimonides, *The Guide of the Perplexed*, I, 57).

The boldness of coming out against all deities, against the sanctities of all nations, had more behind it than the abstraction: "One, not many." Behind that revolutionary statement: "All the gods of the nations are vanities," was a new insight into the relation of the divine to nature: "but He made the heavens" (Psalms 96:5). In paganism the deity was a part of nature, and worship was an element in man's relation to nature. Man and his deities were both subjects of nature. Monotheism in teaching that God is the Creator, that nature and man are both fellow-creatures of God, redeemed man from exclusive allegiance to nature. The earth is our sister, not our mother.

The young lions roar after their prey,
And seek their food from God . . .
Living creatures, both small and great . . .
All of them wait for Thee,
That Thou mayest give them their food in due season.
(Psalms 104:21, 25, 27)

The heavens are not God, they are His witnesses: they declare His glory.

ONE MEANS UNIQUE

One in the meaning of "One, not many," is but the beginning of a series of meanings. Its metaphysical incongruousness with the spiritual idea of God notwithstanding, it stands forever like a barrier to prevent the flow of polytheistic nonsense that always threatens to devastate the minds of men. Yet the true meaning of divine unity is not in His being one in a series, one among others. Monotheism was not attained by means of numerical reduction, by bringing down the multitude of deities to the smallest possible number. One means *unique*.

The minimum of knowledge is the knowledge of God's uniqueness.[1]
His being unique is an aspect of His being ineffable.

To say He is more than the universe would be like saying that
eternity is more than a day.

Of this I am sure: His essence is different from all I am able to
know or say. He is not only superior, He is incomparable. There is no
equivalent of the divine. He is not "an aspect of nature," not an
additional reality, existing along with this world, but a reality that is
over and above the universe.

He is One, and there is no other
To compare to Him, to place beside him.

(Yigdal)

With whom will ye compare Me
That I should be similar?
Saith the Holy One.

(Isaiah 40:25)

The Creator cannot be likened to what He created:
Lift up your eyes on high,
And see: who hath created these?

(Isaiah 40:26)

ONE MEANS ONLY

God is one means He alone is truly real. One means exclusively,
no one else, no one besides, alone, only. In I Kings 4:19, as well as
in other biblical passages, *ehad* means "only." Significantly the ety-
mology of the English word "only" is one-ly.

"What are we?   What is our life? What is our goodness? What
our righteousness? What our helpfulness? What our strength? What
our might? What can we say in Thy presence, Lord our God and God
of our fathers? Indeed, all the heroes are as nothing before Thee, the
men of renown as though they never existed, the wise as if they were
without knowledge, the intelligent as though they lacked understanding; for most of their doings are worthless, and the days of their life
are vain in Thy sight" (Morning Service).

God is One; He alone is real. "All the nations are as nothing
before Him; they are accounted by Him as things of nought, and
vanity" (Isaiah 40:17).

"For we must needs die, and as water spilt on the ground which
cannot be gathered up again" (II Samuel 14:14).

ONE MEANS THE SAME

The speculative mind can only formulate isolated questions, asking at times: What is the origin of all being? and at other times: What is the meaning of existence? To the sense of the ineffable there is only one question, extending beyond all categories of expression, aspects of which are reflected in such questions as: Who created the world? Who rules the history of man? And Israel's answer is: One God. One denotes inner unity: His law *is* mercy; His mercy *is* law.

"One" in this sense signifies "the same." This is the true meaning of "God is One." He is a being who is both beyond and here, both in nature and in history, both love and power, near and far, known and unknown, Father and Eternal. The true concept of unity is attained only in knowing that there is one being who is both Creator and King; "I am the Lord, thy God, who brought thee out of the land of Egypt" (Exodus 20:2). It is this declaration of the *sameness,* of the identity of the Creator and the Redeemer, with which the Decalogue begins.[2]

They depicted Thee in countless visions;
Despite all comparisons Thou art One.
                              (*The Hymn of Glory*)

His is only a single way: His power is His love, His justice is His mercy. What is divergent to us is one in Him. This is a thought to which we may apply the words of Ibn Gabirol:

Thou art One
And none can penetrate . . .
The mystery of Thy unfathomable unity . . .
                              (Ibn Gabirol, *Keter Malhut*)

GOOD AND EVIL

Moral sentiments do not originate in reason as such. A most learned man may be wicked, while a plain unlettered man may be righteous. Moral sentiments originate in man's sense of unity, in his appreciation of what is common to men. Perhaps the most fundamental statement of ethics is contained in the words of the last prophet of Israel: "Have we not all one Father? Has not one God made us? Then why do we break faith with one another, every man with his fellow, by dishonouring our time-honoured troth?" (Malachi 2:10). The ultimate principle of ethics is not an imperative but an ontological fact. While it is true that what distinguishes a moral attitude is the consciousness of obligation to do it, yet an act is not good because we feel obliged to do it; it is rather that we feel obliged to do it because it is good.

The essence of a moral value is neither in its being valid independent of our will nor in its claim that it ought to be done for its own sake. These characteristics refer only to our attitude to such values rather than to their essence. They, furthermore, express an aspect that applies to logical or esthetic values as well.

Seen from God, the good is identical with life and organic to the world; wickedness is a disease, and evil identical with death. For evil is *divergence,* confusion, that which *alienates* man from man, man from God, while good is *convergence,* togetherness, *union.* Good and evil are not qualities of the mind but relations within reality. Evil is division, contest, lack of unity, and as the unity of all being is prior to the plurality of things, so is the good prior to evil.

Good and evil persist regardless of whether or not we pay attention to them. We are not born into a vacuum, but stand, *nolens volens,* in relations to all men and to one God. Just as we do not create the dimensions of space in order to construct geometrical figures, so we do not create the moral and the spiritual relations; they are given with existence. All we do is try to find our way in them. The good does not begin in the consciousness of man. It is being realized in the natural cooperation of all beings, in what they are for each other.

Neither stars nor stones, neither atoms nor waves, but their belonging together, their interaction, the relation of all things to one another constitutes the universe. No cell could exist alone, all bodies are interdependent, affect and serve one another. Figuratively speaking, even rocks bear fruit, are full of unappreciated kindness, when their strength holds up a wall.

HE IS ALL EVERYWHERE

Rabbi Moshe of Kobrin said once to his disciples: "Do you want to know where God is?" He took a piece of bread from the table, showed it to everybody and said: "Here is God."

In saying God is everywhere, we do not intend to say He is like the air, the parts of which are found in countless places. One in a metaphysical sense means wholeness, indivisibility. God is not partly here and partly there; He is all here and all there.

Lord, where shall I find thee?
High and hidden is thy place;
And where shall I not find thee?
The world is full of thy glory.

(Jehudah Halevi)

"Can any hide himself in secret places that I shall not see him? saith the Lord. Do not I fill heaven and earth? saith the Lord" (Jeremiah 23:24).

God is within all things, not only in the life of man. "Why did God speak to Moses from the thornbush?" was a question a pagan asked of a rabbi. To the pagan mind He should have appeared upon a lofty mountain or in the majesty of a thunderstorm. And the rabbi answered: "To teach you that there is no place on earth where the Shechinah is not, not even a humble thornbush" (Exodus Rabba 2:9; cf. Song of Songs Rabba 3:16). Just as the soul fills the body, so God fills the world. Just as the soul carries the body so God carries the world.

The natural and the supernatural are not two different spheres, detached from one another as heaven from earth. God is not beyond but right here; not only close to my thoughts but also to my body. This is why man is taught to be aware of His presence, not only by prayer, study and meditation but also in his physical demeanor, by how and what to eat and drink, by keeping the body free from whatever sullies and defiles.

"An idol is near and far; God is far and near" (Deuteronomy Rabba 2:6). "God is far, and yet nothing is closer than He." "He is near with every kind of nearness" (Jerushalmi Berachot 13a).

It is His otherness, ineffable and immediate as the air we breathe and do not see, which enables us to sense His distant nearness. "For thus saith the high and lofty One that inhabiteth eternity, whose name is Holy; I dwell in the high and holy place, with him also that is of a contrite and humble spirit, to revive the spirit of the humble, and to revive the heart of the contrite ones" (Isaiah 57:15).

UNITY IS CONCERN

Unity of God is power for unity of God with all things. He is one in Himself and striving to be one with the world. Rabbi Samuel ben Ammi remarked that the Biblical narrative of creation proclaims: "One day . . . a second day . . . a third day," and so on. If it is a matter of time reckoning, we would expect the Bible to say: "One day . . . two days . . . three days" or: "The first day . . . the second day . . . the third day," but surely not one, second, third! ̄

Yom ehad, one day, really means the day which God desired to be *one* with man. "From the beginning of creation the Holy One, blessed be He, longed to enter into partnership with the terrestrial world." The unity of God is a concern for the unity of the world.

FOOTNOTES

1. In Hebrew the word *ehad* means both one and unique. It is in the latter sense in which *ehad* is to be understood in the passage of II Samuel 7:23, incorporated in the afternoon service for the Shabbath: "Thou art One and Thy name is One; and who is like Thy people Israel unique *(ehad)* on earth." This was also the understanding of the rabbis, cf. Bechorot 6b. The Targum renders *ehad* with "unique" in Genesis 26:10. *Ehad* is taken in the sense of *meyuhad,* i.e., "unique," unlike other beings, in Megillah 28a. In rabbinic literature God is sometimes called *Yehido shel olam,* the Unique of the universe, or *Yahid be-olamo,* cf. Tanhuma Buber I, 49a: "because God is unique in the universe, He knows the character of every single creature and their minds!" Compare also Hullin 28a, 83b; Bechorot 17a.
2. The Decalogue does not represent, as some scholars assert, a tribal henotheism in the sense that the tribe of Israel should recognize Him alone without denying the reality of the deities that other tribes continued to worship; a God, of whom no image should be made, who created "heaven and earth, the sea, and all that in them is" (Exodus 20:11), cannot admit the reality of other deities.

GOD AND MAN

Contemporary people suppose that the problem of religious belief begins with man, with whether or not he believes there is a God. The relationship between God and man is seen, therefore, as defined at the outset by man. But classical Judaism turns things around. The Hebrew Scriptures tell the story of a long, sometimes sad, often frustrating search. It is the search beginning with the question, "Man, where are you?" And it is God who asks the question, Adam—that is, man—who answers it.

The Hebrew Bible depicts the search of God for man, indeed his pursuit of man. What does this mean for the Judaic conception of the relationship between God and man? It means classical Judaism saw it as a relationship of concern and love. God sought man, wanted him.

Abraham Joshua Heschel describes the relationship between God and man in these terms. He therefore argues that man's yearning for God begins not with man but with God. Before faith, the question of faith itself adumbrates concern on God's part. The presence of the question—is there a God?—testifies to God.

It is fair, then, to ask Heschel these questions: What is the basis of faith? Where is its origin? What is the meaning and effect of faith?

Is faith a declaration? Is it a matter of creed, of intellectual affirmation? What is the dimension of faith? What happens thereafter within the context of Judaic belief?

Why do we find so little definition of what we *mean* by "God"? Is not the philosophical inquiry into the meaning of belief in God central to Judaic theology?

What is the origin of faith? Does it begin with each individual? Or are there earlier origins, a longer chain of believers?

II

GOD IN SEARCH OF MAN

ABRAHAM JOSHUA HESCHEL

(From *God In Search of Man*, by Abraham Joshua Heschel. Philadelphia, 1955: Jewish Publication Society of America, pp. 136-144.)

"WHERE ART THOU?"

Most theories of religion start out with defining the religious situation as man's search for God and maintain the axiom that God is silent, hidden and unconcerned with man's search for Him. Now in adopting that axiom, the answer is given before the question is asked. To Biblical thinking, the definition is incomplete and the axiom false. The Bible speaks not only of man's search for God but also of *God's search for man*. "Thou dost hunt me like a lion," exclaimed Job (10:16).

"From the very first Thou didst single out man and consider him worthy to stand in Thy presence."[1] This is the mysterious paradox of Biblical faith: *God is pursuing man*.[2] It is as if God were unwilling to be alone, and He had chosen man to serve Him. Our seeking Him is not only man's but also His concern, and must not be considered an exclusively human affair. His will is involved in our yearnings. All of human history as described in the Bible may be summarized in one phrase: *God is in search of man*. Faith in God is a response to God's question.

> Lord, where shall I find Thee?
> High and hidden in Thy place;
> And where shall I not find Thee?
> The world is full of Thy glory.
> I have sought Thy nearness;
> With all my heart have I called Thee,
> *And going out to meet Thee*
> *I found Thee coming toward me.*
> Even as, in the wonder of Thy might,

In holiness I have beheld Thee,
Who shall say he hath not seen Thee?
Lo, the heavens and their hosts
Declare the awe of Thee,
Though their voice be not heard.[3]

When Adam and Eve hid from His presence, the Lord called: *Where are thou* (Genesis 3:9). It is a call that goes out again and again. It is a still small echo of a still small voice, not uttered in words, not conveyed in categories of the mind, but ineffable and mysterious, as ineffable and mysterious as the glory that fills the whole world. It is wrapped in silence; concealed and subdued, yet it is as if all things were the frozen echo of the question: *Where are thou?*

Faith comes out of awe, out of an awareness that we are exposed to His presence, out of anxiety to answer the challenge of God, out of an awareness of our being called upon. Religion consists of *God's question and man's answer.* The way *to* faith is the way *of* faith. The way to God is a way of God. Unless God asks the question, all our inquiries are in vain.

The answer lasts a moment, the commitment continues. Unless the awareness of the ineffable mystery of existence becomes a permanent state of mind, all that remains is a commitment without faith. To strengthen our alertness, to refine our appreciation of the mystery is the meaning of worship and observance. For faith does not remain stationary. We must continue to pray, continue to obey to be able to believe and to remain attached to His presence.

Recondite is the dimension where God and man meet, and yet not entirely impenetrable. He placed within man something of His spirit (see Isaiah 63:10), and "it is the spirit in a man, the breath of the Almighty, that makes him understand" (Job 32:8).

FAITH IS AN EVENT

Men have often tried to give itemized accounts of why they must believe that God exists. Such accounts are like ripe fruit we gather from the trees. Yet it is beyond all reasons, beneath the ground, where a seed starts to become a tree, that the act of faith takes place.

The soul rarely knows how to raise its deeper secrets to discursive levels of the mind. We must not, therefore, equate the act of faith with its expression. The expression of faith is an affirmation of truth, a definite judgment, a conviction, while faith itself is *an event,* something that happens rather than something that is stored away; it is *a* *moment* in which the soul of man communes with the glory of God.*

Man's walled mind has no access to a ladder upon which he can, on his own strength, rise to knowledge of God. Yet his soul is endowed with translucent windows that open to the beyond. And if he rises to reach out to Him, it is a reflection of the divine light in him that gives him the power for such yearning. We are at times ablaze against and beyond our own power, and unless man's soul is dismissed as an insane asylum, the spectrum analysis of that ray is evidence for the truth of his insight.

For God is not always silent, and man is not always blind. His glory fills the world; His spirit hovers above the waters. There are moments in which, to use a Talmudic phrase, heaven and earth kiss each other; in which there is a lifting of the veil at the horizon of the known, opening a vision of what is eternal in time. Some of us have at least once experienced the momentous realness of God. Some of us have at least caught a glimpse of the beauty, peace, and power that flow through the souls of those who are devoted to Him. There may come a moment like a thunder in the soul, when man is not only aided, not only guided by God's mysterious hand, but also taught how to aid, how to guide other beings. The voice of Sinai goes on for ever: "These words the Lord spoke unto all your assembly in the mount out of the midst of the fire, of the cloud, and of the thick darkness, with *a great voice that goes on for ever."*5

A FLASH IN THE DARKNESS

The fact that ultimately the living certainty of faith is a conclusion derived from acts rather than from logical premises is stated by Maimonides:

"Do not imagine that these great mysteries are completely and thoroughly known to any of us. By no means: sometimes truth flashes up before us with daylight brightness, but soon it is obscured by the limitations of our material nature and social habits, and we fall back into a darkness almost as black as that in which we were before. We are thus like a person whose surroundings are from time to time lit up by lightning, while in the intervals he is plunged into pitch-dark night. Some of us experience such flashes of illumination frequently, until they are in almost perpetual brightness, so that the night turns for them into daylight. That was the prerogative of the greatest of all prophets (Moses), to whom God said: *But as for thee, stand thou here by Me* (Deuteronomy 5:28), and concerning whom Scripture said: *the skin of his face sent forth beams* (Exodus 32:39). Some see a single flash of light in the entire night of their lives. That was the state of those concerning whom it is said: *they prophesied that time and never again* (Numbers 11:25). With others again there are long or short intermissions between the flashes of illumination, and lastly there are those who are not granted that their darkness be illuminated by a flash of lightning, but only, as it were, by the gleam of some polished object or the likes of it, such as the stones and [phosphorescent] substances which shine in the dark night; and even that sparse light which illuminates us is not continuous but flashes and disappears as if it were the *gleam of the ever-turning sword* (Genesis 3:24). The degrees of perfection in men vary according to these distinctions. Those who have never for a moment seen the light but grope about in their night are those concerning whom it is said: *They know not, neither will they understand; they walk on in darkness* (Psalms 82:5). The Truth is completely hidden from them in spite of its powerful brightness, as it is also said of them: *And now men see not the light which is bright in the skies* (Job 37:21). These are the great mass of mankind . . ."⁶

Only those who have gone through days on which words were of no avail, on which the most brilliant theories jarred the ear like mere slang; only those who have experienced ultimate not-knowing, the voicelessness of a soul struck by wonder, total muteness, are able to enter the meaning of God, a meaning greater than the mind.

There is a loneliness in us that hears. When the soul parts from the company of the ego and its retinue of petty conceits; when we cease to exploit all things but instead pray the world's cry, the world's sigh, our loneliness may hear the living grace beyond all power.

We must first peer into the darkness, feel strangled and entombed in the hopelessness of living without God, before we are ready to feel the presence of His living light.

"And it shall come to pass, when I bring a cloud over the earth, that the bow shall be seen in the cloud" (Genesis 9:14). When ignorance and confusion blot out all thoughts, the light of God may suddenly burst forth in the mind like a rainbow in the sky. Our understanding of the greatness of God comes about as an act of illumination. As the Baal Shem said, "like a lightning that all of a sudden illumines the whole world, God illumines the mind of man, enabling him to understand the greatness of our Creator." This is what is meant by the words of the Psalmist: "He sent out His arrows and scattered (the clouds); He shot forth lightnings and discomfited them." The darkness retreats, "The channels of water appeared, the foundations of the world were laid bare" (Psalms 18:15-16).⁷

The essence of Jewish religious thinking does not lie in entertaining a concept of God but in the ability to articulate a memory of moments of illumination by His presence. Israel is not a people of definers but a people of witnesses: "Ye are My witnesses" (Isaiah 43:10). Reminders of what has been disclosed to us are hanging over our souls like stars, remote and of mind-surpassing grandeur. They shine through dark and dangerous ages, and their reflection can be seen in the lives of those who guard the path of conscience and memory in the wilderness of careless living.

Since those perennial reminders have moved into our minds, wonder has never left us. Heedfully we stare through the telescope of ancient rites lest we lose the perpetual brightness beckoning to our souls. Our mind has not kindled the flame, has not produced these principles. Still our thoughts glow with their light. What is the nature of this glow, of our faith, and how it is perceived?

RETURN TO GOD IS AN ANSWER TO HIM

We do not have to discover the world of faith; we only have to recover it. It is not a *terra incognita,* an unknown land; it is a forgotten land, and our relation to God is a palimpsest rather than a *tabula rasa* [a blank tablet]. There is no one who has no faith. Every one of us stood at the foot of Sinai and beheld the voice that proclaimed, I am the Lord thy God.[8] Every one of us participated in saying, We shall do and we shall hear. However, it is the evil in man and the evil in society silencing the depth of the soul that block and hamper our faith. "It is apparent and known before Thee that it is our will to do Thy will. But what stands in the way? The leaven that is in the dough (the evil impulse) and the servitude of the kingdoms."[9]

In the spirit of Judaism, our quest for God is a return to God; our thinking of Him is a recall, an attempt to draw out the depth of our suppressed attachment. The Hebrew word for repentance, *teshuvah,* means *return. Yet* it also means *answer.* Return to God is an answer to Him. For God is not silent. "Return O faithless children, says the Lord" (Jeremiah 3:14).[10] According to the understanding of the Rabbis, daily, at all times, "A Voice cries: in the wilderness prepare the way of the Lord, make straight in the desert a highway for our God" (Isaiah 40:3). "The voice of the Lord cries to the city" (Micah 6:9).[11]

"Morning by morning He wakens my ear to hear as those who are taught" (Isaiah 50.4). The stirring in man to turn to God is actually a "reminder by God to man."[12] It is a call that man's physical sense does not capture, yet the "spiritual soul" in him perceives the call.[13] The most precious gifts come to us unawares and remain unnoted. God's grace resounds in our lives like a staccato. Only by retaining the seemingly disconnected notes do we acquire the ability to grasp the theme.

Is it possible to define the content of such experiences? It is not a perception of a thing, of anything physical; nor is it always a disclosure of ideas hitherto unknown. It is primarily, it seems, an enhancement of the soul, a sharpening of one's spiritual sense, an endowment with a new sensibility. It is a discovery of what is in time, rather than anything in space.

Just as clairvoyants may see the future, the religious man comes to sense the present moment. And this is an extreme achievement. For the present is the presence of God. Things have a past and a future, but only God is pure presence.

A SPIRITUAL EVENT

But if insights are not physical events, in what sense are they real?

The underlying assumption of modern man's outlook is that objective reality is physical: all non-material phenomena can be reduced to material phenomena and explained in physical terms. Thus, only those types of human experiences which acquaint us with the quantitative aspects of material phenomena refer to the real world. None of the other types of our experience, such as prayer or the awareness of the presence of God, has any objective counterpart. They are illusory in the sense that they do not acquaint us with the nature of the objective world.

In modern society, he who refuses to accept the equation of the real and the physical is considered a mystic. However, since God is not an object of a physical experience, the equation implies the impossibility of His existence. Either God is but a word not designating anything real or He is at least as real as the man I see in front of me.

This is the premise of faith: Spiritual events are real. Ultimately all creative events are caused by spiritual acts. The God who creates heaven and earth is the God who communicates His will to the mind of man.

"In Thy light we shall see light" (Psalms 36:10). There is a divine light in every soul, it is dormant and eclipsed by the follies of this world. We must first awaken this light, then the upper light will come upon us. In Thy light which is within us will we see light (Rabbi Aaron of Karlin).

We must not wait passively for insights. In the darkest moments we must try to let our inner light go forth. "And she rises while it is yet night" (Proverbs 31:15).

FOOTNOTES

1. The liturgy of the Day of Atonement.
2. "Said Rabbi Yose: Judah used to expound, *The Lord came from Sinai* (Deuteronomy 33:2). Do not read thus, but read, *The Lord came to Sinai.* I, however, do not accept this interpretation, but, *The Lord came from Sinai,* to welcome Israel as a bridegroom goes forth to meet the bride." *Mechilta, Bahodesh* to 19:17. God's covenant with Israel was an act of grace. "It was He who initiated our delivery from Egypt in order that we should become His people and He our King," *Kuzari* II, 50. "The first man would never have known God, if He had not addressed, rewarded and punished him. . . . By this he was convinced that He was the Creator of the world, and he characterized Him by words and attributes and called Him *the Lord*. Had it not been for this experience, he would have been satisfied with the name God; he would not have perceived what God was, whether He is one or many, whether He knows individuals or not." *Kuzari,* IV, 3.
3. See *Selected Poems of Jehudah Halevi,* translated by N. Salamon. Philadelphia, 1928, pp. 134-135.
4. *Man is Not Alone,* p. 87f.
5. Deuteronomy 5:19, according to the Aramaic translation of Onkelos and Jonathan ben Uzziel and to the interpretation of *Sanhedrin,* 17b; Sotah, 10b; and to the first interpretation of Rashi.
6. *More Nebuchim,* introduction, ed. J. Ibn Shmuel, Jerusalem, 1947, pp. 6-7. *The Guide of the Perplexed,* translated by Ch. Rabin, London, 1952, p. 43f. In a somewhat similar vein, we read in the Zohar, the Torah reveals a thought "for an instant and then straightway clothes it with another garment, so that it is hidden there and does not show itself. The wise, whose wisdom makes them full eyes, pierce through the garment to the very essence of the word that is hidden thereby. Thus when the word is momentarily revealed in that first instant those whose eyes are wise can see it, though it is soon hidden again." *Zohar,* vol. II, p. 98b. See also Plato, *Epistles,* VII, 341.
7. Rabbi Yaakov Yosef of Ostrog, *Rav Yevi,* Ostrog, 1808, p. 43b.
8. *Tanhuma,* Yitro, I. The words according to the Rabbis, were not heard by Israel alone, but by the inhabitants of all the earth. The divine voice divided itself into "the seventy tongues" of man, so that all might understand it. *Exodus Rabba,* 5, 9.

9. *Berachot,* 17a.
10. According to Rabbi Jonathan, "Three and a half years the *Shechinah* abode upon the Mount of Olives hoping that Israel would return, but they did not, while a voice from heaven issued announcing, Return, O faithless sons." *Lamentations Rabba,* proemium 25.
11. According to *Masechet Kallah,* ch. 5, ed. M. Higger, New York, 1936, p. 283, these passages refer to a perpetual voice.
12. "This call of God comes to him who has taken the Torah as a light of his path, attained intellectual maturity and capacity for clear apprehension, yearns to gain the Almighty's favor, and to rise to the spiritual heights of the saints, and turns his heart away from worldly cares and anxieties." Bahya, *The Duties of the Heart, Avodat Elohim,* ch. 5 (vol. II, p. 55).
13. Rabbi Mordecai Azulai, *Or Hachamah,* Przemysl, 1897, vol. III, p. 42b.

TORAH AS REVELATION

Classical Judaism stands upon the affirmation that God revealed the Torah to Moses at Mount Sinai. The Torah therefore contains and conveys God's will for man, and especially, for Israel, the Jewish people.

But these words refer not merely to specific, historical events. Their claim is not a historical allegation about the origins of a particular book. They are saying something rather different from the assertion, "John Milton wrote *Paradise Lost.*" That difference in intent is self-evident. Given the awesome and mysterious character of God, such as is delineated in the foregoing writing of Abraham Joshua Heschel, one can hardly suppose the classical Judaic theologians maintained something so mundane as the view that somehow the Ground of Being and Creator of the World dictated a little collection of histories and laws to his secretary, Moses.

But if something more is alleged, what is that additional and transcendent assertion? Jakob J. Petuchowski, a theologian at Hebrew Union College-Jewish Institute of Religion, Cincinnati, addresses this question. He takes his place in a long line of Judaic theologians to ask about the meaning of revelation. While he addresses the modern Jew, his analysis accurately represents the classical issues, formulated in the classical way, and answered in dialogue with the classical sources.

He compares the allegation that God gave the Torah to Moses— the image is, "who brought forth the Torah from heaven"—with the belief that God is to be thanked for bringing bread forth from the earth. This analogy is important in two ways.

First, it provides a means of interpreting the image of God's giving the Torah.

Second, it entirely removes the burden of literalism from the concept of revelation, for no one claims, when he thanks God for bringing bread forth from the earth, that God himself ploughed the field, milled the grain and baked the bread.

We want to know how one may justify interpreting the concept of revelation in this way. On what basis does the Judaic theologian argue that the biblical image is an analogy? What is the authority behind his argument?

In dealing with these questions, we enter the framework of discourse characteristic of classical Judaic theology. We want to understand how a Judaic theologian does his work. Does he appeal only to Scripture? Or is the liturgy part of the theological corpus? Is he able to draw upon the normative, legal literature, or only on the extra-legal sayings and traditions?

Above all, are we able to *explain* the analogy between bread from earth and Torah from heaven? Is this merely a device for apologetics, or can we show that the analogy rests upon more fundamental foundations? Do the Scriptures themselves recognize the relationship between "bread" and "Torah?"

III

NOT BY BREAD ALONE

JAKOB J. PETUCHOWSKI

(From *Heirs of the Pharisees,* by Jakob J. Petuchowski. N.Y., 1970: Basic Books, pp. 100-109.)

Bread, the "staff of life," the staple of man's sustenance in symbol and in fact, is regarded in the Jewish Tradition as a gift from God. Partaking of it, the pious Jew engages in what is quite consciously seen to be an imitation of a sacrificial act. His hands must have been washed so that he breaks bread in a state of ritual purity similar to that demanded of the priests in the Jerusalem Temple. He says a prayer before breaking bread, and prior to eating it, he dips his slice of bread in salt—even as salt was an absolute prerequisite in the ancient sacrificial cult.[1] A lengthy grace concludes those of his meals during which bread is eaten. And even after the meal, bread continues to be treated with respect. A pious Jew will guard the leftovers and crumbs from willful destruction almost with the same care which a Roman Catholic priest bestows upon the leftovers of the eucharistic wafer.

While the Talmud recognizes the validity of even a simple doxology like "Praised be the Merciful One, the Master of this bread,"[2] the standard form of the Jewish "Grace before Meals" has long been the following: "Praised art Thou, O Lord our God, Ruler of the Universe, who bringest forth bread from the earth." The idea that it is God who brings forth bread from the earth is one at which even liberal religious Jews do not take umbrage. They do not suspect it of primitive anthropomorphism. They do not feel that their knowledge of the natural sciences has taught them better. And why should there be an objection to this simple prayer? Were not the Jews who first uttered it themselves engaged in agricultural pursuits knowing full well man's own share in the production of bread? God was indeed the Heavenly Provider, but man had to do the plowing, the reaping, the grinding,

35

and the baking. Man may even have to spread manure over his fields before they will yield their produce! And yet, there is the recognition of what moderns might call man's dependence on natural processes, and of what the ancients more readily saw as man's dependence on Nature's God.

When, therefore, it became known, some years ago, that in some of the Israeli settlements they had substituted for the old prayer the phrase, "Praised be the farmer who brings forth bread from the earth," there was a feeling of annoyance by no means confined to Orthodox circles. No, with all his knowledge of the workings of Nature, the modern liberal Jew can still share his ancestors' gratitude to the God "who brings forth bread from the earth."

What the liberal religious Jew finds difficult, if not impossible, to do is to share his ancestors' conviction that the God who brings forth bread from the earth also brings forth His Torah from Heaven. Now, it may seem curious that we should have introduced a discussion of the doctrine of Revelation with a brief disquisition on the Jewish attitude toward bread. But the two subjects happen to be more closely related than might appear at first sight.

Grammatically, the phrase, "bread from the earth" (*lechem min ha-aretz*), has the same structure as the traditional name for Revelation (*torah min hashamayim,* literally: "Torah from Heaven"); and there is a beautiful symmetry in the thought that the God who supplies our material needs from the earth also nourishes our spiritual needs from above. It may, of course, be argued that the word "Heaven" is merely a metonym for God Himself. As such, it does, in fact, frequently occur in Rabbinic literature.[3] There is, then, ample support for David Hoffmann's view[4] that, when the *Mishnah*[5] denies a share in the World-to-Come to him who says that "the Torah is not from Heaven," it is thinking of one who claims that "the Torah is not from *God.*" On the other hand, "Heaven" was surely not understood as a mere metonym for God in that version of the "Blessing over the Torah" which is recorded in the Tractate *Sopherim,*[6] and which reads:

> Praised art Thou, O Lord,
> Who hast given us a Torah from Heaven
> And eternal life on high.
> Praised art Thou, O Lord, Giver of the Torah.

To say to God in a direct address: "Thou hast given us a Torah from God" is not a very likely liturgical phrase; nor, were we to accept such an interpretation, would the poetic parallelism be preserved that matches the "Torah from Heaven" with the "eternal life on high." Besides, the idea that God reveals Himself "from Heaven" is certainly a biblical one![7] Nevertheless, while admitting that the parallel present by *torah min hashamayim* to *lechem min ha-aretz* first inspired these meditations, we do not want to press the point too far nor wish it to be regarded as the crux of our argument.

We are on firmer ground in drawing attention to the *halakhic* (i.e., legal) relation between the blessing over bread and that over the Torah. The Rabbis were aware of the fact that the only blessing explicitly commanded in the Torah itself is the "Grace after Meals." It is found in Deuteronomy 8:10, "And thou shalt eat, and thou shalt be satisfied, and thou shalt bless the Lord thy God for the good land which He hath given thee." The Torah does not explicitly prescribe a blessing to be recited before or after the reading of the Torah. But in the words, "He hath given thee," in the law relating to the "Grace after Meals" the Tosephta[8] sees a reference to the blessing to be recited over the Torah and the performance of the commandments. This is based on the fact that the same word, "give" occurs in Exodus 24:12, where God says to Moses: "Come up to Me into the mount, and be there; *and I will give thee* the tables of stone, and the law and the commandment, which I have written, that thou mayest teach them." Similar arguments occur in other parts of Rabbinic literature.[9]

Perhaps the most detailed form of the argument deriving the obligation to recite a blessing over the Torah from the biblical commandment to say "Grace after Meals" is to be found in Karaite literature. Rejecting the Rabbinic hermeneutics, the Karaites were forced to employ their own, above all the kiyyas (the argument by analogy), in all cases where they wished to retain a Rabbinic observance and had to find their own support for it in the Bible. Thus we find Anan, the founder of the sect, reasoning as follows, in his *Sepher Ha-Mitzwoth*:[10]

Scripture commands the blessing over food in Deuteronomy 8:10. In Ezekiel 3:1 we read about the Prophet's being bidden to "eat this scroll." Now, "this scroll" could only have been the Torah, which is further proved by Ezekiel's report (3:3) that "it was in my mouth as honey for sweetness," seeing that, in Psalm 19:11, the Torah itself is described as "sweeter also than honey." With this analogy between eating and Torah study thus established, it follows, - of course, that Torah reading must be accompanied by benedictions just as eating is. No doubt, Anan was more "Rabbinical" here than he would have cared to admit!

The modern mind will find the Rabbinic and the Karaite arguments equally strange, and will wonder whether the venerable institution of thanking God for the Torah really has nothing more solid to rest on than farfetched analogies between Torah reading and eating. Such skepticism is wholesome. We would indeed be doing the ancient Rabbis an injustice were we to imagine them as meditating on the words of Deuteronomy 8:10, and suddenly coming up with the discovery that what is implied here is a blessing over the Torah. It is much more likely that the blessing over the Torah was instituted on its own merits,[11] and that only afterward did the Rabbis look for a "proof-text" in the Bible.

Yet, if the sequence was indeed such as we have tried to indicate, and as the modern reader would naturally be inclined to assume, if, that is to say, we are in a position to look above and beyond the mere formal structure of Rabbinic hermeneutics, there is still a question to which an answer must be attempted. Supposing that the Rabbis were looking for a biblical basis for the blessing over the Torah, why, of all things, did they go to the "Grace after Meals"? Surely, they should not have found it too difficult to come across something more apropos, something more explicitly and intrinsically related to the institution of the Torah blessing which they were trying to promote!

In other words, we suspect that, over and above the merely formal analogy they discovered between the eating of bread and the reading of the Torah, they were aware of a deeper underlying connection. Could it have been the verse in Deuteronomy 8:3, "Man doth not live by bread alone, but by everything that proceedeth out of the mouth of the Lord doth man live"? Or take the beginning of the fifty-fifth chapter of the Book of Isaiah:

Ho, every one that thirsteth, come ye for water,
And he that hath no money;
Come ye, buy and eat;
Yea, come, buy wine and milk
Without money and without price.
Wherefore do ye spend money for that which is not bread?
And your grain for that which satisfieth not?
Hearken diligently unto Me, and eat ye that which is good,
And let your soul delight itself in fatness.

Not only are the traditional Jewish commentators unanimous in regarding this as an invitation to the people to avail itself of *spiritual* sustenance, but, in the light of the context, it is hard to assume that the Prophet could have meant anything else. The hunger and the thirst he had in mind was that, as Amos had asserted before him,[12] "of hearing the words of the Lord."

It is, therefore, not simply a matter of an arid legalism if the Rabbis established a relationship between bread and Torah. It was part of Israel's Prophetic tradition. It was also implied in the Festival of *Shavuoth* [Pentecost], with its twofold aspect of harvest festival and feast of Revelation. As Theodor H. Gaster aptly remarks, "If, in the primitive argricultural rite, man offers God two loaves of the new bread as a symbol of cooperation, in the historical counterpart—by a fine and inspired inversion—God offers to man the two tablets of the Law."[13]

The connection between bread and Torah is of more than historical interest to us. In it may be found the solution of a very modern theological problem. We have already noted that the modern liberal Jew is not deterred by his knowledge of natural processes and agricultural "know-how" from regarding God as the One "who brings forth bread from the earth." But, when it comes to the old doctrine of "Torah from Heaven," the modern liberal Jew balks.

Having been made aware of the human element which went into the composition of the Bible, having learned to prefer the laborious process of *Quellenscheidung* (separation of the various sources and strata) to the "naive" belief in a Sinaitic Revelation which was *einmalig* (once and for all time), he feels that he can no longer accept the "primitive" dogma of *torah min hashamayim*. Perhaps the responsibility is not altogether his own. He may have been driven to this position by Orthodox intolerance. The Orthodox rabbinate of the nineteenth century was apt to see in the slightest demand for external reforms an evidence of apostasy, a denial of fundamental Jewish dogma. Of course, according to the Rabbinic interpretation of Numbers 15:31, the slightest reservation about the complete divine origin of the entire Torah was sufficient to place one in the category of those who "despise the word of the Lord." And this includes him who believes in the divine origin of the whole Torah, but has reservations about certain laws not explicitly stated there, but merely derived from the text by means of one or another of the Rabbinic hermeneutic rules.[14]

The anti-Sadducean point of such remarks is very obvious, and though such an extremist interpretation of the divine origin of the Torah may have been justified in its time, it is, to say the least, questionable whether it should have been pressed against the Reformers of the nineteenth century. The effect was what in Rabbinic idiom might be described as "a thrusting away with both hands" and as a "closing of the door in front of the potential penitents." The time was to come when the Reformers would accept the Orthodox accusations—and feel proud of them!

That, however, is only one side of the coin. The other has to do with the inner development of the Reform movement itself. Just as in the case of the Rabbinic derivation of the Torah blessing from the law of Deuteronomy 8:10 the practice itself preceded the finding of a basis in Scripture, so, in the case of the Reformers, it will have to be admitted that, by and large, the theological foundations came *after* the practical reforms. In other words, we are not to imagine that an Orthodox Jew studied the Prophets and, on that basis alone, came to the conclusion that the dietary laws were of no religious consequence —whereupon he bit into a ham sandwich. Rather was it the man, already lax in ritual observance, who found support for his deviations from Tradition in what he called "Prophetic Religion."

Seen in this light, the incorporation of the Higher Criticism of the Bible into the theological foundations of Reform Judaism in the twentieth century (though, be it noted, not before, and not by the original apostles of Classical Reform!) becomes intelligible as a kind of "Occam's Razor" for the purpose of dealing with Judaism's adjustment to the practical problems of modern life. Instead of arguing *within* the framework of the traditional *Halakhah* (Jewish Law), which is not always easy, and which, as Conservative Jews well know, always invites the fierce opposition of the Orthodox who can play at the same game, Reform cut the Gordian knot by denying the very premise on which *Halakhah* is predicated, namely the doctrine of "Torah from Heaven."

The Bible became a human, instead of a divine, document. It was read as a record of man's quest for God, rather than as a statement of God's demands on man. In this manner, the detection of the human element became synonymous with disproving the divine authorship.

"For the basis of the old legalism has crumbled away," wrote Claude G. Montefiore.[15] "We no longer believe in the Mosaic and divine origin of the *whole* Pentateuchal law; we no longer believe that all the ordinances date from the same period, and that they are *all* perfect, immutable, and divine. Some of the ceremonial laws may be, in their ultimate origin, much older than Moses, resting as they do upon primordial conceptions, and even upon superstitions or taboos, which have wholly passed away, while others of the ceremonial laws are undoubtedly much later than Moses."

Yet the late Claude G. Montefiore would hardly have approved of the following statement: "For the basis of the old *motzi* [blessing over the bread] has crumbled away. We no longer believe that God is personally concerned with the production of each and every slice of bread, so that the very sandwich we eat could be thought of as a direct gift from God. Some of the ideas behind the *motzi* may be, in their ultimate origin, much older than Judaism, resting as they do upon primordial conceptions, and even upon superstitions and remnants of animism and the worship of fertility gods, which have wholly passed away, while, unlike the ancient Israelite, the modern Jew is fully aware of the processes from gestation through packaging which bring the bread upon his table." Claude G. Montefiore would not have approved of this because, as a deeply religious soul, he was able to perceive the hand of the Creator behind the physical aspects of His creation.

We suggest that a similar view could be taken of the doctrine of "Torah from Heaven"—even by those who feel quite confident that they are able to determine precisely who wrote what, and when, in the post-Mosaic literary history of the so-called Law of Moses. As Franz Rosenzweig wrote to Jakob Rosenheim:

Even if Wellhausen would turn out to be right in all his theories, . . . it would not make the slightest difference to our faith. . . . We, too, translate the Torah as *one* book. For us, too, it is the work of *one* spirit. We do not know who it was; that it was Moses we cannot believe. Among ourselves we call him by the sign which the Higher Criticism uses to designate the final redactor assumed by it, "R." But we resolve this sign not into "Redactor," but into *"Rabbenu"* [Our Teacher]. For, whoever he was, and whatever sources he might have utilized, he is our Teacher, and his theology is our Teaching.[16]

The time is past when the mere denial of the doctrine of "Torah from Heaven" was deemed capable of solving all the practical problems of Reform Judaism. The assumption of the existence of various strata in the composition of the Pentateuch is no longer such a novelty. Many Conservative Jews share it; and the Protestants, who had originally discovered it, have long since proceeded to listen again for the "Word," and to transcend, though not to ignore, the multifarious stratification of sources in a higher "unity of the Bible."

It is, of course, very likely that a modern interpretation of the doctrine of "Torah from Heaven" is going to make somewhat less sweeping demands than the Rabbinic interpretation of Numbers 15:31, which we discussed above. On the other hand, a doctrine of "progressive revelation"—as preached by Reform Judaism—which does not confine the Word of God to the Written Text might not, after all, be so adverse to finding Revelation in the Oral Torah as well. At any rate, the time may well have come when the doctrine of "Torah from Heaven" should be taken seriously again.

Taking "Torah from Heaven" seriously may not be easy for the modern liberal Jew, but it is not impossible. At least, it is not impossible. At least, it is not impossible as long as his rationalism does not prevent him from thanking God for bringing forth bread from the earth. For unless this tribute to Nature's God merely covers up for an apotheosis of Nature herself, the Jew who believes in God's power to produce bread from the soil cannot very well remain deaf to the admonition that "man doth not live by bread alone, but by every thing that proceedeth out of the mouth of the Lord doth man live."

FOOTNOTES

1. Cf. Leviticus 2:13.
2. B. *Berakhoth* 40b.
3. Cf. A. Marmorstein, *The Old Rabbinic Doctrine of God* (London 1927), I, 105ff.
4. David Hoffmann, ed., *Mischnaiot, Seder Nesikin* (Berlin, 1898), p. 189, Note 9.
5. *Mishnah Sanhedrin* 10:1
6. *Sopherim* 13:8 (ed. Mueller, p. xxii).
7. Cf., for example, Deuteronomy 4:36.
8. *Tosephta Berakhoth* 7:2 (ed. Zuckermandel, pp. 15f.).
9. Cf. j. *Berakhoth*, ch. VII (11a, b); and *Abudraham*, beginning of ch. III.
10. *Sepher Hamitzvoth*, in Likkute Kadmonioth, ed. Harkavy (St. Petersburg, 1903), II, 17.
11. Cf. the blessing before the reading from the Torah as described in Nehemiah 8:5-8.
12. Amos 8:11.
13. Theodor H. Gaster, *Festivals of the Jewish Year* (New York, 1953), p. 63.
14. B. *Sanhedrin* 99a; and cf. *Sifré* to Numbers 15:31 (ed. Friedmann, p. 33a).
15. Claude G. Montefiore, *Outlines of Liberal Judaism* (London, 1912), pp. 218f.
16. Franz Rosenzweig, *Briefe* (Berlin, 1935), pp. 581f. (My translation from the German.)

TORAH AS TRADITION

In the theological description of classical Judaism, "Torah" not only refers to the revealed will of God, but also, and especially, serves as the synonym for tradition. Classical Judaism views God's will as contained in the revelation at Sinai, but also in the *record* of that revelation handed down through the ages. Revelation does not happen every day. "God speaks" when and to whom he chooses. One must, therefore, take very seriously the literature—written and oral—which preserves those moments of revelation, contains their message and conveys their meaning.

Classical Judaism posits two revelations—Torahs—from Sinai. The first is contained within the Five Books of Moses. The second comprises the teachings of the sages—the rabbis—orally handed on and then memorized, it is alleged, from Moses to Joshua, the prophets, men of the Great Assembly, the rabbis of the early centuries of the Common Era, and finally written down in the pages of the Talmud. These two Torahs are to be regarded as the authoritative record of God's will.

But having such a record raises more problems than it solves. What of the later generations, subject to the authority of the tradition formed long ago? How are they to have room for their religious creativity, their new insights, their own contribution? And what of the new issues to be addressed to the old tradition? How are these to be investigated?

If "Torah" is wholly historical, it cannot become relevant to the newest questions of the living age. If it is solely contemporary, then how does it relate to the belief in Torah as the once-for-all-time revealed will of God?

These are the issues of religious vitality. Classical Judaism above all sought to enlist within the tradition the best efforts, the great minds, of each successive generation. It made room for all that was to come by means of commentary, the process by which revelation is explained to the new generations and at the same time rendered supple and responsive to the newest concerns.

Here Gershom G. Scholem, Hebrew University of Jerusalem, the great scholar of the history of Jewish mysticism and of the history of

Judaism, explains the process of the creative, free acceptance of tradition and of its authority. We bring to him these questions:

What do we mean by "tradition"? How does tradition take shape? When does a tradition become "traditional"?

Is not tradition going to suppress creativity? If the truth already is known, what room is there for new ideas? Will not innovation become subversive? But if so, how then can the tradition remain vital?

What was the function of the "Oral Torah"—the belief that even the latest rabbis might participate in the process of uncovering the substance and meaning of the Sinaitic revelation?

What is the relationship between one-time revelation and the ongoing course of history?

Does the concept of revelation leave space for disagreement and diverse opinions? Or will it not produce a monolithic structure, incapable of supporting difference?

IV

TRADITION AND COMMENTARY

Gershom G. Scholem

(From "Tradition and Commentary as Religious Categories in Judaism," by Gershom G. Scholem. *Judaism,* Vol. 15, No. 1, Winter 1966, pp. 23-39.)

In considering the problem of tradition, we must distinguish between two questions. The first is historical: How did a tradition endowed with religious dignity come to be formed? The other question is: How was this tradition understood once it had been accepted as a religious phenomenon? For the faithful promptly discard the historical question once they have accepted a tradition; this is the usual process in the establishment of religious systems. Yet for the historian the historical question remains fundamental: in order to understand the meaning of what the faithful simply accept, the historian is not bound to accept fictions that veil more than they reveal concerning the origins of the accepted faith. Thus, tradition as a special aspect of revelation is historically a product of the process that formed rabbinic Judaism between the 4th or 3rd pre-Christian centuries and the 2nd century of the Common Era.

In all religions, the acceptance of a Divine revelation originally referred to the concrete communication of positive, substantive and expressible content. It never occurred to the bearers of such a revelation to question or to limit the specific quality and closely delineated content of the communication they had received. Where, as in Judaism, such revelation is set down in holy writings and is accepted in that form, it initially constitutes concrete communication, factual content, and nothing else. But in as much as such revelation, once set down in holy scriptures, takes on authoritative character, an essential change takes place. For one thing, new historical circumstances require that the communication, whose authoritativeness has been granted, be applied to ever changing conditions. Furthermore, the spontaneous force of human productivity seizes this communication and expands it beyond its original scope. "Tradition" thus comes into being. It embodies the realization of the effectiveness of the Word in every concrete state and relationship entered into by a society.

At this point begins the process in which two questions gain importance: How can revelation be preserved as a concrete communication, i.e., how can it be passed on from generation to generation? (This is a virtually impossible undertaking by itself). And, with ever greater urgency: Can this revelation be applied at all, and if so, how? With this second question, spontaneity has burst into the nascent tradition. In the process of this renewed productivity, holy scriptures themselves are sometimes enlarged; new written communications take their place alongside the old ones. A sort of no-man's-land is created between the original revelation and the tradition. Precisely this happened in Judaism, for example, as the Torah, to which the quality of revelation was originally confined, was "expanded" to include other writings of the Biblical canon that had at first been subsumed, completely and emphatically, under the heading of tradition and considered merely repositories of this. Later, the boundaries often shifted: the canon, as Holy Writ, confronted tradition and within the tradition itself, similar processes of differentiation between written and oral elements were repeated.

From now on tradition asserts itself ever more emphatically as a new religious value and as a category of religious thinking. It becomes the medium through which creative forces express themselves. By the side of the Written Torah tradition arraigns itself, and it is called Oral Torah from approximately the first Christian century on. Tradition is not simply the totality of that which the community possesses as its cultural patrimony and which it bequeaths to its posterity; it is a specific selection from this patrimony, which is elevated and garbed with religious authority. It proclaims certain things, sentences, or insights to be Torah, and thus connects them with the revelation. In the process, the original meaning of revelation as a unique, positively established, and clearly delineated realm of propositions is put in doubt —and thus a development as fruitful as it is unpredictable begins which is highly instructive for the religious problematic of the concept of tradition.

The unfolding of the truths, statements and circumstances that are given in or accompany revelation becomes the function of the Oral Torah, which creates in the process a new type of religious person. In the history of religion, this type has evoked admiration as much as rejection and derision, and not without reason. The Biblical scholar perceives revelation not as a unique and clearly delineated occurrence, but rather as a phenomenon of eternal fruitfulness to be unearthed and examined: "Turn it and turn it again, for everything is in it." Thus the achievement of these scholars, who established a tradition rooted in the Torah and growing out of it, is a prime example of spontaneity in receptivity. They are leaders because they know themselves to be led. Out of the religious tradition they bring forth something entirely new, something that itself commands religious dignity: commentary. Revelation needs commentary in order to be rightly understood and applied—this is the far from self-evident religious doctrine out of which grew both the phenomenon of Biblical exegesis and the Jewish tradition which it created.

This inner law of development of the concept of revelation is also traceable in other religions which accept the authority of revelation. The process under discussion here is therefore of general significance for the phenomenology of religion. Judaism experienced this process in a peculiarly vigorous and consequential form, and its agents examined it with great thoroughness. This will make our consideration of the present complex of problems especially illuminating and far-reaching.

A creative process begins to operate which will permeate and alter tradition—the Midrash: the more regulated Halachic and the somewhat freer Aggadic exegesis of scriptures, and the views of the Biblical scholars in their various schools, are regarded as implicitly contained in the Written Torah. No longer only old and carefully guarded sentences but now also the analyses of scriptures by the scholars themselves lay claim to being tradition. The desire for historical continuity which is of the very essence of tradition is translated into an historical construction whose fictitious character cannot be doubted but which serves the believing mind as a crutch of external authentication. Especially peculiar in this historical construction is the metamorphosis of the prophets into bearers of tradition—a very characteristic, albeit to our minds a very paradoxical, transformation. Originally only the last of the prophets, Haggai, Zechariah, and Malachi, had been meant by this proposition, for they possess special importance in the doctrine of the uninterrupted chain of tradition: the last of the prophets are, not without all justification, regarded as the first of the scribes and "men of the Great Assembly." Subsequently, also the older prophets are designated as links in the chain, which would otherwise have had to be invisible.

This leads to the viewpoint expressed daringly in Talmudic

writings, namely, that the total substance of the Oral Torah, which had in fact been the achievement of the scholars, comes from the same source as the Written Torah, and that it was therefore basically always known. The saying "turn it . . ." reflects this viewpoint. But underneath this fiction, the details of which do not concern us here, there lies a religious attitude which is interesting and which had significant results. I refer to the distinctive notion of revelation including within itself as sacred tradition the later commentary concerning its own meaning. This was the beginning of a road which, with a full measure of inherent logic, was to lead to the establishment of mystical theses concerning the character of revelation as well as the character of tradition.

Here we immediately encounter a significant tension in the religious consciousness of the scholars themselves, between the process by which the tradition actually developed and the interpretation of that process. On the one hand, there was the blossoming productivity of the academies where the Scriptures were explored and examined in ever greater detail—the spontaneous achievement of the generations upon whom, in turn, was bestowed such authority as was transmitted by the great teachers and the tradition. On the other hand, there arose the claim apparently flowing from the dogma of the revealed nature of the Oral Law. What this claim amounted to was that all this was somehow part of revelation itself—and more: not only was it given along with revelation, but it was given in a special, timeless sphere of revelation in which all generations were, as it were, gathered together; everything really had been made explicit to Moses, the first and most comprehensive recipient of Torah. The achievement of every generation, its contribution to tradition, was projected back into the eternal present of the revelation at Sinai. This, of course, is something which no longer has anything in common with the notion of revelation with which we began, namely, revelation as unequivocal, clear, and understandable communication. According to this doctrine, revelation comprises within it everything that will ever be legitimately offered to interpret its meaning.

The patent absurdity of this claim reveals a religious assumption that must be taken all the more seriously. The Rabbis did not hesitate to express this assumption in rather extravagant formulations. In the forty days that Moses spent on Mount Sinai (Ex. 34:28), he learned the Torah with all its implications. Rabbi Joshua ben Levi (a third-century Palestinian teacher) said: "Torah, Mishnah, Talmud, and Aggadah—were already given to Moses on Mount Sinai"—and even the questions that such a bright student will some day ask his teacher! In our context, statements such as these are highly suggestive. They make absolute the concept of tradition in which the meaning of revelation unfolds in the course of historical time—but only because everything that can come to be known has already been deposited in a timeless substratum. In other words, we have arrived at an assumption concerning the nature of truth which is characteristic of rabbinic Judaism (and probably of every traditional religious establishment): Truth is given once and for all, and it is laid down with precision. Fundamentally, truth merely needs to be transmitted. The originality of the exploring scholar has two aspects. In his spontaneity, he develops and explains that which was transmitted at Sinai, no matter whether it was always known or whether it was forgotten and had to be rediscovered. The effort of the seeker after truth consists not in having new ideas but rather in subordinating himself to the continuity of the tradition of the Divine word and in laying open what he receives from it in the context of his own time. In other words: not system but *commentary* is the legitimate form through which truth is approached.

This is a most important principle indeed for the kind of productivity we encounter in Jewish literature. Truth must be laid bare in a text in which it already preexists. We shall deal later with the nature of this preexistent givenness. In any case, truth must be brought forth from the text. Commentary thus became the characteristic expression of Jewish thinking about truth, which is another way of describing the rabbinic genius. Under the influence of Greek thought, there were also explications and attempts at system-construction within Judaism. But its innermost life is to be found where holy texts received commentary, no matter how remote from the text itself these commentaries and their ideas may appear to the present-day critical reader. There is, of course, a striking contrast between the awe of the text, founded on the assumption that everything already exists in it, and the presumptuousness of imposing the truth upon ancient texts. The commentator, who is truly the Biblical scholar, always combines both attitudes.

Tradition as a living force produces in its unfolding another problem. What had originally been believed to be consistent, unified, and self-enclosed now becomes diversified, multifold, and full of contradictions. It is precisely the wealth of contradictions, of differing views, which is encompassed and unqualifiedly affirmed by tradition. There were many possibilities of interpreting the Torah, and tradition claimed to comprise them all. It maintains the contradictory views with astounding seriousness and intrepidity, as if to say that one can never know whether a view at one time rejected may not one day become the cornerstone of an entirely new edifice. In Jewish tradition the views of the schools of Hillel and Shammai, two teachers who lived shortly before Jesus, play an important part. Their mutually contradictory attitudes toward theoretical and practical problems are codified by the Talmud with great thoroughness, although the rule is that in the application of the law the views of Hillel's school are decisive. But the rejected views are stated no less carefully than the accepted ones. The Talmudists formulated no ultimate thesis concerning the unity of these contradictions, concerning dialectical relationships within the tradition. It was only one of the latest Kabbalists who formulated the daring and, at first blush, surprising thesis, which has since been often reiterated, that the *Halachah* would be decided according to the now rejected view of the school of Shammai in the Messianic era. That is to say, the conception of the meaning and of the applicability of the Torah which is unacceptable at any given time within history in reality anticipates a Messianic condition in which it will have its legitimate function—and thereby the unity of the Torah, which embraces all of this, is fully sealed.

Thus, tradition is concerned with the realization, the enactment of the Divine task which is set in the revelation. It demands application, execution, and decision, and at the same time it is, indeed, "true growth and unfolding from within." It constitutes a living organism, whose religious authority was asserted with as much emphasis as is at all possible within this system of thought.

The question remains: Does tradition keep its freshness in such a view, or does it lose its organic ability to grow when too much is demanded of it? At what point does deadly decay lurk? The question is as important as it is hard to answer. As long as there is a living relationship between religious consciousness and revelation there is no danger to the tradition from within. But when this relationship dies tradition ceases to be a living force. To be sure, this looks very different to an outside observer. Everyone who studies the tradition of any religious community is aware of this antinomy. For example: For the Church Fathers the Rabbinical students of Scripture were still guardians of a valuable tradition; to later Christendom, they appeared incomprehensible and rather terrifying—and this at a time when the tradition enjoyed a very active inner life. For tradition omnipotence and impotence dwell closely together; all is in the eye of the beholder.

In Judaism, tradition becomes the reflective impulse that inter-

venes between the absoluteness of the Divine word—revelation—and
its receiver. Tradition thus raises a question about the possibility of
immediacy in man's relationship to the Divine, even though it has been
incorporated in revelation. To put it another way: Can the Divine
word confront us without mediation? And, can it be fulfilled without
mediation? Or, given the assumption of the Jewish tradition which we
have formulated, does the Divine word rather not require just such
mediation by tradition in order to be apprehensible and therefore
fulfillable? For rabbinic Judaism, the answer is in the affirmative.
Every religious experience after revelation is a mediated one. It is the
experience of the voice of God rather than the experience of God.
But all reference to the "voice of God" is highly anthropomorphic—a
fact from which theologians have always carefully tried to escape.

TORAH AS A WAY OF FORMING CULTURE

A group of people who live by an integrated religious doctrine, indeed by a single religious law, is apt to form a society and create a culture which will express the social and cultural effects of that doctrine and law. If you believe that God expects you to do certain things, the pattern of actions resulting from that belief will produce important results in ordinary life.

Now it is already clear that the Jews believe God wants them to study and live by the Torah. One absolutely inevitable consequence for their culture will be emphasis on intellectualism, on study and thinking. People within a culture formed by Judaism are going to lay stress on the virtues of the mind—upon heedfulness and thoughtfulness, consciousness, liveliness, interest in the reasons behind obvious things.

In the communities of Eastern Europe—Poland, Russia, Rumania, Hungary, Lithuania, Latvia, and their neighbors—the Jews came most completely and profoundly to embody the ideal of study of the Torah. The Yiddish-speaking world from the Baltic to the Black Sea and from the Oder to the Dneiper and beyond—the world wiped out by the German Nazis between 1939 and 1945—embodied better, more completely, than any Jewish world before or afterward the belief that man was made to become learned in the Torah, the traditions and laws of Judaism. That world, therefore, allows us to see exactly how the ideal of study of Torah would shape other aspects of the common life: how children were raised, how people achieved importance within society, how ordinary folk shaped their ideals of life and understood their place on this earth.

Shortly after World War II, when the full tragedy of European Jewry became known in the world, Abraham Joshua Heschel composed an account of the inner life of the lost world. He himself had grown up in Poland and had lost nearly his entire family in the Holocaust. Rather than speak about the tragedy, he addressed himself to the spiritual achievement of East European Jewry. Here he describes the role of study of Torah in the culture of the Yiddish-speaking

53

world. Later on, Joseph Landis will tell us about the religious values of the Yiddish language itself.

First, Heschel tells us, What was required to make possible the universal devotion to study of Torah on the part of the masses, not merely of the religious virtuosi? He credits the cultural achievement to the availability of commentaries, which explained for everyone the abstruse and difficult words of the Talmud and the Bible.

What in fact did "study of Torah" mean? How did the ideal affect and shape peoples' lives? What did the masses do when they studied Torah? How did they make their living? And what was the result for ordinary everyday affairs of this knowledge?

How could they afford it? In the West, learning is an aristocratic venture. One must have not only ability, but also the leisure, to study. East European Jewry was a very poor community. Where did it find the time to learn, since everyone had to work for a living?

How did the ideal of Torah enter into the home? What ways were available to communicate the ideal to children? How did "study of Torah" influence the choice of a marriage-partner? Did it produce the capacity to earn a better living, as people claim is the result of a college-education?

V

THE STUDY OF TORAH

ABRAHAM JOSHUA HESCHEL

(From *The Earth Is the Lord's. The Inner World of the Jew in East Europe*, by Abraham Joshua Heschel. N.Y., 1950, pp. 39-55, under the chapter headings, "For the People", "The Luxuries of Learning", and "Pilpul".)

An inestimable factor in the development of Ashkenazic Jewry was the democratization of Talmudic learning to a degree unknown before.

In the first five centuries following the completion of the Talmud,[1] the Babylonian academies had hegemony over Jewish life. The Jews of all lands were accustomed to consult the Geonim, the celebrated heads of the academies of Sura and Pumbeditha[2] on all points of earnest difficulty. Whenever they encountered an equivocal or obscure passage in the Talmud or a debatable issue of law, or a problem of belief, they would send their question to Babylonia. The decisions, rulings, and interpretations of those eminent scholars were both authoritative and indispensable.

It was not until the twelfth century that the Occident began to emancipate itself. In that period, two epoch-making literary events changed the intellectual conditions of Jewish learning: Rashi composed his comprehensive commentary on the Talmud, and Maimonides published his Code of Jewish Law. They rendered the Jewish masses independent of the Geonim, whose office at the time began to decline. No longer was it necessary to refer questions to Babylonia. Maimonides created for the first time a compendium that covered the entire field of law, a masterpiece of construction, unsurpassed in the profundity of its decisions and implications, ingenious in the conciseness and simplicity of its style and brilliant in its omitting the argumentative and dialectical.

But it was particularly Rashi who brought intellectual emancipation to the people. Without a commentary, the Hebrew Scripture and particularly the Talmud are accessible only to the enlightened few. The

55

old commentaries offered interpretations of isolated passages and were mostly limited to single sections of the Talmud. Rashi's Commentary, explaining with exquisite simplicity almost every word of the immense text, unraveling the involved complexities of Talmudic dialectics, is a faithful companion who attends the student to whatever part of the text he may turn. Humbly, unobtrusively, he communes with the student, conveying by a minimum of words a maximum of meaning. With the help of a short phrase or even one word, he frequently illumines what seems to be thick darkness. Instead of offering abstract dissertations on principles, methods, and legal decisions, he explains only what immediately concerns the student, the meaning of a term, the implication of a statement, the gist of an intricate argument.

Rashi democratized Jewish education, he brought the Bible, the Talmud, and the Midrash[3] to the people. He made the Talmud a popular book, everyman's book. Learning ceased to be the monopoly of the few. It spread increasingly with the passing of time. In many communities, the untutored became the rare exception.

In almost every Jewish home in Eastern Europe, even in the humblest and the poorest, stood a bookcase full of volumes; proud and stately folio tomes together with shy, small-sized books. Books were neither an asylum for the frustrated nor a means for occasional edification. They were furnaces of living strength, timeproof receptacles for the eternally valid coins of spirit. Almost every Jew gave of his time to learning, either in private study or by joining one of the societies established for the purpose of studying the Talmud or some other branch of rabbinic literature. To some people, it was impossible to pray without having been refreshed first by spending some time in the sublime atmosphere of Torah.[4] Others, after the morning prayer, would spend an hour with their books before starting to work. At nightfall, almost every one would leave the tumult and bustle of everyday life to study in the *beth ha-midrash*. Yet the Jews did not feel themselves to be "the People of the Book." They did not feel that they possessed the "Book," just as one does not feel that one possesses life. The Book, the Torah, was their essence, just as they, the Jews, were the essence of the Torah.

A typical Jewish township in Eastern Europe was "a place where Torah has been studied from time immemorial; where practically all the inhabitants are scholars, where the Synagogue or the House of Study is full of people of all classes busily engaged in studies, townfolk as well as young men from afar . . . where at dusk, between twilight and evening prayers, artisans and other simple folk gather around the tables to listen to a discourse on the great books of Torah, to interpretations of Scripture, to readings from theological, homiletical, or ethical writings like *Hovoth Ha-Levavoth*[5] and the like . . . where on the Sabbath and the holidays, near the Holy Ark, at the reading stand, fiery sermons are spoken that kindle the hearts of the Jewish people with love for the Divine Presence, sermons which are seasoned with words of comfort from the prophets, with wise parables and keen aphorisms of the sages, in a voice and a tone that heartens one's soul, that melts all limbs, that penetrates the whole being."[6]

Poor Jews, whose children knew only the taste of "potatoes on Sunday, potatoes on Monday, potatoes on Tuesday," sat there like intellectual magnates. They possessed whole treasures of thought, a wealth of information, of ideas and sayings of many ages. When a problem came up, there was immediately a host of people, pouring out opinions, arguments, quotations. One raised a question on a controversial passage in Maimonides' work, and many vied with one another in attempts to explain it, outdoing one another in the subtlety of dialectic distinctions or in citing out-of-the-way sources. The stomachs were empty, the homes barren, but the minds were crammed with the riches of Torah.

There were many who lived in appalling poverty, many who were pinched by never-ending worries, and there were plenty of taverns with strong spirits. But drunkards were rarely seen among Jews. When night came and a man wanted to pass away time, he did not hasten to a tavern to take a drink, but went to pore over a book or joined a group which—either with or without a teacher—indulged in the enjoyment of studying revered books. Physically worn out by their day's toil, they sat over open volumes, playing the austere music of the Talmud's groping for truth or the sweet melodies of exemplified piety of ancient sages.

"Once I noticed," writes a Christian scholar, who visited the city of Warsaw during the First World War, "a great many coaches on a parking place with no drivers in sight. In my own country I would have known where to look for them. A young Jewish boy showed me the way: in a courtyard, on the second floor, was the *shtibl* of the Jewish drivers. It consisted of two rooms: one filled with Talmud-volumes, the other a room for prayer. All the drivers were engaged in fervent study and religious discussion. . . . It was then that I found out and became convinced that all professions, the bakers, the butchers, the shoemakers, etc., have their own *shtibl* in the Jewish district; and every free moment which can be taken off from their work is given to the study of the

Torah. And when they get together in intimate groups, one urges the
other: *'Sog mir a shtickl Torah*—Tell me a little Torah.' "

An old book saved from the countless libraries recently burned in
Europe, now at the Yivo[7] Library in New York, bears the stamp, "The
Society of Wood-Choppers for the Study of Mishnah[8] in Berditshev."

They were a people whose most popular lullaby chants: "The
Torah is the highest good." Mothers at the cradles crooned: "My
little child, close your eyes; if God will, you'll be a rabbi." The state
did not have to compel the Jews to send their children to school.
Joshua had commanded the children of Israel to study the Torah "day
and night."

At the birth of a baby, the school children would come and chant
the *Shema Israel* in unison around the cradle. When taken for the first
time to the *heder*[9], the child was wrapped in a prayer shawl like a
scroll. Schoolboys were referred to as "the holy flock," and a mother's
tenderest pet name for a boy was "my little *zaddik*," my little saint.
Parents were ready to sell the pillow from under their heads to pay
tuition for their children; a poorly educated father wanted at least his
children to be scholars. Women toiled day and night to enable their
husbands to devote themselves to study. When economic exigencies
made it impossible for people to give most of their time to the Torah,
they tried at least to support the students. They shared their scanty
food to give board to a wandering student. And when the melancholy,
sweet chanting of Talmudic study coming from the *beth ha-midrash*
penetrated the neighboring streets, exhausted Jews on their pallets felt
sweet delight at the thought that by their acts of support they had a
share in that learning. In small towns, the sexton would go at dawn
from house to house, knocking at the shutters and chanting:

Get up, Jews,
Sweet, holy Jews,
Get up and worship the Creator!
God is in exile,
The *Shekinah*[10] is in exile,
The people is in exile.
Get up to serve the Creator!

The ambition of every Jew was to have a scholar as a son-in-law,
and a man versed in the Torah could easily marry a well-to-do girl
and obtain *kest*[11] for a few years or even permanently, and thus have
the good fortune of being able to study in peace. Nowadays we
speak disparagingly of this custom. But few institutions have done
more to promote the spiritual development of large masses of people.

Their learning was essentially nonutilitarian, almost free of direct pragmatic designs, an aesthetic experience. They delved into those parts of the law that had no relevance to daily life no less eagerly than into those that had a direct bearing on it. Detached in their learning from interests in mundane affairs, they grappled with problems which were remote from the banalities of the normal course of living. He who studied for the purpose of receiving a rabbinical diploma was the object of ridicule. In the eyes of these people, knowledge was not a means for achieving power, but a way of clinging to the source of all reality. In the eyes of Hasidim, study for the sake of acquiring scholarship was considered a desecration.

The aim was to partake of spiritual beauty, or to attain by osmosis a degree of self-purification. Carried away by the mellow, melting chant of Talmud reading, one's mind would soar high in pure realm of thought, away from this world of facts and worries, away from the boundaries of here and now, to a region where the Shekinah listens to what the children of men create in the study of His Word. There was holiness in their acumen, the cry "my soul thirsteth for God, the living God"[12] in their wrestling with the Lore. They were able to feel heaven in a passage of Talmud.

Rabbi Zusya[13] of Hanipol once started to study a volume of the Talmud. A day later, his disciples noticed that he was still dwelling on the first page. They assumed that he must have encountered a difficult passage and was trying to solve it. But when a number of days passed and he was still immersed in the first page, they were astonished, but did not dare to query the master. Finally one of them gathered courage and asked him why he did not proceed to the next page. And Rabbi Zusya answered: "I feel so good here, why should I go elsewhere?"

Enamored of learning, they put their entire being into the study of the Talmud. Their intellectual effort was stirred by a blazing passion. It is an untold, perhaps incommunicable, story of how mind and heart could merge into one. Immersed in complicated legal discussions, they could at the same time feel the anguish of Shekinah that abides in exile. Endeavoring to solve an antinomy or contradiction raised by a seventeenth-century super-commentary on the Talmud, they were able in the same breath to throb with sympathy for Israel and all people afflicted with distress. Study was a technique of sublimating feeling into thought, of transposing dreams into syllogisms, of expressing grief in formulating keen theoretical difficulties and joy in finding a solution to a difficult passage in Maimonides. Tension of the soul found an outlet in contriving sagacious, almost insoluble riddles. They invented new logical devices in explaining the word of God, thrilled with yearning after the Holy. To figure out an answer to gnawing doubts was to them supreme pleasure. Indeed, a world of subdued gaiety and frolic quivered in the playful subtleties of their *pilpul.*

Pilpul, the characteristic method of study developed in the East European period, had its origin at the ancient academies in Babylonia in the first centuries of the common era. Its goal was not to acquire information about the Law, but rather to examine its implications and presuppositions; not just to absorb and to remember but to discuss and to expand. All later doctrines were considered to be tributaries of the ancient never-failing stream of tradition. One could debate with the great sages of bygone days. There was no barrier between the past and the present. If disagreement was discovered between a view held by Rabbi Akiba Eiger of Posen, who lived in the nineteenth century, and Rabbi Isaac Alfassi of Morocco, who lived in the eleventh century, a Warsaw scholar of the twentieth century would intervene to prove the consistency in the learning carried on throughout the ages.

The power of the *pilpul* penetrated even into the *Kabbalah.* Dialectic joined with mysticism. The late Ashkenazic *kabbalists* constructed symbolic labyrinths out of mystic signs so involved that only *Kabbalists* endowed with both mystic passion and intellectual keenness could safely venture into them.

The plain meaning of words, the straight line of a general rule seemed too shallow, too thin, too narrow to hold the expanding power of their minds. In the light of the *pilpul,* the nature and force of words and concepts underwent a radical change. The simplest principle was disclosed to rest upon a complex of concepts and involved in a mass of relations to other principles. New conclusions of old rules heretofore unnoticed were thus deduced, offering guidance in cases which had not been provided for in old works. At the same time, inconsistencies and divergencies were revealed by applying an even more penetrating and minute analysis of the subject matter.

At times, the *pilpul* degenerated into hairsplitting dialectics and grappled with intellectual phantoms. Deviating from the conventional forms of logical soundness, it was bitterly attacked by some of the great rabbis. Yet, not only did the *pilpul* infuse new vitality into the study of the Talmud, it stimulated ingenuity and independence of mind, encouraging the students to create new out of old ideas. Over and above that, the storm of the soul that was held in check by rigorous discipline, the inner restlessness, found a vent in flights of the intellect. Thinking became full of vigor, charged with passion. The mind melted the metal of Talmudic ideas and forged it into fantastic molds, zigzags, in which thought at first became startled, lost its way, but at the end succeeded in disentangling itself. They did not know how to take anything for granted. Everything had to have a reason, and they were more interested in reasons than in things.

Ideas were like precious stones. The thought that animated them reflected a wealth of nuances and distinctions, as the ray of light passing through a prism produces the colors of the rainbow. Upon rotation, many-faceted ideas shed a glittering brilliance that varied in accordance with the direction in which they were placed against the light of reason. The alluring gracefulness, the variety of the polished ideas enlightened the intellect, dazzled the eye. Concepts acquired a dynamic quality, a color and meaning that, at first thought, seemed to have no connection with one another. The joy of discovery, the process of inventing original devices, of attaining new inventions and new insights, quickened and elated the heart. This was not realistic thinking; but great art likewise is not a reproduction of nature, nor is mathematics an imitation of something that actually exists.

It is easy to belittle such an attitude of mind and to call it unpractical, unworldly. But what is nobler than the unpractical spirit? The soul is sustained by the regard for that which transcends all immediate purposes. The sense of the transcendent is the heart of culture, the very essence of humanity. A civilization that is devoted exclusively to the utilitarian is at bottom not different from barbarism. The world is sustained by unworldliness.

FOOTNOTES

1. The body of Jewish law, legend and thought comprising the Mishnah, or text, and the Gemara, or commentary. It was completed in the fifth century.
2. Town in Babylonia.
3. Works of exposition on the Bible, written during the first millennium.
4. Divine instruction or guidance; Scripture; Jewish lore.
5. "The Duties of the Heart," a work on Jewish piety, written by Rabbi Bahya ibn Pakuda in the eleventh century.
6. From "Shloime Reb Hayim's" by Mendele Moher Sefarim, one of the great Hebrew and Yiddish writers.
7. Yiddish Scientific Institute.
8. The earliest part of the Talmud, containing the fundamentals of Jewish law.
9. Elementary Hebrew school.
10. "Indwelling." Divine hypostasis indwelling in the world and sharing the exile of Israel; Divine Presence among men; a synonym for God.
11. The part of the dowry which consisted of a promise to provide food and board for a specified number of years after the marriage.
12. Psalm 42:2.
13. A Hasidic leader.

ISRAEL AS THE CHOSEN PEOPLE

The third element in the trilogy of fundamental categories in Judaic theology is "Israel," meaning not the State of Israel created in 1948, or the land of Israel on the eastern shores of the Mediterranean, but the *people* of Israel, the Jewish people. Classical Judaic theology never supposed "man"—without traits, ties, distinctions—came into relationship with God. It understood from the biblical record that God had sought "man" and had found Abraham, Isaac, Jacob. He had wanted to give his Torah to "man" but ended up revealing it to a single man, Moses, and through him, to one, unique people, "Israel." Israel is therefore something more than an ethnic group or a particular society. It is defined in a way other than that which will mark off any other group. The concept, "Israel" functions within Judaism somewhat as does the concept, "church" in Christianity.

The Jews are *Israel* because of the Torah, because of the love of God. Israel is defined as such not in the natural way in which other peoples are defined, that is, because they possess a common culture or a common set of customs. A person becomes part of "Israel" not through ethnic or territorial assimilation, that is, by marrying a Jew or by taking up residence in a Jewish settlement.

A person becomes part of "Israel" by taking on the Torah, by acknowledging the unity of God and accepting his will—that is, by conversion to a religious assertion. The idea of religious conversion, brought to the larger part of mankind by Christianity, began in the pre-Christian period in the history of Judaism. It meant that a change in beliefs rendered a person utterly different in his social and ethnic characteristics—a most unnatural, but rather, theological event.

Clearly, classical Judaic theology regarded Israel as the beloved of God. From the time of Amos onward, to be sure, that love was understood not as preference or as the source of privilege, all the more so not as a reason for arrogance or superiority over others. It was the occasion for special responsibilities.

"Only you have I known among the families of man. Therefore I shall visit upon you all your iniquities." From Amos' time onward, the history of Israel, the Jewish people, was interpreted in terms of divine concern. When the Second Temple was destroyed in 70 A.D., the people were comforted by the rabbis of that time with this message: Just as God was trustworthy in punishing you for your sins, so you may have confidence that he will respond to your regeneration.

Here we shall consider an account of the view of Israel as God's people derived from the sayings of the rabbis of the Talmud. Solomon Schechter, a great scholar of the Talmud, who died more than half-a-century ago, expounds the ideas of Israel's relationship to God and of the election of Israel through early rabbinic sayings on the subject.

The first question he answers is this: What was the relationship between men and God, as perceived by the rabbis? Was it formal and distant, guided only by an "external" law? Or was it intimate and full of love?

Is Israel alone in the world? Is the suffering of the people their own affair? Or does God suffer with them? Does he care for them?

Can God ultimately reject Israel? Is it possible that they may sin so grievously that he will finally and completely give up on them? What is the nature of divine forebearance and forgiveness in relationship to Israel?

What is the meaning of God's choosing Israel, Israel's "election"? How do the classical Judaic theologians explain that belief? Is this not a too-particularistic, too-tribal notion? What does it have to say to the rest of mankind?

VI

GOD, ISRAEL, AND ELECTION

Solomon Schechter

(From *Some Aspects of Rabbinic Theology*, by Solomon Schechter. N.Y., 1936: Behrman House, Inc., pp. 46-64, under the chapter headings, "God and Israel," and "Election of Israel.")

Neither the terms of space nor heaven as applied to God, nor the imaginary descriptions placing his particular abode on high, meant for the Rabbis remoteness from the world. Whatever the faults of the Rabbis were, consistency was not one of them. Neither speculation nor folklore was ever allowed to be converted into rigid dogma. When the Rabbis were taught by experience that certain terms meant for superficial proselytes only a reflex of their former deities, they not only abandoned them for a time, but substituted for them even the Tetragrammaton itself; a strong measure, taken in contradiction to ancient custom and tradition, and thus proving how anxious the Rabbis were that nothing should intervene between man and God.

We shall now proceed to show how still more intimate and close was the relation maintained and felt between God and Israel. He is their God, their father, their strength, their shepherd, their hope, their salvation, their safety; they are his people, his children, his first-born son, his treasure, dedicated to his name, which is sacrilege to profane. In brief, there is not a single endearing epithet in the language, such as brother, sister, bride, mother, lamb, or eye, which is not, according to the Rabbis, applied by the Scriptures to express this intimate relation between God and his people. God is even represented by the Rabbis as saying to Moses, "As much as thou canst exalt this nation (Israel) exalt it, for it is as if thou wert exalting me. Praise it as much as thou canst, glorify it as much as thou canst, for in them I will be glorified, as it is said, 'Thou art my servant, O Israel, in whom I will be glorified' " (Isaiah 49:3). "What is his (God's) name? *El* Shaddai, Zebaoth. What is the name of his son? Israel!" Nay, more, though a king of flesh and blood would resent to hear one of his subjects arrogating his title (as Caesar Augustus), the Holy One, blessed be he, himself confers on Israel the names by which he is himself distinguished, as wise, holy, the chosen ones, and does not even deny them the title of gods, as it is written, "I have said, Ye are gods" (Psalms 82:6).

This intimacy of relationship is reciprocal. "He (God) needs us even as we need him" was a favourite axiom with certain mystics. In the language of the Rabbis we should express the same sentiment thus, "One God through Israel, and one Israel through God. They are his selected people, and he is their selected portion." "God is the help and the support of all mankind, but still more of Israel." "They recognized in him the King, and he recognized in them the masters of the world. . . . Israel declares (his unity) in the words, 'Hear, O Israel: The Lord our God, the Lord is *one*' (Deuteronomy 6:4); and the holy spirit (or word of God) proclaims their election (in the words), 'And who is like thy people Israel, a nation that is *one* (or alone) in the earth' " (I Chronicles 17:21). "He glorified them when he said, 'Israel is my son, even my first-born,' whilst they sang a song unto him in Egypt." Israel brought him down by their praise (from all the seven heavens to earth, as it is said, "And let them make me a sanctuary, that I may dwell among them") (Exodus 25:9), and he lifted them by his praise above (to the heaven), as it is said, "That the Lord thy God will set thee on high above" (Deuteronomy 28:1). "Blessed be his (God's) name for ever," exclaims a Rabbi, enthusiastically, "who left those above and chose those below to dwell in the Tabernacle because of his love of Israel." Indeed, the Holy One, blessed be he, says to Israel, "You are my flock and I am the shepherd, make a hut for the shepherd that he come and provide for you; you are the vineyard and I am the watcher, make a tent for the watcher that he guards you; you are the children and I am the father,—it is a glory for the father when he is with his children and a glory for the children when they are with their father; make therefore a house for the father that he comes and dwells with his children."

Israel bears in common with the angels such names as gods, holy ones, children (of God). But God loves Israel more than the angels. Israel's prayer being more acceptable to him than the song of the angels, whilst the righteous in Israel are in closer contact with the Deity than the angels, and are consulted by them as to "what God hath wrought."

Again, "He who rises up against Israel rises up against God; hence the cause of Israel is the cause of God; their ally is also his." For God suffers with them in their suffering and is with them in their distress.

Their subjection implies his subjection, and his presence accompanies them through their various captivities among the Gentiles. Therefore their redemption is his redemption, their joy is his joy, their salvation his salvation, and their light his light.

Their cause is indeed so closely identified with God's cause that on the occasion of the great historical crisis at the Red Sea, God is supposed rather to resent the lengthy prayer of Moses, and says unto him, "Wherefore criest thou to me? (Exodus 14:15). I need no asking for my children, as it is said, 'Wilt thou ask me concerning my children?' " (Isaiah 45:11). The recognition of this fatherhood is all that God wants from Israel. "All the wonders and mighty deeds which I have done for you," says God unto Israel, "were not performed with the purpose of being rewarded (by you), but that you honour me like children and call me your father." The filial relationship suffers no interference, whether for good or evil, of a third person between Israel and God. Israel loves him and loves his house, no man indeed knowing the love which is between Israel and their Maker. And so does the Holy One, blessed be he, love them. He wants to hear Israel's voice (as expressed in prayer), and is anxious for them to listen unto his voice. According to another explanation (of Exodus 14:15), Moses was given to understand that there was no need for his prayers, the Holy One by his intimate relation to Israel being almost himself in distress.

This paternal relation, according to the great majority of the Rabbis, is unconditional. Israel will be chastised for its sins, even more severely than other nations for theirs; but this is only another proof of God's fatherly love. For it was only through suffering that Israel obtained the greatest gifts from heaven, and what is still more important to note is, that it was affliction which "reconciled and attached the son to the father (Israel to God)." "The Israelites are God's children even when full of blemishes," and the words, "A seed of evildoers, children that are corrupt" (Isaiah 1:4), are cited as a proof that even corruption cannot entirely destroy the natural relation between father and child. Indeed, when Isaiah received the call, "the Holy One, blessed be he, said unto him, 'Isaiah! my children are troublesome and rebellious. If thou dost take upon thyself to be insulted and beaten by my children thou wilt be sent as my messenger, not otherwise!' Isaiah answered, 'Yes, on this condition.' As it is said, 'I gave my back to smiters and my cheeks to them that plucked off the hair' (Isaiah 50:6), I am not even worthy to carry messages to thy children.' " But Elijah, the Rabbis say, who in his zeal denounced Israel, saying, "I have been very jealous for the Lord God of hosts; because the children of Israel have forsaken thy covenant, thrown down thine altars, and slain thy prophets with the sword" (I Kings 19:14), was dismissed with the answer, "I have no desire in thy prophecy"; and his prophetic office was transferred to the milder Elisha, the son of Shaphat, who was anointed in Elijah's place (19:16). Likewise is the Prophet Hosea rebuked for his refraining from praying for Israel, God saying unto him, They are my beloved ones, the sons of my beloved ones, the sons of Abraham, Isaac, and Jacob. For this is indeed the glory of both patriarchs and prophets, that they are prepared to give themselves (as an atoning sacrifice) for Israel; as, for instance, Moses, who said in case God would not forgive the sin of Israel, "Blot me, I pray thee, out of thy book which thou hast written" (Exodus 23:32). Jeremiah, however, who proved himself just as jealous for the glory of the son (Israel) as for the glory of the father (God), saying as he did, "We have transgressed and have rebelled: thou hast not pardoned" (Lamentations 3:42) (thus though confessing Israel's guilt, still reproaching God, so to speak, for his declining to forgive), was rewarded by the continuation of his gift of prophecy, as it is said, "And *he adds* besides unto them many like words" (Jeremiah 36:32). And, it is on the strength of this view of childship that some of the prophets pleaded with God on behalf of Israel. "Behold," they said to the Holy One, blessed be he, "thou sayest (because of their transgressions) they are not any longer thy children, but they are recognisable by their countenances as it is said, 'All that see them shall acknowledge them that they are the seed, which the Lord has blessed' (Isaiah 61:9). As it is the way of the Father to be merciful with his children though they sin, so thou wilt have mercy with them (notwithstanding their relapses). This is (the meaning of the verse): 'But now, O Lord, thou art our father. . . . Be not wroth very sore, O Lord, neither remember iniquity forever'" (Isaiah 64:8, 9). Indeed, God says, after you (Israel) stood on the mount of Sinai and received the Torah and I wrote of you that I love you; and since I loved you, how could I hate you (considering that I loved you as children)?

The only opponent to the view of the majority regarding the paternal relation is R. Judah, who limits it to the time when Israel acts as children should act. When R. Akiba, in a time of great distress, opened the public service with the formula, "Our father, our king, we have sinned against thee; our father, our king, forgive us." he only expressed the view of the great majority, that Israel may claim their filial privileges even if they have sinned. The formula of the daily confession, "Forgive us, O our Father, for we have sinned," points in the same direction. In fact, the term "Father," or "Our Father, who is in heaven," or "My Father, who is in heaven," is one of the most frequent in the Jewish Prayer Book and the subsequent liturgy. The latter seems to have been a favourite expression with the Tanna of the school of Elijah, who very often introduces his comments on the Bible (a mixture of homiletics and prayer) with the words, "My Father in heaven, may thy great name be blessed for all eternity, and mayest thou have delight in thy people Israel." Another consequence of this fatherly relation is that Israel feels a certain ease and delight in the fulfilment of the Law which to slaves is burdensome and perplexing. For "the son who serves his father serves him with joy, saying, 'Even if I do not entirely succeed (in carrying out his commandments), yet, as a loving father, he will not be angry with me'; whilst the Gentile slave is always afraid lest he may commit some fault, and therefore serves God in a condition of anxiety and confusion." Indeed, when Israel feels uneasy because of their having to stand in judgment before God, the angels say unto them, "Fear ye not the judgment. . . . Know ye not him? He is your next of kin, he is your brother, but what is more, he is your father."

The quotations in the preceding [pages] will suffice to show the confidence which the Rabbis felt in the especially intimate relations existing between God and Israel. This renders it necessary to make here some reference to the doctrine of Israel's election by God, which in fact is only another term for this special relation between the two. "To love means in fact, to choose or to elect." The doctrine has found no place in Maimonides' Thirteen Articles of the Creed, but still even a cursory perusal of Bible and Talmud leaves no doubt that the notion of the election always maintained in Jewish consciousness the character of at least an unformulated dogma.

The Rabbinic belief in the election of Israel finds, perhaps, its clearest expression in a prayer which begins as follows: "Thou hast chosen us from all peoples; thou hast loved us and taken pleasure in us, and hast exalted us above all tongues; thou hast sanctified us by thy commandments and brought us near unto thy service; O our King, thou hast called us by thy great and holy name." These words, which still breathe a certain scriptural air, are based, as may be easily seen, on the Biblical passages of Deuteronomy 10:15, 14:2, Psalms 149:2; and Jeremiah 14:27. There was thus hardly any necessity for the Rabbis to give any reasons for their belief in this doctrine, resting as it does on ample Biblical authority; though, as it would seem, they were not quite unconscious of the difficulties which such a doctrine involves. Thus Moses is represented by them as asking God: "Why out of all the seventy nations of the world dost thou give me instructions only about Israel?" the commandments of the Torah being mostly addressed to the "children of Israel" (*e.g.* Exodus 3:15, 31:30, 33:5; Leviticus 24:2); whilst in another place we read, with reference to Deuteronomy 7:7, that God says to Israel, "Not because you are greater than other nations did I choose you, nor because you obey my injunctions more than the nations; for they (the nations) follow my commandments, even though they were not bidden to do it, and also magnify my name more than you, as it is said, 'From the rising of the sun, even unto the going down of the same, my name is great among the Gentiles'" (Malachi 1:11). The answers given to these and similar questions are various. According to some Rabbis, Israel's election was, as it would seem, predestined before the creation of the world (just as was the name of the Messiah), and sanctified unto the name of God even before the universe was called into existence. Israel was there before the world was created and is still existing now and will continue to exist in the future (by reason of its attachment to God). "The matter is to be compared to a king who was desiring to build; but when he was digging for the purpose of laying the foundations, he found only swamps and mire. At last he hit on a rock, when he said, 'Here I will build.' So, too, when God was about to create the world, he foresaw the sinful generation of Enosh (when man began to profane the name of the Lord), and the wicked generations of the deluge (which said unto God, 'Depart from us'), and he said, 'How shall I create the world whilst these generations are certain to provoke me (by their crimes and sins)?' But when he perceived that Abraham would one day arise, he said, 'Behold, I have found the *petra* (rock) on which to build and base the world.'" The patriarch Abraham is called the rock (Isaiah 51:1, 2); and so Israel are called the rocks (Numbers 33:9). They are an obstinate race and their faith in God is not a shifting one, and, as a later author expresses it, if you leave them no alternative but apostasy or crucifixion, they are certain to prefer the latter. "Hence the thought of Israel's creation preceded the creation of the world."

According to other Rabbis, Israel's claim to the election is because they declared God as king on the Red Sea, and they said, "The Lord shall reign for ever and ever" (Exodus 15:18). According to others again, it was on account of their having accepted the yoke of his kingdom on Mount Sinai. Why did the Holy One, blessed be he, choose Israel? Because all the other nations declared the Torah unfit and refused to accept it, whilst Israel agreed and chose God and his Torah. Another opinion maintains that it was because of Israel's humbleness and meekness that they were found worthy of becoming the chosen people. This may perhaps be connected with the view expressed that God's reason for the election of Israel was the fact that they are the persecuted ones, all the great Biblical characters such as Abraham, Isaac, Jacob, Moses, David, having been oppressed and especially chosen by God. From another place it would seem that it is the holiness of Israel which made them worthy of the election. It is worth noting, however, that the passage in which the reason of Israel's meekness is advanced concludes with the reminder that God says, "My soul volunteered to love them, though they are not worthy of it," quoting as a proof from the Scriptures the verse, "I will love them freely" (Hosea 14:5). This suggests that even those Rabbis who tried to establish Israel's special claim on their exceptional merits were not altogether unconscious of the insufficiency of the reason of works in this respect, and therefore had also recourse to the love of God, which is not given as a reward, but is offered freely. When an old Roman matron challenged R. Jose (b. Chalafta) with the words, "Whomsoever your God likes he brings near unto him (elects)," the Rabbi answered her that God indeed knows whom to select: in him whom he sees good deeds he chooses him and brings him near unto him. But the great majority of the Rabbis are silent about merits, and attribute the election to a mere act of grace (or love) on the part of God. And he is represented as having answered Moses' question cited above, "I give these instructions about Israel (and not about the nations) because they are beloved unto me more than all other nations; for they are my peculiar treasure, and upon them I did set my love, and them I have chosen." "Praised be the Omnipresent" (*makom*), exclaims the Tanna of the school of Elijah, "blessed be he, who chose Israel from among all the nations, and make them verily his own, and called them children and servants unto his name . . . and all this because of the love with which he loved them, and the joy with which he rejoiced in them."

It must, however, be noted that this doctrine of election—and it is difficult to see how any revealed religion can dispense with it—was not quite of so exclusive a nature as is commonly imagined. For it is only the privilege of the first-born which the Rabbis claim for Israel, that they are the first in God's kingdom, not the exclusion of other nations. A God "who had faith in the world when he created it," who mourned over its moral decay, which compelled him to punish it with the deluge, as a father mourns over the death of his son, and who, but for their sins, longed to make his abode among its inhabitants, is not to be supposed to have entirely given up all relations with the great majority of mankind, or to have ceased to take any concern in their well-being. "Though his goodness, loving-kindness, and mercy are with Israel, his right hand is always stretched forward to receive *all* those who come into the world, . . . as it is said, 'Unto me every knee shall bow, every tongue shall swear' " (Isaiah 45:23). For this confession from the Gentiles the Holy One is waiting. In fact, it did not escape the composers of the Liturgy that the same prophet by whom they established their claim to election called God "the King of the Gentiles" (Jeremiah 10:7), and on this the Rabbis remark that God said to the prophet, "Thou callest me the King of the Gentiles. Am I not also the King of Israel?" The seeming difference again between "I am the Lord, the God of *all* flesh" (Jeremiah 32:27), and "the Lord of hosts, *the God of* Israel" (ver. 15), or between the verse "Three times in the year all thy males shall appear before *the Lord God*" (Exodus 23:17) and another passage enjoining the same law, but where God is called "the Lord God, the God *of Israel*" (34:23), is explained by the Rabbis to indicate the double relation of God to the world in general, and to Israel in particular. He is the Lord of all nations, while his name is especially attached to Israel. Of more importance is the interpretation given to Deuteronomy 6:4, "Hear, O Israel," etc. (the *Shema*), which runs as follows: "He is *our* God by making his name particularly attached to us; but he is also the one God of *all* mankind. He is *our* God in this world, he will be the only God in the world to come, as it is said, And the Lord shall be King over all the earth; in that day there shall be one Lord, and his name one" (Zechariah 14:9). For, "in this world, the creatures, through the insinuations of the evil inclination, have divided themselves into various tongues, but in the world to come they will agree with one consent to call only on his name, as it is said, 'For then I will restore to the people a pure language, that they may all call upon the name of the Lord, to serve him with one consent' " (Zephaniah 3:9). Thus the *Shema* not only contains a metaphysical statement (about the unity of God), but expresses a hope and belief—for everything connected with this verse has a certain dogmatic value—in the ultimate universal kingdom of God.

THE HOLY LAND IN JUDAIC THEOLOGY

The modern world has witnessed the creation of the State of Israel in the ancient land of the Jewish people. This is powerful testimony to the importance of that particular place on earth, "the holy land," "the promised land," in the historical religious experience of Israel. Indeed, the return of the Jews to that land after so many centuries tells us that the land forms one of the chief components in the religious imagination of Judaism.

But what was its place in classical Judaic theology? Is the concern for a particular state, a nation, merely a response on the part of the Jews to the nationalism of modern life?

One might claim, for example, that when nationalism became a force in the formation of nineteenth-century society and culture, the Jews took over the common concern for having a nation but endowed their nationalism with a religious significance which the classical tradition did not, to begin with, recognize.

When in the late nineteenth century Theodor Herzl proposed the creation of a Jewish state, Reform rabbis opposed him on the grounds that "Judaism is a religion" and has nothing to do with "nationalism." Herzl himself was prepared to accept any land, not only what was then called Palestine, for the building of a Jewish refuge. The British government at the turn of the century offered to the World Zionist Organization the use of Uganda for the building of a Jewish state. Herzl was prepared to accept it. The Jewish masses, particularly in Eastern Europe, successfully opposed him. "Only the land of Israel (Palestine)" was their view.

Arthur Hertzberg, who teaches Jewish history at Columbia University, here describes the place of the holy land in the Judaic religious tradition. He shows that while Zionism was born in an age of nationalism, it is not like other nationalisms of the time or afterward. For it takes up an age-old theme in Judaic belief, the conviction that one particular land has been made holy and belongs to the chosen people.

That conviction is not "Zionist propaganda." It derives from biblical literature. It was elaborated and developed in Talmudic Judaism.

Through the Middle Ages philosophers and poets, mystics and ordinary believers alike looked to the holy land and prayed for its welfare. Jewish worship, like Jewish thought, centered upon the land. The Jew asked God for many things, but never omitted to seek the welfare of the land.

What are the connections between Judaism and the land of Israel? How have the Judaic theologians explained those connections? Are these sporadic, or continuing? Do they represent something superficial? Or do they speak out of the depths of the soul of Judaism?

VII

JUDAISM AND THE LAND OF ISRAEL

Arthur Hertzberg

(From *Judaism*, Vol. 19, No. 4, Fall, 1970, pp. 423-434.)

As a political fact the State of Israel is a unique creation. Though its legal existence has been recognized by all the major powers and by most other states, all of its immediate neighbors, the six Arab states on its borders, continue to insist that its presence in the Middle East is a political and moral affront of such magnitude that it entitles them to try to effect its destruction. There have been many revolutions in the twentieth century in the name of national self-determination; Israel is the only example of a new state created by a largely non-resident people returning to the homeland of its ancestors.

In our century the tendency of political states, both old and new, has been to conceive of themselves as secular arrangements which represent no particular religious tradition. The State of Israel is indeed largely secular. For that matter, one of the avowed purposes of its creators was to make it possible for Jews to lead completely secular lives as Jews, within their own polity. Nonetheless, Israel was created by Jews to be, and to remain, an essentially Jewish State, that is, to represent something more than a conventional, secular, political arrangement to serve the needs of its individual citizens of whatever condition or provenance. This mystique pervades even the secularists in Israel and is deeply felt among the majority of the Jews of the world, regardless of the nature of their religious convictions or commitments. The multiplicity of often clashing forms of life and value appears, from this perspective, to be the confusion of creativity, the necessary turmoil which attends the effecting of a synthesis between the old and the new. The present is seen as an age of becoming, and the sometimes even bitter internal conflicts of the moment are part of some larger harmony. The national mood in Israel is one of attempting to encounter the twentieth century in terms of its own historic tradition.

The most unusual characteristic of the life of Israel today is its connection with the Jewish community of the world. This theme was stated by one of its earliest constitutional acts, the Law of Return, under which any Jew is a citizen of the State of Israel from the moment of his arrival as an immigrant. Such a law is not entirely unprecedented among modern irredentist movements, but the whole complex of connections between the State of Israel and the world Jewish community is, indeed, unique. Support, both moral and financial, by the majority of the Jews outside of its borders is critically necessary to the development of Israel. The State of Israel regards itself, and is universally regarded, as the spokesman for some Jewish interests, such as the rights of the Jews of the Soviet Union, which are not immediately related to its own position and which, sometimes, in terms of narrowest self-interest, Israel would be best off avoiding. The leadership of Jerusalem remains dedicated to the task of helping to preserve Jewish loyalty and consciousness among the Jews on all five continents.

It is too narrow and even unjust to view this concern as the desire of an embattled nation to keep alive a maximum reservoir of good will and support or even, ultimately, of potential new immigrants. The preservation of the Jewish spirit is the fundamental purpose for which the State was conceived by its founders, and this commitment is even more important than the immediate needs which the Jewish settlement in the Holy Land has served during this tragic century, as the major place to which Jewish refugees from persecution could come as of right and not as an act of foreign grace. In turn, the Jews of the world look upon Israel as the major contemporary incarnation of many of their own hopes for continuity. The depth of the emotion which Israel evokes among them is, to be sure, affected by recent memories of Auschwitz. Israel is, indeed, in its very strength, a symbol of the end of Jewish passivity and lack of power to resist slaughter; it does represent an open door for Jews with the keys to their safety. At the very root, however, Israel, and the world Jewish concerns which help sustain it, are both based on some of the grand and ancient themes of Jewish religion and of Jewish history. One cannot understand the present unless it is viewed as both a contemporary re-evocation of elements of faith and hope peculiar to Judaism and, paradoxically, as a contemporary tension between this older outlook and newer modes of thought and life.

II

All of the elements of Jewish religious consciousness were present and, indeed, defined, in the very first encounter, in the Biblical narrative, between the One God and Abraham. The account needs to be recalled, both for what it affirms and for what it excludes: "And God said to Abram, go forth from your land and from your place of birth and from the house of your father to the land which I will show you. And I will make of you a great people and I will bless you and make your name great; and be a blessing." In the next verse the last promise is amplified: "and all the families of the earth will be blessed through you." Abraham obeyed the command and entered the land, where the One God appeared to him, reiterating and amplifying the promise: "and to your children I will give this land" (Genesis 12:1-3). In these encounters Abraham was taken away from all of his original relationships. Community, land and even the family within which he arose, all represent ties which were broken for a fresh beginning, a covenant with the Lord, in which a new community was to be created which Abraham was to found. It was to arise in a particular place, the land of Canaan, which had been set aside for the authentic encounter between the seed of Abraham and the God who founded their community. The life of this community in this land was to exist for a purpose: to demonstrate to all other people how human life is to be lived at its most moral. The implication already exists in the original sending that any falling away from such a standard will represent a breach in the covenant and a defilement of holy soil. Exile is already conceivable as punishment and the ultimate return is already in view as laden with messianic meaning, of redemptive quality for Jews and for mankind.

One can skip the centuries and quote a modern writer from almost our own time, to find these most ancient themes reappearing essentially as they were first pronounced. Solomon Schechter wrote in 1906, in New York: "The selection of Israel, the indestructibility of God's covenant with Israel, the immortality of Israel as a nation, and the final restoration of Israel to Palestine, where the nation will live a holy life on holy ground, with all the wide-reaching consequences of the conversion of humanity and the establishment of the Kingdom of God on earth—all these are the common ideals and the common ideas that permeate the whole of Jewish literature extending over nearly four thousand years."

Both as a fact and as a promise the relationship of Jews to the land of Israel thus appeared as an indispensable element in the original covenant. Jerusalem appears later, at the time of David. It is clear from both of the Biblical accounts of its conquest, in Samuel and in Chronicles, that making the city into the capital is the act which set the seal on the creation of the Jewish Kingdom. The city did not belong to any individual tribe, not even to the tribe of Judah: "And David and all Israel went to Jerusalem" (I Chronicles 14:4), thus acquiring it by action of the entire people and making of it the place to which all Israel would turn. It certainly does not need to be demonstrated that all of the Biblical writers looked to Jerusalem as the essence of the meaning of their faith, life and hope. In the later years of the existence of the Second Temple, Jerusalem was the center of pilgrimage not only for the Jews in the Land of Israel but also for the increasingly scattered Diaspora. The evidence for this is to be found in all the literature of the period, in Josephus (Wars I, 4, 13), Philo (Laws I, 68) and the New Testament (Acts of the Apostles 2:5). The literature of the Talmud is, of course, laden with accounts of masses from all the Jewish world coming to the Temple, especially to celebrate the Passover. There is a tale, no doubt exaggerated, that on one Passover, King Agrippa had the priests count the number of paschal lambs that had been offered up and he found that the total exceeded 1,200,000 (*Pesaḥim* 64b). It is well known that in those days, in the century before its destruction by the Romans, the Temple was visited by gentiles as well as by Jews and there is Talmudic evidence that in the sacrificial cult there was regular provision for acts of prayer and atonement for all of the "seventy nations" of the world.

The connection between Jews and the land was not broken by the Exile. By the third century, the Babylonian Jewish community had begun to overshadow the one which remained in the land under the Romans, and yet Babylonian authorities ruled, as firmly as those in the Holy Land, that either party to a marriage could force the other, by appeal to Rabbinic courts, to move from the Diaspora to the Land of Israel (*Ketubot* 110b). Dwelling in the land remained, in the view of most of the later Rabbinic authorities, a Biblical commandment of continuing validity, and those of the medieval writers who did not insist on this as a religious good absolved themselves and the people of their generation because of the dangers to life that the journey involved (*Responsa* of R. Isaiah Trani II, 25). This point is perhaps best made by quoting a tale from the third century: Two rabbis were once on their way out of the Land of Israel to Nisibis, where the great teacher, R. Judah ben Batyrah, dwelt, to learn Torah from him. They got as far as Sidon and there they remembered the Land of Israel. They began to weep, they rent their garments, and they remembered the Biblical verses which promised the land to the seed of Abraham. The rabbis turned around and went back to their place in the land, pronouncing that dwelling in the Land of Israel is, in itself, an act equal of religious significance to all of the Commandments in the Torah (*Sifrei, Re'eh*).

In aspiration and in memory the connection of Jews with the land was, thus, not broken by the Exile. On the contrary, the destruction of the Temple and of the Holy City, Jerusalem, and the absence of Jews from their land, were regarded as a punishment. Life outside of the Holy Land was possible for Jews, but it was less than the full life, in perfect obedience to God, which could happen only with physical restoration. What has increasingly appeared with the progress of historical research in the last century is that these religious commitments were more than merely visionary. Some Jews continued to remain in the land even during the most dangerous and disastrous times and in every century there were returns to it, sometimes by small handfuls of leading spiritual figures and, on occasion, by substantial communities.

In the early centuries of the common era, access to Jerusalem, itself, was denied to Jews, though there is some evidence that the Roman emperors of the second century and the one thereafter did permit them to visit the city and to worship on the Mount of Olives and, sometimes, even on the Temple Mount itself. The situation became even more difficult by the fourth century, and there is contemporary evidence from Christian sources that Jews had the greatest difficulty in buying the right to come to pray near the Western Wall, at least on the Ninth of Ab, the anniversary of the destruction of the Temple. The Pilgrim from Bordeaux, the earliest Christian visitor whose written account of his visit to Jerusalem has survived, tells that in the year 333 Jews came every year to that site to "bewail themselves with groans, rend their garments, and so depart" (*The Bordeaux Pilgrim*, pp. 21-22). There are comparable accounts by the Church Father, Gregory of Nazianzus (*Orat VI de pace*, p. 91), and by Jerome, in his commentary to Zephaniah written in the year 392 (Migne, *Patrologia*, XXV, Col. 1354). But with the end of Roman rule in Palestine the prohibition against Jews living in Jerusalem was lifted, and after that there is evidence for an often flourishing Jewish community in that city. During the Crusades the great traveler, Petahiah of Regensburg, was in Jerusalem in the years 1180-1185, and he reports that at the time there was only one Jew, a dyer, resident there, but after the era of the Crusades the community began to rebuild.

It is instructive in this connection that, ever since 1844, a half-century before the first stirrings of modern Zionism, Jerusalem has been the one city in the Holy Land which has consistently had a Jewish majority in its population. According to the 1844 edition of the Encyclopedia Britannica the population figures of the time were 7,120 Jews,

5,530 Moslems and 3,390 Christians, and all of them lived within the walled city. By 1896, when much of the Jewish population was already outside the wall but the city as a whole was still a unit, there were more than 28,000 Jews and some 17,000 Christians and Moslems, combined into roughly equal halves (*Luah Eretz Yisrael*, 1896). The first government census by the British, that of October, 1922, found almost 34,000 Jews and about 38,000 Moslems and Christians in the whole of the city. Even at that point, with the Jewish population growth taking place entirely outside the wall, there were still 5,639 Jews in the Old City itself. In 1931, Jews were a majority of 51,000 in the city out of a total population of 90,000, while by 1939 the Jewish population of all of Jerusalem was an even more pronounced majority. However, almost two decades of riots and pogroms by Arabs against Jews in the Old City had made it a dangerous place in which to live, and Jewish numbers in the Old City itself had declined to something over 2,000.

In the last two millennia of its history Jerusalem has been the most dangerous and difficult place for Jews to dwell in of any of the cities of the Holy Land, yet this sampling of population figures is evidence that physical connection to the city remained so precious to Jews that they were willing, throughout the ages, to risk the dangers and to submit to the suffering. All of the chronicles and contemporary accounts of the Middle Ages substantiate the import of the figures for the last century: whenever the barest possibility existed, even under hostile powers, enough Jews were to be found to cleave to Jerusalem so that, across the centuries, theirs was the largest continuing presence there. Memories of the past, messianic hopes for the future, and modern Zionism in all its contemporaneity are, indeed, the heirs of the major continuing physical connection with that city.

This clinging by Jews to Jerusalem, even more than to the whole of the rest of the Holy Land, is no accident; it has the deepest roots in the continuing religious tradition and folk consciousness of Jews. It is "the city which I have chosen unto me" (I Kings 11:36) and the one "upon which my name is called" (II Kings 21:4). It was, of course, the place where the Temple stood, the seat of God's presence, even though the heaven and the heaven of heavens could not contain Him. In the imagery of prophecy Zion and Jerusalem are often parallel to all of Israel; both these names are often used to represent not only the whole of the people but also all of its land. For example, "Speak unto Zion, you are my people" (Isaiah 51:16) or "Comfort ye, comfort ye, my people; speak to the heart of Jerusalem" (Isaiah 40:1). The synagogue poets of late ancient and medieval times made much of these themes, and of the hundreds of examples that could be given, the most famous is also the most characteristic. Writing in Spain in the eleventh century, Judah Halevi cries out: "Zion, wilt thou not ask after the peace of thy captive children?" Ironically, this poet and philosopher ended his life as a pilgrim in the Holy Land, where he was killed soon after his arrival.

In the daily prayers of Jews to this day, one of the benedictions of the silent devotion is a prayer for the rebuilding of Jerusalem; that paragraph represents the hope for the restoration of Jews to the Holy Land as a whole. In the grace which Jews say after every meal, morning, noon, and night, the third benediction reads: "And rebuild Jerusalem, the holy city, speedily and in our day; blessed art thou, O Lord, who builds Jerusalem." All synagogues throughout the Jewish world, from the first one in antiquity to those being erected this very day, have been built in such fashion that they face towards Jerusalem. Its very name has always evoked the memory of a time when all was well, when Jews lived on their land and worshipped God in His holy temple, and the hope for the day when some of this glory would return. To be buried on the Mount of Olives, no matter where one dies, has been regarded for two millennia as the surest hope of the Resurrection, and bodies were being returned from Rome some 2,000 years ago for that purpose. To kiss the stones of Jerusalem, even in its destruction, was to be as close to God as man could be. To participate in its rebuilding was the hope of the ages.

In the Holy Land, as a whole, the Jewish presence after the fourth century was, in terms of numbers, of relatively lesser importance. Nonetheless, the realities of Jewish history during the nineteen centuries of the Exile are misstated if there is no emphasis on the important existence of Jewish communities in the land itself throughout the centuries. The Talmud of Jerusalem was created by important schools of Jewish learning in the Holy Land, and these declined only in the fourth and fifth century under Christian persecution. The fixing of the vocalization of the Hebrew Bible, the Masoretic Text, was done by Jewish scholars in Tiberias between the eighth and tenth centuries. At that time, and for the next century or so, both the Karaites and the followers of the Talmudic tradition had important communities in the Holy Land, and, for a while around the year 1000, academies of rabbinic learning were reconstituted in Jerusalem and Ramleh. These were of such consequence that they shared leadership in the Jewish world, as a whole, with the schools in Babylonia, though the Babylonian academies had by then, enjoyed an uninterrupted tradition of almost a millennium. Even under the Crusaders, Jewish communities continued to exist in the cities of Acre and Ashkelon as well as in a variety of other places, particularly a number of villages in the Galilee, in several of which Jews have dwelt without interruption since before the destruction in the year 70 C.E.

At the beginning of the thirteenth century there came the first organized attempt by Jews in Europe to return to the Holy Land, when three hundred rabbis of France and England came there. Some of these men were of the highest intellectual rank. Naḥmanides left Spain after an unfortunate disputation in Barcelona, which was forced upon him by Pablo Christiani, and spent the last three years of his life from 1267 to 1270, reconstituting a Jewish community in Jerusalem. Towards the end of the fifteenth century, the almost equally important Obadiah of Bartinora, the author of the standard commentary on the Mishnah, left Italy for the Holy Land and he, too, reinvigorated the Jewish community in Jerusalem.

From the beginning of the sixteenth century, there was an important growth of the Jewish population in the Galilee and, especially, in the town of Safed. Exiles from Spain, after the final expulsion of Jews in 1492, arrived in the country in some numbers and within a century there were no less than eighteen academies of Talmudic studies and twenty-one synagogues in Safed alone. Indeed, the most important spiritual stirring and creativity within Jewry during the sixteenth century took place there. There was even an abortive attempt to reconstitute the authority of the ancient patriarchate, which had lapsed under Roman persecution. The studies of both Kabbalah and Talmud were pursued with renewed creative élan, and it was in Safed, in 1567, that Josef Karo published the *Shulḥan Arukh* which was almost immediately accepted by the bulk of world Jewry as the authoritative summation of Jewish law and practice.

Until the end of the seventeenth century, the overwhelming majority of the Jews in the Holy Land were either Sephardim, of Spanish extraction, or Orientals. Central and East European influence, however, became prominent in the year 1700, and has existed in unbroken continuity into the contemporary era. A group of several hundred people arrived from Poland under the leadership of Rabbi Judah the Pious, and even though the destiny of this community was not a happy one, these immigrants were followed by others. Toward the end of the eighteenth century there were disciples of Elijah of Wilno, the greatest Talmudic scholar of the age, as well as a major group of relatives and other followers of his great antagonist, the founder of Ḥasidism, Israel

Baal Shem Tov. Both legalists and ecstatics within East European Jewry could not then imagine the continuity of Judaism without a living link to the soil of the Holy Land.

Throughout these centuries economic conditions in the country were generally difficult, and the Jews suffered perhaps more than did other communities. Those in the Holy Land were constantly sending letters and even personal emissaries to their brethren in the Diaspora asking for support, and one of the prime sources of our knowledge of medieval and early modern Jewish history is in what remains of these exchanges. It was a well established tradition throughout the Jewish world that these continuing requests from their brethren in the Holy Land took priority even over local charitable needs.

The Jews in the Holy Land were, to be sure, living largely from foreign alms, and in this they were seemingly parallel to Christian pilgrims and monastic orders in the land during that era. But there were two important points of difference: Jews who came to the Holy Land did not cluster around a variety of holy places, for from Jewish perspective, dwelling in the land, anywhere, was the fulfillment of religious commandment. In the second place, their very presence in the land had radically different resonance among the Jews of the world than the Christian or Moslem presences had among their brethren elsewhere. This often embattled and struggling Jewish community, repeatedly reinforced by new arrivals and always in connection with the whole of the Diaspora, was a constant reminder to the majority that it was living less than the ideal religious life and that return to the land was the ultimate goal. Maimonides, in the twelfth century, had defined this consummation as not necessarily an eschatological event attended by miracles and cataclysms. The restoration would happen in a natural way, by a change in the political situation which would allow Jews to return to their homeland as part of a universal process ushering in a final age of justice and peace. This view did not become the dominant one, for Messianists continued to dream of a cataclysmic "end of days."

Hopes of immediate return were aroused more than once through the ages. For a brief moment in the sixteenth century, when the melodramatic David Reubeni appeared in Rome to offer some supposed military support to Pope Clement VII against the Turks, there was even talk of such a restoration in the highest Christian quarters. The false messiah Shabbetai Zvi had half the Jewish world, and even some Christians, convinced that the miraculous restoration would take place in the year 1666. During Napoleon's campaign in the Middle East in 1799, he summoned the Jews to rally to his banner with the promise that he would help restore them to their land. We know that this offer resulted from some conversation with younger elements of Jewry in the Holy Land. For that matter, the first stirrings towards making an end of living essentially on alms began before the middle of the nineteenth century. Sir Moses Montefiore, the leader of English Jewry, and various forces of the French Jewish community, especially the Rothschild family, worked to teach Jews in Palestine to become artisans and even farmers. Central European philanthropists even created a school for these purposes in 1854 in Jerusalem. It was followed in 1870 by the founding of an agricultural school, Mikveh Israel, and within the next two years two Jewish farm colonies were established. The career of modern Zionism began in 1881, as a direct result of large scale pogroms in Russia, but already in that year, before any of the new immigration to the land began, the American Consul in Jerusalem, Warder Cresson, wrote to his government that there were then a thousand Jews in the country who were deriving their livelihood from agriculture.

III

This ancient and ongoing connection to the land and the messianic hopes which this connection both exemplified and helped to keep in being were the spiritual and emotional climate within which modern Zionism arose. In the immediate situation of the last decades of the nineteenth century the bulk of the world Jewish community, which was then to be found in Europe, found itself confronted by three situations. The most searing and immediate was virulent hatred of Jews, and not only in their major place of settlement in Russia. While millions were on the move from that country after 1881, it occurred to several of the intellectual leaders of Russian Jewry that in their newer homes these emigrants might ultimately be as much in danger as they had been in the places from which they were fleeing. Such phenomena as French and German anti-Semitism towards the end of the century raised the question whether the more liberal part of Europe, in which Jews had been formally emancipated, would honor, in bad times, the promise of equality for all.

In the second place, what seemed then to be the most hopeful of contemporary political ideas was the example of those peoples who were working toward their own national independence. Liberal nationalism was being proclaimed, not in the name of dominance over others, but of a creative future for all the historic communities which would be both autonomous and live in concert with each other. This was the great dream of Mazzini, and the earliest major theoretician of Zionism, Moses Hess, responded to it as early as 1860 with acceptance and profound emotion.

The third situation, and the one perhaps most difficult to define, was the inner spiritual estate of Jewry itself. The dissolution of older values and identities, and especially of the religious, which was engulfing the younger intellectuals of all the traditions of the Western world, was felt with particular poignancy among Jews. The new age was revolutionary and upsetting of the older faiths, but for the Christian majority the continent of Europe, its monuments and most of what men had built on that soil, and its very languages represented the continuity of Christendom. The revolution was occurring for Christians in a context which could ultimately assimilate even these tensions into some new synthesis. But from the Jewish viewpoint, though Western secularity required an act of personal conversion to the mode of life which descended from the majority tradition, those Jews who were willing to undergo this conversion, such as Heine and Disraeli, found themselves less than completely accepted. The nineteenth century, thus, taught some Jews that it had been possible for them to be authentically themselves in the century before, while still in the ghetto, apart from society, whereas in the new, half-emancipated age that followed, it was much more difficult to find their own mode of encountering modernity, either as individuals or as part of their own historic community. The nineteenth century was sufficiently open to Jews, intellectually, for them to experience all of its problems; it was sufficiently closed to deny them the possibility, even if they had wished, to disappear as individuals in modern society. They remained sufficiently rooted in their own older heritage to regard their community as an ultimate spiritual good, worthy of both survival and inner refreshing. They were sufficiently men of their day to feel that their own involvement in their particular past and in the land sacred to their spiritual tradition was in keeping with the contemporary belief that historic communities and peoples were worthy of preservation, for their own sake and for the service of humanity.

The tragedies and torments of the twentieth century and the achievements of the Jews of Israel have confirmed the direst of these predictions and some of the greatest of these hopes.

It cannot be emphasized enough that even the greatest of opportunities that the open society made available to Jews raised for them severe questions of spiritual survival. The rights of equality, wherever they have substantial meaning, were given to Jews as individuals, and the continuity of their community perforce had to be defined as a matter of private belief or, at its most organized, as a religious association parallel to that of contemporary Christian churches. From the Jewish perspective such redefinition, enshrined in the modern slogans of the separation of Church and State or of religion and culture, was a far more difficult and devastating change than it was for the Christian majority in the Western world. For Jews, the holy congregation of all Israel, which means the reality in this world of all that Jews do in community, is the fundamental premise of their identity and tradition.

Classic Jewish interpretation of the Bible has always insisted that Israel "according to the flesh" is what is meant by Isaiah's prophecies concerning "the suffering servant." It is the individual Jew's experience of the Jewish people, of its corporate life, way and history which mediates for him between the individual and God. When the richness and inner integrity of the life of that community is attenuated by either persecution or assimilation, or when belonging to the tradition becomes so privatized as to represent a bewildering variety of personal choices, that which is specifically Jewish in the consciousness of Jews will act, as it had acted in the last century, to recreate a living Jewish community on the land of Israel. For the rest of world Jewry this community represents the indispensable contemporary center which ties Jews to one another and which encourages them to believe that their own lives, though cast in different molds and under minority circumstances, are viable. Its very creation some two decades ago represented a turning away from despair in the aftermath of the Nazi Years and the rekindling among Jews of belief in the future. To use one of the cliches of the contemporary "theology of hope," the Jewish people in the 1940's had ceased believing in either the *humanum* or the *futurum*. It regained belief in both in 1948, when the State of Israel was established.

IV

There can be no doubt that the Zionist reconstitution of a national Jewish community in Palestine in our time was an act which derived both from the ultimate well springs of the historic Jewish faith and from the immediate necessities of a stormy contemporary age. This does not mean that all the trappings of political statehood and all the acts of sovereign power are here being presented as commanded, valid or necessary. On the contrary, what saves any nationalism, any sense of historic community and kinship, from becoming exclusivist, from the arrogance of "blood and soil," is conscience. It is even more wicked to assert that there is no salvation outside one's own nation than to pronounce that there is no salvation outside one's own church. The conscience which protects us from both such assertions has become manifest in the modern age both in secular forms, such as the United Nations Declaration on Human Rights, and in religious pronouncements by all of the major Western faiths. This most fundamental of our moral convictions has as its source Biblical prophecy. It was Amos who said to the Jewish people of his time that in the eyes of God, chosen though they were by Him, they had no more rights than the children of the Ethiopians, and that his bringing the Jews from Egypt was paralleled by his bringing the Philistines from Caftor and the Arameans from Kir. Here we are confronted by the universal element, the command of the living God of all the world, which enters as a radical demand into the midst of every human particularity and keeps it under judgment. Indeed, the meaning of community for Jews is that they live in the real world of action and choice, in this world, and the meaning of their chosenness is that they are subject to the most severe and searching of moral judgments: "Only you have I known from all the nations of the world; therefore, I will visit upon you all your iniquities" (Amos 3:2). For men of religion, indeed for all men of conscience, both elsewhere and in Israel, its acts, like those of any other people, are under judgment.

It needs to be remembered in this connection that the Zionist movement has itself, at least during part of its history, been of two minds about the demand for a sovereign Jewish state. Statehood, as such, was not even in the Zionist program from the days of the Balfour Declaration in 1917 until almost all the Zionists, with the doors of Palestine completely closed to Jews, had little choice but to opt for sovereignty in 1948.

In accepting, in 1917, the last reformulation of the Balfour Declaration, Weizmann and his colleagues knew that they were agreeing to some form of bi-national existence with the Arabs in Palestine. This was all clearer in the exchanges of 1919 between the Emir Feisal and both Felix Frankfurter and Chaim Weizmann. It was against any increase in Jewish numbers in Mandate Palestine, and not against a Jewish State, that Arabs made riots in 1921. For that matter, the repeated stoppages in Jewish immigration by the British authorities under Arab pressure, especially during the 1930's while Hitler was becoming an ever more murderous menace, was what made it clear to the Jews that any increase in their numbers, any possibility of having the legal right to buy land, or even the ultimate safety of their community could not be left to the good will of others, of which there was all too little. From the Jewish perspective, partition, and even statehood, were not hoped-for consummations but, rather, dire necessities. For that matter, even the very military might of Israel is less a source of pride and of national chauvinism than of fear of the constantly threatened destruction. It is certainly beyond doubt that the present choice of Israel is either its own sovereignty or its ceasing to exist, not only as a state, but also as a community. What is equally true is that, for the continuity of Judaism and of Jews, the State of Israel is today a prime necessity for all men who care that the Jewish ethos should flourish and make its own kind of contribution to all of mankind.

PART II

TORAH: A WAY OF LIVING

The theological foundations of classical Judaism support a great structure of law and ethics, a way of living always mindful of the will of God as expressed in the Torah to the people of Israel.

Concrete, everyday actions embody and express the theological convictions of Judaism. These actions are in accord with *halakhah*, the way things are to be done in nearly every situation of life. Torah is not solely a statement *about* reality. It is primarily a way of living. That is to say, Torah is theology, but, even more, it is *halakhah*. And the two cannot be set against one another, for the *halakhah* is the concrete and practical expression of theology, while theology is the abstract and theoretical statement of *halakhah*.

We are what we do: This is the perspective of Judaism. And in the service of God Jews do a great many things. Some of these things concern relations between God and man. Many more express the relationship between man and his fellow man. Still others are about man in his inner life, between man and himself.

The first may be called "ritual," though, if ritual is understood as something external and formal, then the spirit of Jewish ritual, of the practical commandments, is not going to be understood. For nothing could be less ritualistic, less external and formal, than the many practical deeds of religious significance called forth by the *halakhah*.

The second may be called "ethical," though for Judaism one cannot fairly distinguish between "ethics" and "law," as though the first were not defined by the second, and as if the second were not given suppleness and universality by the first. The contrary is the case. Ethics and law reciprocally enrich one another, are so essentially interrelated as to form a single entity.

Finally, we allude to the relationship between man and himself, but this relationship is defined just as are the others, by the ethics and morality of the law.

What is the meaning, first, of Jewish observance, of Torah as a way of life? This is a general question, comprehending not only ritual and ethics, but also the private reflections of the individual, his perceptions, not of an abstraction such as "man," but of the concrete, highly private individual.

How does the law speak of the world of the mind and the soul? What are the ways in which law corresponds to theology? That is our second question.

What of the world beyond the law? The infinite possibilities of daily action cannot be limited and prescribed within a law-code. They are to be worked out through the guidance of ethical principles, applied by the individual to his unique situation. What are the characteristics of Judaic ethical literature?

Having considered ethical literature, we turn to the greatest legal literature of Judaism, its *halakhic* classic, the *Shulhan Aruk*. Who wrote the work? Why did he do so? What did he hope to accomplish?

We begin with theology and end with the legal literature, all the time concentrating attention on the way in which Judaism expresses "Torah" in the mode and manner of life of the ordinary person. This expression constitutes the nexus, the link, between the religious guides and the people as a whole. *Halakhah* is what transforms the normal into the normative.

ROUTINE AND SPONTANEITY IN THE
LIFE OF TORAH

What does it mean to live according to the way of Torah? Torah is not something merely to be studied, but rather a guide to everyday life. So Judaism has taught for thousands of years.

But if that is the case, you have to ask about life under the Torah. That life might be perceived as mechanical, formalistic, the pattern of a robot who always knows what to do and always does what he is told. You might suppose that, with so many laws and traditions, so many religious actions to be done, there will be no room for conscience, for the individual and his own perplexities. You might imagine that there is nothing to be decided, for everything seems already determined.

Nothing could be further from the truth. Here Abraham Joshua Heschel describes his own life within Torah, particularly in regard to prayer.

Now the one thing most people take for granted is that prayer must be spontaneous. You may pray anywhere you feel like doing so. But if you do not feel like doing so, you should pray no where. Now this view stands quite contrary to the position of the Torah, which teaches that you should pray at certain times and in certain ways. You should say certain words, in a prescribed order and formula. There can be no greater contrast than that between the view of prayer widely held within the Western culture and the ideal of prayer within the Torah.

But take an even more striking paradox. The first *mitzvah,* or commandment, of Judaism is to love God with all your heart, with all your soul, and with all your might. That is what the *Shema* says. But how can you *command* love? How is the love of God a command-ment, a religious requirement? Nothing, after all, more fully depends upon the heart, upon the conscience of the private person, than love. It is something you give freely, of your own will, or not at all. You cannot make someone else love you. You cannot force yourself to love God.

Now when prayer has to be said at a certain time and in a certain way, it may easily become routine, a habit, not an expression of the heart at all. But then it may hardly be called prayer. But if prayer is not called forth on particular occasions and for prescribed purposes, there may be no praying at all. For prayer is the most difficult and most elevated religious action—religious *duty,* Judaism would say.

How do you find a way between pure habit and utter capriciousness? How do you pray when you do not feel like it? Is not prayer submerged by the requirement to pray? In larger terms, is not love destroyed by law? These are the issues to be brought to Rabbi Heschel, for he asks himself these very questions, explaining, out of his years as a Jew in Berlin, what he discovered about the meaning of Jewish observance.

VIII
THE MEANING OF OBSERVANCE

ABRAHAM JOSHUA HESCHEL

[From *The Jewish Frontier*, April, 1954, pp. 22-28.]

While man is attached to the ultimate at the root of his being, he is detached and uncurbed in his thoughts and deeds, free to act and free to refrain; he has the power to disobey. Yet a tree is known by its fruits, not by its roots. There are no ugly trees but there are wormy fruits. Only one question, therefore, is worthy of supreme anxiety. How to live in a world pestered with lies and remain unpolluted, how not to be stricken with despair, not to flee but fight and succeed in keeping the soul unsoiled and even aid in purifying the world?

Such strength, such guidance cannot be wrested from the stars. Nature is too aloof or too old to teach confused man how to discern right and wrong. The sense of the ineffable is necessary, but not sufficient to find the way from wonder to worship, from willingness to realization, from awe to action.

Western philosophy has suffered its tragic defeat as a consequence of the fondness of its great masters for the problem of cognition. Guided by the assumption that he who knows how to think will know how to live, philosophy has, since the days of Socrates, been primarily a quest of right thinking. Particularly since the time of Descartes, it concentrated its attention on the problem of cognition, becoming less and less aware of the problem of living. In fact, the less relevant to living a problem was, the more respectable and worthy of exploration it appeared to philosophers.

However, thinking about ultimate problems is more than a particular skill. It is an act of the total personality, a process into which all faculties of mind and soul are thrown, and is necessarily affected by the personal climate in which it comes to pass; we think the way we live. To think what we sense, we must live what we think. If culture is to be more than the product of a hothouse, then it must grow out of

93

the soil of daily living, and in turn affect the inner stronghold of the human personality. Culture has to grow from within outward, from the concrete existence, conduct and condition of man.

There is darkness in the world and horror in the soul. What is it that the world needs most? Harsh and bitter are the problems which religion comes to solve: ignorance, evil, malice, power, agony, despair. These problems cannot be solved through generalities, through philosophical symbols. Our problem is: Do we believe what we confess? Do we mean what we say?

We do not suffer symbolically. We suffer literally, truly, deeply. Symbolic remedies are quackery. The will of God is either real or a delusion.

This is the most important challenge to us: "We have eyes to see but see not; we have ears to hear but hear not." Any other issue is relevant only as far as it helps us to answer that challenge.

I came with great hunger to the University of Berlin to study philosophy. I looked for a system of thought, for the depth of the spirit, for the meaning of existence. Erudite and profound scholars gave courses in logic, epistemology, esthetics, ethics and metaphysics. They opened the gates of the history of philosophy. I was exposed to the austere discipline of unremitting inquiry and self-criticism. I communed with the thinkers of the past who knew how to meet intellectual adversity with fortitude, and learned to dedicate myself to the examination of basic premises at the risk of failure.

Yet, in spite of the impressive intellectual attainments offered to me, I became increasingly aware of the gulf that separated my views from those held at the University. I had come with a sense of anxiety: how can I rationally find a way where ultimate meaning lies, a way of living where one could never miss a reference to supreme significance? Why am I here at all, and what is my purpose? I did not even know how to phrase my concern. But to my teachers that was a question unworthy of philosophical analysis.

I realized: my teachers were prisoners of a Greek-German way of thinking. They were fettered in categories which presupposed certain metaphysical assumptions which could never be proved. The questions I was moved by could not even be adequately phrased in categories of their thinking.

My assumption was: man's dignity consists in his having been created in the likeness of God. My question was: how must man, a being who is in essence the image of God, think, feel and act? To them, religion was a feeling. To me, religion included the insights of the Torah which is a vision of man from the point of view of God. They spoke of God from the point of view of man. To them God was an idea, a postulate of reason. They granted Him the status of being a logical possibility. But to assume that He had existence would have been a crime against epistemology.

The problem to my professors was how to be good. In my ears the question rang: how to be holy. At the time I realized: There is much that philosophy could learn from Jewish life. To the philosophers: the idea of the good was the most exalted idea, the ultimate idea. To Judaism the idea of the good is pen-ultimate. It cannot exist without the holy. The good is the base, the holy is the summit. Man cannot be good unless he strives to be holy.

In those months in Berlin I went through moments of profound bitterness. I felt very much alone with my own problems and anxieties. I walked alone in the evenings through the magnificent streets of Berlin. I admired the solidity of its architecture, the overwhelming drive and power of a dynamic civilization. There were concerts, theatres, and lectures by famous scholars about the latest theories and inventions, and I was pondering whether to go to the new Max Reinhardt play or to a lecture about the theory of relativity.

Suddenly I noticed the sun had gone down, evening had arrived. "From what time may one recite the Shema in the evening?"

I had forgotten—I had forgotten Sinai—I had forgotten that sunset is my business—that my task is "to restore the world to the kingship of the Almighty."

So I began to utter the words: "With his word brings on the evenings . . ."

And Goethe's famous poem rang in my ear:

Ueber allen Gipfeln ist Ruh
O'er all the hilltops is quiet now.

No, that was pagan thinking. To the pagan eye the mystery of life is Ruh, death, oblivion.

To us Jews, there is meaning beyond the mystery. We would say:

O'er all the hilltops is the word of God
Ueber allen Gipfeln ist Gottes Wort.

Blessed are thou . . . who with his word brings on the evenings.

And His love is manifested in His teaching us Torahs, precepts, laws . . .

Ueber allen Gipfeln is God's love for man—
Thou hast loved the house of Israel with everlasting love
Thou hast taught us Torah, mitzvoth, laws, rules.

How much guidance, how many ultimate insights are found in the *Siddur* [Jewish prayerbook].

How grateful I am to God that there is a duty to worship, a law to remind my distraught mind that it is time to think of God, time to disregard my ego for at least a moment! It is such happiness to belong to an order of the divine will.

I am not always in a mood to pray. I do not always have the vision and the strength to say a word in the presence of God. But when I am weak, it is the law that gives me strength; when my vision is dim, it is duty that gives me insight.

Indeed, there is something which is far greater than my desire to pray. Namely, God's desire that I pray. There is something which is far greater than my will to believe. Namely, God's will that I believe. How insignificant is my praying in the midst of a cosmic process! Unless it is the will of God that I pray, how ludicrous is it to pray.

On that evening, in the streets of Berlin, I was not in a mood to pray. My heart was heavy, my soul was sad. It was difficult for the lofty words of prayer to break through the dark clouds of my inner life.

But how would I dare not to *davn* [worship]? How would I dare to miss a *ma'ariv* [the evening prayer]?

Why did I decide to take *Halacha* seriously in spite of the numerous perplexities in which I became enmeshed?

Why did I pray, although I was not in a mood to pray? And why was I able to pray in spite of being unprepared to pray? What was my situation after the reminder to pray *Ma'ariv* struck my mind? The duty to worship stood as a thought of ineffable meaning; doubt, the voice of disbelief, was ready to challenge it. But where should the engagement take place? In an act of reflection the duty to worship is a mere thought, timid, frail, a mere shadow of reality, while the voice of disbelief is a power, well-armed with the weight of inertia and the preference for abstention. In such an engagement prayer would be fought in *absentia,* and the issue would be decided without actually joining the battle. It was fair, therefore, to give the weaker rival a chance: to pray first, to fight later.

I realized that just as you cannot study philosophy through praying, you cannot study prayer through philosophizing. And what applies to prayer is true in regard to the essentials of Jewish observance.

What I wanted to avoid was not only the failure to pray to God during a whole evening of my life but the *loss of the whole,* the loss of belonging to the spiritual order of Jewish living. It is true that some people are so busy with collecting shreds and patches of the law, that they hardly think of weaving the pattern of the whole. But there is also the danger of being so enchanted by the whole as to lose sight of the detail. It became increasingly clear to me that the order of Jewish living is meant to be, not a set of rituals, but an order of all of man's existence, shaping all his traits, interests and disposition; "not so much the performance of single acts, the taking of a step now and then, as the pursuit of a way, being on the way; not so much the acts of fulfilling as the state of being committed to the task, the belonging to an order in which single deeds, aggregates of religious feeling, sporadic sentiments, moral episodes become a part of a complete pattern."

The ineffable Name, we have forgotten how to pronounce it. We have almost forgotten how to spell it. We may totally forget how to recognize it.

There are a number of ideas concerning Jewish law which have proved most inimical to its survival, and I would like to refer to two. One is the assumption that either you observe all or nothing; all of its rules are of equal importance; and if one brick is removed, the whole edifice must collapse. Such intransigeance, laudable as it may be as an expression of devoutness, is neither historically nor theologically justified. There were ages in Jewish history when some aspects of Jewish ritual observance were not adhered to by people who had otherwise lived according to the law. And where is the man who could claim that he has been able to fulfill literally the *mitzvah* of "Love your neighbor as yourself"?

From a rationalist's point of view it does not seem plausible to assume that the infinite, ultimate supreme Being is concerned with my putting on *Tefillin* [phylacteries] every day. It is, indeed, absurd to believe that God should care whether a particular individual will eat leavened or unleavened bread during a particular season of the year [Passover]. However, it is that paradox, namely that the infinite God is intimately concerned with finite man and his finite deeds, that nothing is trite or irrelevant in the eyes of God, which is the very essence of the prophetic faith.

There are people who are hesitant to take seriously the possibility of our knowing what the will of God demands of us. Yet we all wholeheartedly accept Micah's words: "He has showed you, O man, what is good, and what does the Lord require of you, but to do justice, and to love kindness and to walk humbly with your God." If we believe that there is something which God requires of man, then what is our belief if not *faith in the will of God, certainty of knowing what His will de-*

mands of us? If we are ready to believe that God requires of us to be holy, if we are ready to believe that it is God who requires us "to love kindness," is it more difficult to believe that God requires us to hallow the Sabbath and not to violate its sanctity?

If it is the word of Micah uttering the will of God that we believe in, and not a peg on which to hang views we derived from rationalist philosophies, then "to love justice" is just as much *Halacha* as the prohibition of making a fire on the Seventh Day. If, however, all we can hear in these words are echoes of Western philosophy rather than the voice of Micah, does that mean that the prophet has nothing to say to any of us?

A serious difficulty is the problem *of the meaning of Jewish observance.* The modern Jew cannot accept the way of static obedience as a short-cut to the mystery of the divine will. His religious situation is not conducive to an attitude of intellectual or spiritual surrender. He is not ready to sacrifice his liberty on the altar of loyalty to the spirit of his ancestors. He will only respond to a demonstration that there is meaning to be found in what we expect him to do. His primary difficulty is not in his inability to comprehend the *Divine origin* of the law; his essential difficulty is in his inability to sense the presence of *Divine meaning* in the fulfillment of the law.

Let us never forget that some of the basic theological presuppositions of Judaism cannot be justified in terms of human reason. Its conception of prayer and of the nature of man as having been created in the likeness of God, its conception of God and history and even of morality defy some of the realizations at which we have honestly arrived at the end of our analysis and scrutiny. The demands of piety are a mystery before which man is reduced to reverence and silence. In a technological society, when religion becomes a function, piety, too, is an instrument to satisfy his needs. We must, therefore, be particularly careful not to fall into the habit of looking at religion as if it were a machine which can be worked, an organization which can be run according to one's calculations.

The problem of how to live as a Jew cannot be solved in terms of common sense and common experience. The order of Jewish living is a spiritual one; it has a spiritual logic of its own which cannot be apprehended unless its basic terms are lived and appreciated.

It is in regard to this problem that we must keep in mind three things. a) Divine meaning is *spiritual* meaning; b) the perception of Divine meaning is contingent upon *spiritual preparedness;* c) it is experienced *in acts,* rather than in speculation.

a) The problem of ethics is: what is the ideal or principle of conduct that is rationally justifiable? While to religion the problem of living is: what is the ideal or principle of living that is spiritually justifiable? The legitimate question concerning the forms of Jewish observance is, therefore, the question: Are they spiritually meaningful?

We should, consequently, not evaluate the *mitzvoth* [religious deeds] by the amount of rational meaning we may discover at their basis. Religion is not within but beyond the limits of mere reason. Its task is not to compete with reason, to be a source of speculative ideas, but to aid us where reason gives us only partial aid. Its meaning must be understood in terms compatible with the sense of the ineffable. Frequently where concepts fail, where rational understanding ends, the meaning of observance begins. Its purpose is not essentially to serve hygiene, happiness or the vitality of man; its purpose is to add holiness to hygiene, grandeur to happiness, spirit to vitality.

Spiritual meaning is not always limpid; transparency is the quality of glass, while diamonds are distinguished by refractive power and the play of prismatic colors.

Indeed, any reason we may advance for our loyalty to the Jewish order of living merely points to one of its many facets. To say that the *mitzvoth* have meaning is less accurate than saying that they lead us to wells of emergent meaning, to experiences which are full of hidden brilliance of the holy, suddenly blazing in our thoughts.

Those who, out of their commendable desire to save the Jewish way of life, bring its meaning under the hammer, tend to sell it at the end to the lowest bidder. The highest values are not in demand and are not saleable on the marketplace. In spiritual life some experiences are like a *camera obscura,* through which light has to enter in order to form an image upon the mind, the image of ineffable intelligibility. Insistence upon explaining and relating the holy to the relative and functional is like lighting a candle in the camera.

Works of piety are like works of art. They are functional, they serve a purpose, but their essence is intrinsic, their value is in what they are in themselves.

b) Sensitivity to spiritual meaning is not easily won; it is the fruit of hard, constant devotion, of insistence upon remaining true to a vision. It is "an endless pilgrimage . . . a drive towards serving Him who rings our hearts like a bell, as if He were waiting to enter our lives . . ." Its essence is not revealed in the way we utter it, but in the soul's being in accord with what is relevant to God; in the extension of our love to what God may approve, our being carried away by the tide of His thoughts, rising beyond the desolate ken of man's despair".

"God's grace resounds in our lives like a staccato. Only by retaining the seemingly disconnected notes comes the ability to grasp the
theme."

c) What is the Jewish way to God? It is not a way of ascending
the ladder of speculation. Our understanding of God is not the triumphant outcome of an assault upon the riddles of the universe nor a
donation we receive in return for intellectual surrender. Our understanding comes by the way of *mitzvah*. By living as Jews we attain our
faith as Jews. We do not have faith in deeds; we attain faith through
deeds.

When Moses recounted to the people the laws of the covenant with
God, the people responded: "We will do and we will hear." This statement was interpreted to mean: *In doing we perceive.*

A Jew is asked to take *a leap of action* rather than *a leap of faith*:
to surpass his needs, to do more than he understands in order to understand more than he does. In carrying out the word of the Torah he is
ushered into the presence of spiritual meaning. Through the ecstasy of
deeds he learns to be certain of the presence of God.

Jewish law is a sacred prosody. The Divine sings in our deeds,
the Divine is disclosed in our deeds. Our effort is but a counterpoint in
the music of His will. In exposing our lives to God we discover the
Divine within ourselves and its accord with the Divine beyond ourselves.

If at the moment of doing a *mitzvah* once perceived to be thus
sublime, thus Divine, you are in it with all your heart and with all your
soul, there is no great distance between you and God. For acts of
holiness uttered by the soul disclose the holiness of God hidden in
every moment of time. And His holiness and He are one.

Why should worship be bound to regular occasions? Why impose
a calendar on the soul? Is not regularity of observance a menace to the
freedom of the heart?

Strict observance of a way of life at fixed times and in identical
forms tends to become a matter of routine, of outward compliance.
How to prevent observance from becoming stereotyped, mechanical,
was, indeed, a perennial worry in the history of Judaism. The cry of
the prophet: "Their heart is far from me" was a signal of alarm.

Should I reject the regularity of prayer and rely on the inspiration
of the heart and only worship when I am touched by the spirit?
Should I resolve: unless the spirit comes, I shall abstain from praying?
The deeper truth is that routine breeds attention, calling forth a response where the soul would otherwise remain dormant. One is com-

mitted to being affected by the holy, if he abides at the threshold of its realm. Should it be left to every individual to find his own forms of worship whenever the spirit would move him? Yet who is able to extemporize a prayer without falling into the trap of cliches? Moreover, spiritual substance grows in clinging to a source of spirit richer than one's own.

Inspirations are brief, sporadic and rare. In the long interims the mind is often dull, bare and vapid. There is hardly a soul that can radiate more light than it receives. To perform a *mitzvah* is to meet the spirit. But the spirit is not something we can acquire once and for all but something we must be with. For this reason the Jewish way of life is to reiterate the ritual, to meet the spirit again and again, the spirit in oneself and the spirit that hovers over all beings.

At the root of our difficulties in appreciating the role of *Halacha* in religious living is, I believe, our conception of the very essence of religion. "We are often inclined to define the essence of religion as a state of the soul, as inwardness, as an absolute feeling, and except a person who is religious to be endowed with a kind of sentiment too deep to rise to the surface of common deeds, as if religion were a plant that can only thrive at the bottom of the ocean. Now to Judaism religion is not a feeling for something that is, but *an answer* to Him who is asking us to live in a certain way. *It is in its very origin a consciousness of duty, of being committed to higher ends;* a realization that life is not only man's but also God's sphere of interest."

"God asks for the heart." Yet does he ask for the heart only? Is the right intention enough? Some doctrines insist that love is the sole condition for salvation, stressing the importance of inwardness, of love or faith, to the exclusion of good works. . . .

Faith does not come to an end with attaining certainty of God's existence. Faith is the beginning of intense craving to enter an active relationship with Him who is beyond the mystery, to bring together all the might that is within us with all that is spiritual beyond us. At the root of our yearning for integrity is a stir of the inexpressible within us to commune with the ineffable beyond us. But what is the language of that communion, without which our impulse remains inarticulate?

We are taught that what God asks of man is more than an inner attitude, that He gives man not only *life* but also *a law,* that His will is to be served not only adored, *obeyed* not only *worshipped.* Faith comes over us like a force urging to action. We respond by pledging ourselves to constancy of devotion, committing us to the presence of God. This remains a life allegiance involving restraint, submission, self-control and courage.

Judaism insists upon establishing a unity of *faith* and *creed*, of *piety* and *Halacha,* of *devotion* and *deed.* Faith is but a *seed,* while the deed is its growth of decay. Faith disembodied, faith that tires to grow in splendid isolation, is but a ghost, for which there is no place in our psychophysical world.

What *creed* is in relation to *faith,* the *Halacha* is in relation to *piety.* As faith cannot exist without a creed, piety cannot subsist without a pattern of deeds; as intelligence cannot be separated from training, religion cannot be divorced from conduct. Judaism is lived in deeds, not only in thoughts.

A pattern for living—the object of our most urgent quest—which would correspond to man's ultimate dignity, must take into consideration not only his ability to exploit the forces of nature and to appreciate the loveliness of its forms, but also his unique sense of the ineffable. It must be a design, not only for the satisfaction of needs, but also for the attainment of an end, the end of being *a holy people.*

The integrity of life is not exclusively a thing of the heart, and Jewish piety is therefore more than consciousness of the moral law. The innermost chamber must be guarded at the uttermost outposts. Religion is not the same as spiritualism; what man does in his concrete physical existence is directly relevant to the divine. Spirituality is the goal, not the way of man. In this world music is played on physical instruments, and to the Jew the *mitzvoth* are the instruments by which the holy is performed. If man were only mind, worship in thought would be the form in which to commune with God. But man is body and soul, and his goal is to love so that both "his heart and his flesh" should sing to the living God.

Moreover, worship is not one thing, and living, another. Does Judaism consist of sporadic landmarks in the realm of living, of temples in splendid isolation, of festive celebrations on extraordinary days? The synagogue is not a retreat, and that which is decisive is not the performance of rituals at distinguished occasions, but how they affect the climate of the entire life.

The highest peak of spiritual living is not necessarily reached in rare moments of ecstasy; the highest peak lies wherever we are and may be ascended in a common deed. There can be as sublime a holiness in fulfilling friendship, in observing dietary laws, day by day, as in uttering a prayer on the Day of Atonement.

Jewish tradition maintains that there is no extraterritoriality in the realm of the spirit. Economics, politics, dietetics are just as much as ethics within its sphere. It is in man's intimate rather than public life, in the way he fulfills his physiological functions that character is formed. It is immensely significant that, according to the Book of Genesis, the first prohibition given to man concerned the enjoyment of the forbidden fruit.

"The fate of a people . . . is decided according to whether they begin culture at the right place—not at the soul. The right place is the body, demeanor, diet, physiology; the rest follows . . . contempt of the body is the greatest mishap." Judaism begins at the bottom, taking very seriously the forms of one's behavior in relation to the external, even conventional functions, and amenities of life, teaching us how to eat, how to rest, how to act. The discipline of feelings and thoughts comes second. The body must be persuaded first. "Thou shalt not covet" is the last of the Ten Commandments, even though it may be the first in the case history of the afore-mentioned transgressions. While not prescribing a diet—vegetarian or otherwise—or demanding abstinence from narcotics or stimulants, Judaism is very much concerned with what and how a person ought to eat. A sacred discipline for the body is as important as bodily strength. . . .

BELIEF AND BEHAVIOR: CORRESPONDENCES

Halakhah, "the way," refers to the laws which guide the life of the pious Jew. In classical Judaism theologians find much leeway for argument and disagreement, even about the most fundamental questions.

Granted one is expected to believe in God, in the Torah as the revealed will of God, in the resurrection of the dead. But what do you mean by "God"? Is he like man, or wholly different from man? What is included in "Torah"? What do you mean by "revelation"? Some theologians may stress a mystical interpretation of all of reality, including of the beliefs of Judaism, and others will offer a highly rational view. One philosopher of religion will say that revelation is needed because human reason is inadequate to uncover the truths of God. Another will say that reason would have found out all that the Torah has to teach, but revelation made the process of discovery easier and brought man more rapidly to the will of God.

These disagreements are possible because the norms of the faith are not set within them. The norms are established by law. Argue as you will, differ as you must, at the end you will say your prayers at sunrise, because so the law demands. The most abstruse theological arguments will not affect the prayers you say at sundown.

Yet the laws too contain important ideas, express those ideas in concrete actions. So you cannot suppose that the pious Jew is a religious behaviorist, who does what he is told without thinking, without *meaning something* by what he does.

The contrary is the case. The *halakhah* is normative, is central to the Judaic way of life, precisely because through it are expressed the fundamental convictions of Judaism. The *halakhah* is not a collection of empty prescriptions and meaningless hocus-pocus, but an expression of the heart and soul of the believing Jew. It will not only express what he believes, but shape and mold his perceptions of the world.

David S. Shapiro, who is a rabbi in Milwaukee, Wisconsin, and teaches at the University of Wisconsin-Milwaukee, explains in some detail the correspondence between *halakhah* and theological ideas (he uses the word, "ideology" where other religious thinkers might

105

say "theology"). He shows that it is too simple, too facile, to suppose observance says nothing to, or about, the observant person.

What is the correspondence between belief and behavior? How does the law convey meanings beyond itself? Do forms and gestures bear theological significance? These are the questions to be asked.

IX

THE IDEOLOGICAL FOUNDATIONS
OF THE HALAKHAH

David S. Shapiro

(From *Tradition*. A Journal of Orthodox Jewish Thought, Vol. 9, Nos. 1-2, Spring-Summer, 1967, pp. 100-122. Footnotes have not been reproduced.)

Halakhah is the way of life formulated by the Torah for the guidance of mankind and Israel. But Halakhah is also a vast system of thought that extends over the limitless ranges of human experience, subjecting them to its critical scrutiny in the light of the principles, regulations and laws revealed at Sinai and unfolded in the religious literature of subsequent millenia. The Halakhah is dual in character; it is empirical and ideal, pure and applied, method and legislation. Pure Halakhah contains the *a priori* postulates which subject the world to its quantitative and qualitative norms. For the ideal Halakhah the actuality of its norms or their realizability may be of no consequence. The intellectual preoccupation of the great men of Halakhah has, to a great extent, been the ideal construction rather than its practical application. But, in addition to its ontological character, the Halakhah has its normative side. It seeks to impose its forms on mundane reality. The ethos which derives from the halakhic *a priori* constitutes the goal of the Halakhah. "Great is study for it culminates in practice."

A pertinent question has recently been raised as to whether the characteristics of the "man of Halakhah" could not easily be attributed to personality types known in Roman Catholicism. This writer is not in a position to know to what extent a Roman Catholic "Halakhah" operates in the life of a devout adherent of that faith. After all, did not Paul set out to demolish the authority of the traditional Halakhah in favor of salvation through the "blood of the lamb"? Yet despite the initial anti-nomianism of Gentile Christianity, Roman Catholicism has set up its own "halakhic" forms with its rigorous demands and insistence on precision both in the performance of its sacraments and in its directives for daily conduct in various phases of life. In the long run, however, the question raised about Roman Catholic "Halakhah" may not be too significant, because we may be dealing here with vestiges of Jewish influence, as is probably also true of the "halakhic" counterparts of the Islamic way of life.

More significant is the question whether the Halakhah as such is a specifically Jewish phenomenon. If Halakhah simply stands for a body of rules and regulations that discipline the lives of groups and individuals, then the term could be applied to codes of behavior that control the lives of followers of any religious system (or political structure, for that matter). All societies, from the most primitive to the most advanced, impose upon their constituents norms of conduct, religious taboos, and rules of etiquette which, more or less, approximate halakhic standards. The strictness of primitive taboos in certain areas of life is well known, and has already been noted by various Jewish medieval thinkers. Maimonides states in the *Guide*: "The fourth (purpose of the laws of purity) is to ease unpleasant restrictions and to order things in such a manner that questions of uncleanness and cleanness should not prevent a man from engaging in any of his occupations."

Yet we are convinced that the Halakhah is the uniquely Jewish response to the divine call and that the halakhic act is the truly sacred act. The uniqueness of the Halakhah is not its regulative character, nor even its range, comprehensiveness, intensity and precision. What makes it unique, I believe, are rather the objectives that it has set out to accomplish and the religious principles upon which it is established and which it seeks to further. The Halakhah may be unique also in terms of its methodology, but this quality is primarily of interest to students of logic and comparative thought. For us the uniqueness of Halakhah consists in its contents, in the realm of ends towards which it strives, in the ideology in which it has its genesis and in its mandatory character. The Halakhah is the divine law for man, not merely a tool for the avoidance of misfortune or for the attainment of blessings from on High. It is the supreme concretization of the will of God for mundane existence. Above all else, it seeks for man the achievement of the goal for which he was created: the attainment of his Godlikeness—the unfolding within him of his divine image.

I

The Halakhah is not a mere random collection of rules and statutes. It is a system of thought and conduct based on a classification of six hundred and thirteen commandments. Subdivided into positive and negative commandments, they are categorized into those that pertain to man's relation to God and those that govern his relation to his fellow-man. The commandments also have been classified as *torot* [revelations], *chukkim* [ordinances], *mishpatim* [laws], *edot* [testimonies], and *mitzvot* [religious actions, commandments]. This classification goes back to the Torah itself and is highlighted in the 19th and 119th Psalms.

A comprehensive analysis of the divine commandments was attempted to a large scale by Maimonides. In modern times, the most thorough attempt was made by Rabbi Samson Raphael Hirsch in his *Nineteen Letters, Chorev,* and *Commentary to the Pentateuch.* In these works a total philosophy of the Halakhah is expounded, perhaps the most thorough attempt to achieve this goal in the history of Jewish rational thought. The Kabbalists have, in their own way, constructed thorough and heaven-soaring metaphysical systems whereby every aspect of the Torah and every detail of the Halakhah assume their proper niche in a cosmic framework. But not many of the rationalistic thinkers of Judaism have dared to do the same for the Halakhah within the scope of their own world-outlook.

The Halakhah is a harmonious system, not a monolithic one, and, in spite of differences and apparent discrepancies, it must be viewed as an organic whole. This striving for unity is evident in the presumed harmony behind the disparate halakhic positions maintained by various sages. The Halakhah is a Revelation which emanates from the One Shepherd of Israel. We must endeavor to find the Revealer in the Revelation in all its aspects, ramifications, and divergencies. For students of the Torah the proposition "Both views are the words of the living God" is more than a mere verbalism. It is a principle which directs them to deeper understanding and more penetrating insights. Through discovery of the *reasons for the commandments* one is able to see the unity permeating the entire structure of Halakhah. It becomes the task of every generation to continue in the enterprise of searching for the *reasons of the commandments.* How much more relevant has this task become for our generation when surrender to blind commitment is very difficult for thoughtful people.

The Torah speaks to all generations and to all individuals. Not merely does every person have to apply the practical norms of the Halakhah to his own unique situation, but he must seek to make it meaningful as he performs the act. The actual dissimilarity among human beings (which justifies the right to differences and individuality for thereby God's greatness is manifested) compels a dynamic and flexible view of the character of Halakhah. Our mystics teach us that all the world is in a constant state of flux. In an expanding, growing, and unfolding universe, it is unbelievable that the divine Torah itself does not participate and partake of this dynamic quality. All our sages who wrote *chiddushim* (novellae) [new insights] on all phases of halakhic (as well as aggadic) research were tacitly committed to this concept of novelty. Perhaps for this reason Halakhists continue to deal with problems which have engaged the attention of their predecessors in past generations. Every age looks at the same problems with different eyes, as does every individual. This unique insight which is the divine gift to every individual constitutes that individual's portion in the Torah for the attainment of which he always prays.

The immutability of the Torah is one of the basic tenets of our faith. The Torah represents the eternal will of God. Nevertheless, the application of the will of God cannot remain static. The Torah was given to Israel and its sages who are to serve as co-workers with the Giver of the Torah in everlastingly recreating it under varying circumstances and changing conditions so that it may properly serve the purpose for which it was given. In search for the appropriate application of Halakhah at any given historical moment, the sages of Israel discover that what was revealed at Sinai was waiting to be disclosed at the moment when the need for this discovery became indispensable.

The idea that the Halakhah is historically conditioned should not seem strange. That Halakhah transcends time and space is not a meaningful concept, since it is intended to operate *within* the confines of historical and spatio-temporal reality. However, only the Torah can define the relationship of its laws to time, space and history, and set the conditions under which its commandments are binding. Within these limits its imperatives are absolute.

At the same time the Torah makes possible a wide latitude of personal initiative in the observance of the commandments. These areas of individual aspiration are included in the numerous general commandments among which are those that issue a call to do the good and the right, strive for holiness, walk in the ways of the Creator, seek the ways of pleasantness and peace, go beyond the measure of the law, and aspire to achieve the highest level of piety. This latitude, of course, calls for the assumption of a greater range of responsibilities on a far more intensive level. It challenges man to seek the road that leads to Godlikeness and the sanctification of God's Name.

That the Halakhah is a vast open system of thought and practice imbedded in a powerful and dynamic universe, rather than a fixed and static one, makes it possible for the people bound by it to go from strength to strength in endless search for its God on high. Because of its character, the Halakhah must keep open to the universe and attuned to all currents of thought. Since the Torah derives from the Creator, Who is guiding the universe towards never-ending goals, the openness of the Halakhah and its eternal vitality is made possible.

II

Halakhah is neither theology nor anthropology, but it is obviously based on both. As a phase of Torah, Halakhah is the earthly embodiment of the divine word and derives from the essential character of God. With man its primary concern, the Torah must have a doctrine of God and a theory of man to which its Halakhah corresponds. Theology and anthropology are preconditions of Halakhah. For this reason it would be correct to say that the acceptance of God as the Ultimate Reality cannot be included within the framework of Halakhah, since all of Halakhah is predicated on the truth of this assumption.

In what way does the theology of Judaism find its explication in the Halakhah?

The reality of God is the ground upon which everything in the Torah is based. While there are proponents of non-theistic ethics for whom the goal of human survival is the paramount principle, for the Torah the will of God is the source of all concepts of right and wrong. The Halakhah is the will of God, an expression of His nature. For men this means that there obtains a relationship between God and the universe, a concept which, of course, has a significance for man which it does not have for God.

The relationship of God to the universe involves two concepts: the transcendence of God and His immanence. The doctrine of transcendence proclaims the freedom of God from subjection to inexorable fate. It emancipates Him from any possible limitation by any existent force outside of Him. God is a free agent, limitless in His creative powers, recreating and refashioning the world ever anew. God, Who is Himself unshackled, is the Creator of freedom. Man's freedom is the product of the divine freedom. The very possibility of Revelation is grounded in the divine freedom. It is at this juncture that theology and anthropology intersect. Because this universe has its origin in a Being Who is free and has chosen man to be free, the Halakhah which makes demands upon man as a free agent is made possible. It is God Who has redeemed Israel from the house of bondage, who calls upon Israel to accept His yoke not as slaves subject to a tyrannical master, but as free men who voluntarily choose His service out of reverence and love.

God's transcendence is the ground for the doctrine of *creatio ex nihilo*. An uncreated world would be transcendent in respect to God as He is transcendent in respect to the world. In a pantheistic cosmos no transcendence obtains. God and the universe are co-extensive, even where God is infinite in His attributes. Because God's power over the universe is unlimited, He has made it possible for man to act upon the universe and lead it to higher and higher levels of grandeur. The profound religious significance of *creatio ex nihilo* is not merely that Revelation and a supernatural operation upon history are predicated upon this doctrine, but that a self-sufficient universe (at least in its finite modes) could not possibly be that kind of dynamic universe as the one created by God Who, calling it into being from eternal nothingness, enables it to rise to unimaginably lofty heights limited only by His infinity. The possibilities of man's ascent are likewise unlimited, except for the bounds set by his Creator.

While the doctrine of transcendence makes Halakhah possible, the doctrine of immanence determines the character of the Halakhah. Because God created the world, we conclude that "the earth is the Lord's and the fulness thereof, the world and they that dwell therein" (Psalms 24:1). The universe is His possession in which he finds delight. He is transcendent to it but He also dwells with it because He loves it, and He fills it with His overflowing goodness. The world and all that is therein are, therefore, to be regarded as divine creations to which attaches the sacredness wherewith God has endowed His creation. God's creation may not be employed for purposes not sanctioned by the Creator. Man's control over the world, as well as the rights of all creatures, are determined by Him Who is the Author of all things and has placed the world at man's disposal to bring it to perfection and lift it up to the highest goals of eschatological fulfillment. It is He Who, at the same time, distinguishes between darkness and light, between the holy and the profane, and between the pure and the unclean. In the first chapter of Genesis God reveals Himself in two capacities: as the Creator and the Divider. The two major divisions of Halakhah, the positive and the negative, are based on these two aspects of divine activity. The positive in Halakhah reflects on a human level the creative activity of God. The negative bespeaks the finite and unredeemed character of the universe wherein the evil derived from man's freedom is countered and overcome by means of man's withdrawal from contact with it.

The concept of the unity of God is essential for the undivided commitment demanded by the Halakhah, which formulates the imperatives of God. Any multiplicity of deities is based on an assumption of the bifurcated character of the universe. Under such conditions there can be no undivided commitment to the good. Man would constantly be torn between loyalties. A spiritual concept of God is likewise fundamental for the halakhic outlook. Corporeal characteristics attributed to God would ultimately result in a denial of the divine transcendence. He would then come to be regarded as a superhuman being, partaking both of human frailties as well as virtues. Instead of being the originator of all being, He would be regarded as included within the order of creation. Right and wrong would no longer be determined by Him. As a finite God, He would be a victim of a pre-existent good and evil over which He could exercise no ultimate control. Thus, the goals of Halakhah for never-ending perfection would be impossible. The ideal of *Imitatio Dei* towards which the Halakhah directs the human personality would easily be corrupted.

God, Who is the Creator and the Only One, demands a reverential attitude towards the world He has created. He has created the world out of love. In His goodness He maintains it, and by His grace He provides for its sustenance. Not a single item is excluded from the sphere of divine interest since everything exists for the purpose designated by its Maker. All of creation stands at His service and fulfills His holy will. God has imposed His law and order upon the physical world. All creatures are kept within their bounds by the limits of natural law and thus obey the will of God. Revelation, which at its lowest level represents the imposition of a divine order upon the physical and biological realms, reaches its peak in the demand for law and order in the life of man. It is the character of God as Creator and Sustainer of the world, His transcendence and immanence, that determines man's relationship to the universe. The essence of the Law embodied in His Revelation is determined by the very nature of God, since it has its origin in Him. The Halakhah reflects not merely the will of God, but that which is identical with His will—His essence.

The anthropology of Halakhah is based, as stated above, on the concept of freedom. Man is free to choose, and man's true humanity is achieved in his free submission to the will of God. The Halakhah recognizes fully the animal in man. In some states he may be "similar to the ass." Man's kinship with the beast manifests itself in a number of ways. Man eats and drinks as does the beast but no aspect of his instinctive deportment does he abuse to a greater degree, and with the unhesitating support of his intellect, than the sexual. Even man's propensities toward violence and aggressive behavior are held more in check. Natural man, not ennobled by Halakhah, and dominated by his uncontrolled impulses, degrades himself and lowers himself to the level of an animal.

What renders man human in the eyes of the Halakhah is the voluntary submission to a life of responsibility, and the acceptance of the divine commandments as norms of behavior. One who is bound by divine commandments (*ben mitzvot*) has attained the true status of humanity. It is not his mere possession of reason that enables him to rise to that level, for by itself it can be used to further his irrational and destructive drives. By using reason to achieve a life of service within the scope of the divine commandments, man rises from the sub-human state to the human.

The range of duties is not the same for all. Some are subject to more obligations than others. But one's essential humanity is not minimized by the fact that one has fewer duties to perform, even though the level of "holiness" (*kedushah*) may rise by the increase in duties. Race, color, and other circumstances, irrelevant to the performance of the divine commandments, are of no account. It is the relationship to the divine commandments which determines one's stature as a human being.

All men, within the scope of duties that applies to them, may ascend to higher and higher levels. Perhaps what R. Simeon ben Jochai had in mind when he declared "You are called man" is that the full attainment of humanity is the product of an undivided commitment to that which renders a man a man—the obligation to observe the divine commandments. The less committed a man is, the less human he is. Nevertheless, even he who is farthest removed from the embodiment of true humanity is still not totally deprived of humanity, either because of his own potential virtues or those of his descendants or because he irrevocably bears upon himself even if only faintly, the imprint of the divine image.

The Halakhah is not committed to any particular theory of psychology, except that it vigorously opposes such as will totally deny man's responsibility. It does not concern itself with the various types of souls or phases of the soul. However man's-psyche may be constituted, the Halakhah is content with the assumption that man is a creature that can choose between good and evil and can acquire a knowledge of right from wrong, which makes him capable of acting in the light of this knowledge. It assumes that by concentration on the study of the Torah man can overcome his selfishness, his aggressiveness, and the extremes of his sensual desires. There are times when, in order to achieve this end, the study of the Torah is impotent and only the marshalling of all the spiritual resources at one's disposal, such as the power of faith and the anticipation of death, can give man the strength to overcome the evil forces within him. There may be times when even these media will fail and man will succumb. But he has it within his power to avoid an open desecration of God's name. The Halakhah takes cognizance of the weakness of man, but it does not extenuate the failure to strive to overcome his weakness. While recognizing the role of both heredity and environment—the choosing of good mates, of a good education, and so on—as important factors in the moulding of personality, the ultimate determinant in the case of the undisturbed human being is his free will.

Though primarily concerned with man's life upon earth, Halakhah does not ignore his fate after death. The doctrine of reward and punishment in this life as well as after death are halakhic presuppositions. Acceptance of this doctrine as well as belief in the Resurrection of the dead are halakhic imperatives, even though the manner in which they are to be accepted is not dogmatically formulated.

Halakhah grants reason a significant place in the elaboration of its principles and, sometimes, in serving as a source for halakhic norms. What conscience approves or disapproves is given recognition, because the normal human personality has within it the capacity for distinguishing between right and wrong, and this capacity has priority over Torah in terms of chronology as well as in respect to its binding authority. Nevertheless, the Halakhah derives its norms primarily from the revealed texts. Its processes of thought remain discontent with resort only to reason and conscience as the ultimate arbiters of right and wrong. The Halakhah seeks to transcend reason and conscience by finding standards of behavior imbedded within the very structure of the universe and flowing out of that divine wisdom with which the world was created.

III

The Halakhah, like the Torah, is both particular and universal. There is the Halakhah for all humanity, the Seven Commandments for the Children of Noah. This universal Halakhah requires explication and expansion in every generation in accordance with the specific needs of that generation. Every people and religion carries within it a vestige of this primeval, binding-on-all, Halakhah. But there is also the

particular Halakhah which is the unique possession of Israel and binding upon it alone. The two systems of Halakhah are undoubtedly interrelated and aim toward a common goal. It is to the subject of the
teleology of Halakhah that we must now address ourselves.

It is true that the Halakhah nowhere explicitly states its teleology,
but it is quite obvious that as it locates its source in divine wisdom it
must be related to the divine plan for creation. While formally the
Halakhah is a special schematization of the space-time continuum, the
man of Halakhah is concerned with the transformation of time and
space into a domain of holiness. Certainly the requirement of Halakhah that performance of a divine commandment be preceded by a
specific blessing emphasizes the notion that we achieve sanctification
by means of the fulfillment of the commandment. While one's obligation has been fulfilled even when the divine commandment has been
performed under duress, provided one has not repudiated its divinely
obligatory character, or even has carried it out as a matter of rote,
nevertheless *ab initio* one is required to recite the benediction before
the sacred act, so that one becomes conscious of what he is about to
do and becomes imbued with its goal. Does not the Biblical text state
explicitly: "That ye may remember and do all My commandments, and
be holy unto your God" (Numbers 15:40; cf. Exodus 13:9)? The
performance of the commandments may not require specific intention,
but the act must be performed consciously. A reduction of Halakhah
to orthopraxy and behaviorism, ungrounded in ideology and unmoti-
vated by teleology, renders it nothing but a desiccated skeleton.

Since the study of the Torah is the supreme imperative of the
Halakhah, it may rightly be assumed that within this Halakhah one can
find the key to its teleology. No one, I am certain, will maintain that
the commandment to study the Torah is limited only to the formal or
practical aspects of the Halakhah, whether presently applicable or not.
The commandment includes the study of the narrative portions of the
Torah, as well as the prophetic writings, as well as the wisdom literature, we achieve insight into the reasons for the specific commandments and the Halakhah as a whole. That the commandments are
reasonable is a presupposition of the Torah. That they have meaning
within the scope of mundane human existence is clearly spelled out.
Our duty is only to proceed and study. Our sages have indeed maintained that we are unable to fathom the depth and the ultimate meaning of the commandments, but they have never failed to demonstrate
their rational significance for our daily life.

The question was raised by R. Isaac as to why it was necessary to begin the Torah with an account of the creation of the world rather than with the first commandment. R. Isaac's answer, superficially understood, addressed itself to the specific problem of his day—the right of the Jewish people to the Holy Land. However, as clarified by Nachmanides, there is more to R. Isaac's answer than meets the eye. The Torah of Moses was given by God, as Maimonides states, "to straighten the path way of every creature and to direct every man to the truth, and this purpose includes all nations within its scope." The account of the creation of the world and the early history of mankind is undoubtedly intended not only as background for the history of Israel, but as the preamble to the entire Torah. The purpose of the Torah is made clear in the first eleven chapters of Genesis which deal with the twenty generations that preceded the appearance of Abraham. The Gaon of Vilna has expressed this truth in his own unique way when he asserted that the Torah is the record of the history of all mankind, of every individual, and of every existent being, down to the least blade of grass and grain of sand, from the beginning of time until its end.

While the Halakhah undoubtedly has its own principles of logic and hermeneutic rules, we would be wrong in maintaining that the Halakhah can be divorced from ideology and theology. The ideological ground of the Torah in all its ramifications is clearly set forth at the very beginning of the Book of Genesis. It is not in vain that the Gaon of Vilna states that the entire Torah is included within its very first verse. What the preamble affirms is that this world has been created by God, that He rejoices in His handiwork and delights in its goodness, and that He has created man in His image. In this divine image all human beings share, either as an inherent possession or as potentiality. The image of the divine in man sets him apart from the animal kingdom and endows him with a unique character unparalleled in all creation.

The chapters of Genesis that follow speak to us of God Who reveals His will to man. His desire is that men know Him and that they live in close proximity with Him. When they turn away from Him, He admonishes them, punishes them, and even washes man from the face of the earth, when all hope for his improvement vanishes. But God wants mankind to survive and learn how to know Him and walk in His ways. When Noah's progeny fail to fulfill the divine goal, God selects Abraham and his seed as bearers of the divine blessing to mankind. In the course of the struggle for Israel's emancipation, the ultimate goal to be achieved by this people always remains aloft. We are constantly reminded that the supreme intervention of Almighty God in the history of mankind was to lead to the recognition of the Supreme God, even by the bitterest enemies of Israel, until the day when the glory of God will fill the entire earth.

The concept of paternal blessing, which dominates the narrative portions of the patriarchal period, underscores the profound significance of blessing as the third aspect of *Imitatio Dei* which man is to emulate. The first chapter of Genesis reveals God as the One Who creates, divides, and blesses. In its loyalty to God and His revealed Law, Israel enhances creation, separates the holy from the profane, and distributes blessings to all of existence. These are tasks with which the Jewish individual and people have been entrusted. God has made them the medium of His blessing, until the time when all nations will once more deserve to receive it directly from His hand. "On that day Israel will be the third to Egypt and Assyria in the midst of the earth, whom the Lord God has blessed saying: Blessed be My people Egypt, My handiwork Assyria, and My heritage Israel."

It has been charged that to hope for blessing as a consequence of the observance of the divine commandments represents a materialistic outlook, unworthy of higher religion. There can be nothing farther from the truth. God has created man so that he be worthy of the receipt of His blessings. Man's failure to observe His commandments is not only an act of rebellion against his Creator, but constitutes a disruption of His plan for man and His world. Observance of His commandments is not only an act of surrender to His will, but the means whereby God's blessings are distributed to the world and its creatures.

The *telos* of Jewish existence, and hence the teleology of the Halakhah, can be conceived of in no terms other than the impartation of blessings on all levels of reality. Israel has been charged with the guardianship of the world, and with the task of testifying to its character as a divine creation. Israel is to serve as the preserver of the divine image in the world, and to make clear for all time that man and the world are to be regarded as the handiwork of God is its bounden duty. Maimonides has maintained that through a knowledge of the universe we can achieve the love of God. The obverse is also true— that by means of the love of God we acquire a love for the world He has created. The love for His creatures and the dignity with which they are to be treated is universal in its application.

The concept of the divine image in man is a basic presupposition of the Halakhah. Thus by walking in the ways of God, man becomes Godlike. The divine attributes, by which we can mean nothing other than the modes of His entering into relationship with the world He has created, become the ideal of human behavior. The very term Halakhah itself derives from the Biblical phrase "to walk in the ways of God". A detailed study of the commandments of the Torah and their halakhic ramifications, this writer believes, should demonstrate the character of the Halakhah as a medium for the implementation of Imitatio Dei. The knowledge of the Torah, the correlate of the knowledge of the divine attributes, is thus to be identified with the knowledge of God, that the Lord executes lovingkindness, justice and righteousness in the midst of the earth.

The Halakhah is grounded in the will of God, but there is nothing man can do that can in any way benefit God. Whatever He ordains is for the benefit of the world that He has created. The Torah has been given to us for our benefit; and the commandments are to be fulfilled so that it may be well with us, and that mankind will be purified and ennobled. Through the Torah, whose ways are ways of peace and pleasantness, peace will be achieved in the world, a goal which the Halakhah postulates.

The acceptance of this-worldly goals on the part of the Halakhah need not exclude ultimate metaphysical and mystical goals which transcend those of the rational Halakhah. *Homo Halakhicus* [*Ish ha-Halakhah*] [the man of the halakhah] can be *homo religiosus* as well as *homo mysticus*. The mundane and metaphysical goals of Halakhah or the Torah are not antithetical. They merely apply to different levels of experience, personal or historical. The fact that many of the great Halakhists have at the same time been outstanding protagonists of the Kabbalah and profound mystics confirms the truth that the presumed tension between the Halakhic and the Kabbalistic is not real.

The study of the Torah as the supreme obligation of the Jew is not divorced from *Imitatio Dei,* even if it has no bearing on practical problems. The study of the Torah was never meant to be a mere intellectual exercise, but a means for the ennoblement of the spirit of man. "Whosoever is engaged in the study of the Torah for its own sake will achieve many things. He will become a lover of God and a lover of His creatures. He will bring joy to God and joy to His creatures."

Even the study of the non-practical aspects of the Torah has its effect upon one who studies Torah for its own sake. The study of the Torah is the equivalent of performance where the sacred act cannot be actualized. The moral goal toward which the commandment is directed is implemented in the orientation of the heart toward that goal.

Maimonides maintained that many of the commandments are historically conditioned. At the same time he undoubtedly believed that the Halakhah transcends the conditions from which it may have originated initially, as is clear from his inclusion of what he regards as historically conditioned laws in his great Code. He has, likewise, made it clear from the *Sefer ha-Madda* [Book of Knowledge], with which his Code opens, what he regards as the basic goals of Torah and Halakhah—namely, the fulfillment in our lives of the knowledge of God, His love and fear, the sanctification of His name, *Imitatio Dei,* the rejection of polytheism and idolatry, the ceaseless striving to know His will through study, and the striving to better our ways through repentance. In our study of Torah it is our duty to seek to discover in what way the Halakhah in all its details seeks to embody the goals it has set out to accomplish. In this manner we may enable the Halakhah to rise to new heights and make possible the achievement of its Messianic purposes.

BEYOND THE LAW: ETHICS

No system of law can legislate for each and every situation of life. Men are too varied. The conditions of their everyday affairs posit too many unforeseen choices. Classical Judaic theologians deal with the world beyond the law through ethical treatises. Here they lay down rules and regulations not in detail, but through espousing general moral and ethical principles. Each person will find out how to cope with the unique conditions of his life through reflection upon and application of such principles.

Before us is not a treatise of philosophical ethics, an analysis of the most basic propositions concerning such abstractions as "man", or "the good", or "the truth". Judaic ethics may not be rightly called ethics at all, if you look in an ethical treatise for an inquiry into high abstractions. For Judaic ethics is—as one would by now expect—practical and concrete, an expression not of the philosophical intellect, but of wisdom.

The ethical claim is not to speak about "man" or "the good" but about what you should do in the here-and-now. Classical Judaism is all too concrete, too specific, too much interested in this world, to offer the sort of philosophical discourses characteristic of ethical thinking in other religious traditions.

That is not to suggest, to be sure, that the great Judaic theologians and philosophers did not raise questions transcending concrete matters, for they did. But the ethical literature read by the people and formative of their piety and moral perceptions is best represented in what follows.

Moses Hayyim Luzzatto lived in Italy from 1707 to 1747. His ethical treatise, *Mesillat Yesharim*, "The Way of the Righteous", was translated by Mordecai M. Kaplan, himself a theologian and founder of the Jewish Reconstructionist Movement. Luzzatto takes a saying in the Talmud which lists a progression of virtues: heedfulness leads to cleanness, cleanness leads to holiness, holiness leads to even higher things. He investigates the substance of each of the steps of the ladder.

We shall read part of his account of cleanness. What is interesting is that when the Talmudic saying originally was given, in the first cen-

121

tury A.D., "cleanness" meant *ritual* cleanness. It was the requirement of the Temple in Jerusalem that whoever came to sacrifice and worship be in a state of cleanness as prescribed in the Book of Leviticus, the code of priestly laws. A man became unclean, for instance, by touching a reptile or a corpse. He became clean through a rite of purification. Now cleanness in biblical literature was used not only in a ritual sense, but also as a metaphor for moral and ethical purity. And it was that sense of the word which predominated in later literature. One who was "clean" would have a pure heart—and that did not mean, a heart which has not touched a corpse, but rather, a heart in which was no malice or evil.

But what does it mean to be "clean" in this sense? And what are the sources of "impurity"? Luzzatto will spell it out for us, in terms of everyday life but not in the intimate details governing just exactly what you should do in this specific circumstance or that one. This ethical treatise falls between the detailed precision of law, on the one side, and the abstraction of philosophical ethics on the other.

X

CLEANNESS

Moses Hayyim Luzzatto

(From *Mesillat Yesharim. The Path of the Upright,* by Moses Hayyim Luzzatto.
Translated and edited, with an introduction by Mordecai M. Kaplan, Philadelphia,
1966: Jewish Publication Society of America, pp. 134-233, specifically, pp. 134,
136, 138, 142, 144, 146, 148, 152, 154, 158, 160, 168, 170, 174, 176, 182, 184,
186, 188, 190, 200, 202, and 224.)

The quality of cleanness consists in being free from evil traits as
well as from sin. That applies not only to sin which is flagrant, but also
to such as we are inclined to condone. If we were to look for the true
reason why we condone certain sins, we should find that it is because
the human heart is plagued, as it were, with lust, of which it is with
difficulty ever thoroughly cleansed. Therefore are we inclined to be
indulgent.

Only the man who is entirely free from that plague, and who is
undefiled by any trace of the evil which lust leaves behind it, will see
clearly and judge truly. Desire cannot mislead him; he looks upon the
most trifling sin as an evil to be shunned. Our Sages designated the
perfect men, those whose standard of purity was so high that there
was not the least trace of evil in them, as "The clean-minded men of
Jerusalem" (San. 23a).

You may know the difference between one who is merely self-
watchful and one who is clean, although the two resemble each other
in certain respects. The former is merely watchful of his conduct and
takes care not to commit any flagrant sin. But he has not yet achieved
such mastery of himself as to ignore the voice of inclination when it
tries to prove to him that he may commit certain acts, the evil character
of which is not manifestly flagrant. Although it is true that he endeavors to subue his evil *Yezer,* and to subject his desires to control,
he does not thereby alter his nature, nor is he enabled to dismiss the
gross inclinations from his heart. He only succeeds in overcoming them,
and in following wisdom instead of his inclination. With all that, the

innate evil of his physical nature keeps on doing its work, and seeks to seduce him and lead him astray.

Once a man has so trained himself in being watchful of his conduct that he has taken the first step toward being free from flagrant sin, once he has acquired the habit of zealously performing his religious duties and has developed a love and longing for his Creator, he will, by force of such training, learn to keep aloof from all worldly strivings and fix his mind on spiritual perfection, until he is altogether clean. The fire of physical passion will die out in his heart, and a longing for the divine will awaken in him. Then will his vision become so clear and so pure that nothing will mislead him. He will be beyond the sinister power of his physical being, and his conduct will be free from all possible taint. . . .

The quality of cleanness finds expression in manifold ways. It assumes, indeed, as many forms as there are negative commandments, since to be clean means to be clean of transgression in all its forms.

Although the evil *Yezer* [impulse] endeavors to lead man into sin by all sorts of temptations, there are certain temptations which are stronger than others. Those are the ones to which the evil *Yezer* always helps us find a reason for yielding. Hence, it is against them especially that we must fortify ourselves, if we would overcome the *Yezer* and be free from sin. Thus the sages have said, "The human being has a natural inclination for theft and licentiousness" (Hag. 11b). We see that although most people are not outright thieves, that is, do not actually seize their neighbor's property and transfer it to their own premises, yet in their dealings with one another they have a taste of the sin of theft, insofar as they permit themselves to profit at their neighbor's expense, claiming that profit has nothing to do with theft.

There are, indeed, many laws against theft.

"Thou shalt not steal" (Ex. 20:15).

"Thou shalt not rob" (Lev. 19:13).

"Thou shalt not oppress" (ibid).

"Ye shall not deal falsely, neither lie to one another"
    (Lev. 19:12).

"Ye shall not wrong one another" (Lev. 25:14).

"Thou shalt not remove thy neighbor's boundary" (Deut. 19:14)
All these laws against theft apply to many of the dealings that generally take place in commercial transactions. Each law in itself embraces a number of prohibitions. Not only are those deeds forbidden which are manifestly rapacious and fraudulent, but also those which in the end must lead to fraud.

Our Sages liken the act of underbidding the labor of another to adultery (San. 81a). We find that R. Judah forbids a merchant to distribute parched corn and nuts among children as an inducement to buying. If the other Sages permitted such practice, it is only because it gives no advantage to the trader over his competitors, since they do the same (B. M. 60a). "To defraud a human being," said our Sages, "is a graver sin than to defraud the Sanctuary" (B. B. 88b). They have even exempted the laborer who works on his employer's premises from reciting the benediction when breaking bread, and from all but the first benediction after meals. A laborer may interrupt his work to recite only the first paragraph of the *Shema* (Ber. 16a).

All the more is it forbidden to have any matter of a secular character interrupt the work that one is hired to do. To transgress this law is to commit theft. When Abba Hilkiah was hired to do work, he refused to answer the greetings even of men of learning. He considered it a sin to use for his own purpose the time that belonged to his employer (Ta'an. 23 a, b). Our father Jacob said explicitly, "Thus I was; in the day the drought consumed me, and the frost by night; and my sleep fled from mine eyes" (Gen. 31:40). What excuse can they give who look after their own pleasures, and attend to their own interests, when they should be doing the work for which they are paid?

When a man is paid to do a day's work, his time is not his own for that day. "One who hires himself out to do a day's work," said the Rabbis, "sells himself for that day" (B. M. 56b). Therefore, whatever time he uses in any way for his own purposes is stolen; and if his employer waive not the claim against him, he is not absolved from his sin. As it is said, "The Day of Atonement absolves no man from sins committed against his neighbor, unless his neighbor be conciliated" (Yoma 85b). Even if a man perform a *Mitzvah* during the time when he should be engaged in work, it is not accounted to him as a meritorious deed but as a transgression; for an act initially a transgression cannot be transformed into a *Mitzvah*. . . .

Consider the trait of cleanness in relation to deceit. How we are liable to yield to the temptation of acting deceitfully! For example, it is evidently proper for a man to praise his wares, or, by resorting to persuasion, to earn for his labor as much as he can. We say of such a man that he is ambitious and will succeed (Pes. 50b). "The hand of the diligent maketh rich" (Prov. 10:4). But, unless he is very careful to weigh his actions, the outcome is bound to be evil instead of good. He will sin and act dishonestly in violation of the precept, "Ye shall not wrong one another" (Lev. 25:17). Our Sages said, "It is forbidden to deceive even a non-Jew" (Hul. 94a), and in Scripture we read, "The remnant of Israel shall not do iniquity, nor speak lies; neither shall a deceitful tongue be found in their mouth" (Zeph. 3:13).

"It is not permitted," the Rabbis added (B. M. 60a), "to vamp up old things to make them appear new. It is not permitted, in the sale of one kind of produce, clandestinely to introduce any other kind into it, though what is introduced is as fresh as the rest, and even worth more. Whoever does such things is called an evil-doer. Scripture terms him 'iniquitous, odious, abominable and obnoxious'" (Sifra to Lev. 19:35). They said further, "One who spoils his neighbor, even of a farthing's worth, is as though he had deprived him of his life" (B. K. 119a). You see, therefore, how grave is this sin even when only a small amount is involved. "The rains are withheld," our Sages said, "mainly for the sin of robbery" (Ta'an. 7b). "The decree against the generation of the flood would not have been sealed, were it not for their rapacity" (San. 108a). "But", you will say, "how, in the course of bargaining, can we avoid trying to convince our neighbor that the articles we want to sell him is worth the price we are asking?" There is an unmistakable distinction between fraudulent and honest persuasion. It is perfectly proper to point out to the buyer any good quality which the thing for sale really possesses. Fraud consists in hiding the defects in one's wares and is forbidden. This is an important principle in the matter of business honesty. . . .

The laws against unchastity are second in importance only to those against theft. "The majority of men commit theft; a smaller number commit unchastity" (B. B. 165a). Whoever desires to be free from the latter sin must exert himself not a little. It is not the forbidden act alone that constitutes unchastity, but whatever approaches it in character. Thus Scripture states explicitly, "None of you shall approach any woman near of kin to you to uncover her nakedness" (Lev. 18:6). In the words of our Sages, "Do not imagine that where cohabitation is sinful, it is no sin to fondle, caress or kiss." As a Nazirite who has taken the vow is commanded to abstain not only from wine but also from grapes, whether they be fresh or dried, and from any product of grapes, so is it forbidden even to touch any woman except one's wife, and whoever touches a woman not his wife brings death upon himself (Ex. R. 16:2). Note the aptness of the analogy. For, although the Nazirite is forbidden primarily to drink wine, yet the Torah has also commanded him to abstain from everything that bears any relation to wine. This illustrated to the Sages the way they were to set up a fence around the Torah by means of prohibitions which they were authorized to institute, in order to forestall violation of the prohibitions in the Torah. Thus what the Torah did in the case of the law of the Nazirite authorized the Sages to do in the case of the other laws. We thus note it to be the will of God that, when He forbids anything expressly, we should infer that whatever resembles it is likewise forbidden. . . .

We have thus far spoken of the two principal grave sins into which men often fall because of the many guises which those sins assume, and the strong leaning which the human heart has toward them. In degree of appetite, the craving for forbidden food and drink comes third after theft and unchastity. The food may be forbidden because it is entirely *terefah* or mixed with *terefah*. It may contain a mixture of meat and milk, or it may contain suet, or blood, or it may have been prepared by a Gentile. The drink may be wine which has been used in libations, or ordinary wine handled by Gentiles. To abstain from all such forbidden things demands great care and great self-control, for we must contend with the natural appetite for delectable dishes, with the monetary loss that may be incurred through observance of the dietary laws, and with similar factors.

The details of observance in the prohibition of certain foods are many, as may be seen from the well-known laws which are set forth in the works of the codifiers. Whoever is prone to be lenient in those matters wherein the Rabbis have urged us to be exacting inflicts harm upon himself. Thus have our Sages said in the *Sifra,* " 'Neither shall ye make yourselves unclean by eating of forbidden animals, thus defiling yourselves' (Lev. 11:43). If you make yourselves unclean with them, you will in the end become defiled" (*Sifra* to Lev. 11:43). By this they imply that forbidden food actually introduces impurity into the heart and soul of man, so that the holiness of God, blessed be He, departs far from him. Our Sages also said, "Transgression stupefies the heart of man" (Yoma 39a), by depriving him of the powers of understanding and reason which the Holy One, blessed be He, bestows upon the saints, as it is said, "For the Lord giveth wisdom" (Prov. 2:6). Man becomes coarse and beastlike, steeped in the grossness of this world. And this is more true of one who partakes of forbidden food than of one who commits any other transgression, because food enters the body and becomes part of its very substance. . . .

Now we shall speak of the common sins that we commit in our social life, as when we taunt, or insult, or mislead, or slander, or hate our neighbor, or nurse revenge, or swear, or lie, or act sacrilegiously. Who can say, "I am free from such sins; I am clear of all such guilt?"

These are sins that take on so many various and subtle forms that only by great effort may we be on our guard against them.

Do not taunt your neighbor. This means that you must neither do nor say to him that which might shame him, though there be no one else present. "If a man has repented of his sins," says the Talmud (B. M. 58b), "no one should say to him, 'Remember thy former doings'." A man who has been afflicted with disease must not be spoken to as was Job by his friends, who said, "Remember, I pray thee, whoever perished, being innocent?" (Job 4:7). When a person is asked whether he has any grain to sell, he must not refer the applicant to his neighbor, if he knows that his neighbor never dealt in grain. Our Sages said (B. M. 58b) that to taunt one's neighbor is worse than to deceive him, as is shown by the fact that the admonition, "And thou shalt fear thy God" (Lev. 25:17), comes immediately after the law against taunting, and not after the law against deceiving one's neighbor. . . .

Slander and tale-bearing. It is well known how grave a sin this is. It assumes so many forms that our Sages long ago stated the general rule that "everyone is guilty of a modicum of the sin of slander" (B. B. 165a). What constitutes a modicum of slander? When, for instance, we say of some one, "He is a man whose hearth fires are always burning" (Arak. 15b), or when we enumerate a man's virtues in the presence of his enemies (Arak. 16a). Such remarks, however unimportant and far removed from slander they may seem, actually partake of its character. Know for a rule that the Yezer is resourceful. So that, to make any remark which is apt to cause injury or disgrace to one's neighbor, whether in his presence or in his absence, is to commit slander, a sin which is hateful and abominable to the Lord. "Whoever makes a habit of speaking slander," say our Sages, "acts as though he denied the existence of God" (Arak. 15b). And in Scripture we read, "Whoso slandereth his neighbour in secret, him will I destroy" (Ps. 101.5).

Hatred and revenge. These the human heart, in its perversity, finds it hard to escape. A man is very sensitive to disgrace, and suffers keenly when subjected to it. Revenge is sweeter to him than honey; he cannot rest until he has taken his revenge. If, therefore, he has the power to relinquish that to which his nature impels him; if he can forgive; if he will forbear hating anyone who provokes him to hatred; if he will neither exact vengeance when he has the opportunity to do so, nor bear a grudge against any one; if he can forget and obliterate from his mind a wrong done to him as though it had never been committed; then he is, indeed, strong and mighty. So to act may be a small matter to angels who have no evil traits, but not to "those that dwell in houses of clay, whose foundation is in the dust" (Job 4:19). Yet such is the sovereign decree. Scripture declares it with the utmost clearness, so that further comment is unnecessary. "Thou shalt not hate thy brother in thy heart. Thou shalt not take vengeance nor bear any grudge against the children of thy people" (Lev. 19:17, 18).

The difference between taking revenge and bearing a grudge is well known. To take revenge is to return evil for evil. To bear a grudge is to remind a man of the evil he has done to you though you repay him with good (Yoma 23a). The evil *Yezer* always wants to excite us to anger, and continually attempts to have us retain at least some remembrance of the evil that our neighbor may have done to us. If the *Yezer* is not able to keep alive a vivid image of the wrong done to us, he strives to have at least a faint impression of it cling to the memory. He argues thus, "If you want to grant that man the favor which he refused you when you were in need, you do not have to grant it to him cheerfully. You may refuse to retaliate, but you do not have to be his benefactor or to offer him help. If you insist upon extending considerable help to him, do so at least without his knowledge. It is not necessary for you to associate with him and again become his friend. If you have forgiven him, it is enough that you do not show yourself to him as his enemy; if you are willing to go further and associate with him once more, at least do not display as much love as formerly." With these and similar sophistries, the evil *Yezer* endeavors to seduce men's hearts. The Torah therefore lays down a general rule which takes all these possibilities into account. "Thou shalt love thy neighbour as thyself" (Lev. 19:18), as thyself, without difference or distinction, without subterfuge and mental reservation, literally as thyself. . . .

Lying is another disease that is very prevalent. It exists in various degrees. There are some who actually make it their business to tell lies. They go about inventing stories without any foundation in truth, in order to have material for gossip, or to be considered clever and conversant. Of them it is said, "Lying lips are an abomination to the Lord" (Prov. 12:22). "Your lips have spoken lies, your tongue muttereth wickedness" (Isa. 59:3). Our Sages have described the fate that awaits such men in the following: "There are four groups of human beings who are forever excluded from the Divine Presence; liars constitute one of those groups" (Sotah 42a).

There are others who, though they approximate the type of liars described above, are not so corrupt. They are in the habit of introducing some untruth into everything they say. While they do not make it their business to go about inventing stories concerning things that never were, they always add something fictitious which occurs to them while they are speaking. This has become so much a habit with them as to be second nature. Such liars it is impossible ever to believe. In the words of our Sages, "The liar is punished by not being believed even when he speaks the truth" (San. 89b). This practice has become so much a part of their character that nothing they utter is free from falsehood. It is this evil trait that the prophet denounces when he says, "They have taught their tongue to speak lies; they weary themselves to commit iniquity" (Jer. 9:4). . . .

Cleanness is as necessary a quality of character as it is of conduct. In fact, it is more difficult to have a clean character than to act cleanly; for our physical nature exerts a greater influence upon our inward traits than upon our outward actions. Our physical constitution and its disposition may prove either a great help or a great hindrance in the development of character. The struggle that we have to wage against our natural inclinations is very strenuous. Thus our Sages said, "Who is mighty? He who subdues his *Yezer*" (Ab. 4:1).

The traits of which human nature is compounded are very many and every one of man's actions may be traced to some particular trait. But just as we have discussed only those *Mitzvot* in the observance of which men are negligent, so we shall now speak somewhat at length only of the principal traits with which we are familiar, namely, pride, anger, envy, and lust. That all of these traits are manifestly evil does not require any proof. They are pernicious both inherently and by reason of their consequences. They are foreign to reason and common sense, and each one by itself is enough to involve man in the gravest sins. . . .

Avarice fetters a man with worldly cares, and makes of toil and traffic thick ropes about his arms, as it is written, "He that loveth silver shall not be satisfied with silver" (Eccl. 5:9). The love of money distracts him from the performance of religious duties, for under the pressure of his mighty business he will omit prayers, and forget many a *Mitzvah*. That he will neglect the study of the Torah goes without saying. Commenting upon the verse which says of the Torah, "It is not beyond the sea" (Deut. 30:13), our Sages added, "The knowledge of the Torah is not to be found among those who cross the seas to engage in commerce" (Er. 55a). Similarly, in the Mishnah, "Not he who is engrossed in business can grow wise" (Ab. 2:5).

Greed it is which exposes a man to many dangers and weakens him with the anxiety it causes, even after he has acquired wealth. We thus read in the Mishnah, "The more possessions, the more anxiety" (Ab. 2:7). And greed frequently brings a man to transgress not only the precepts of the Torah, but also the natural laws of reason.

Even worse than greed is the lust for honor. A man may control his craving for wealth and for pleasure, but the craving for honor is irresistible because it is almost impossible to endure being inferior to one's fellows. This is why so many people stumble and perish.

THE LITERATURE OF THE LAW

So far we have considered the law and the ideas associated with it—the way of Torah as expressed in the minds of the philosophers of the *halakhah*. But what about the maker of the law, the man who achieves sufficient learning so as to be able to guide others in the practice of the religious life?

In *Way of Torah* we read the ethical will of an ordinary Jew, who expresses the highest ideals of a representative common man. In that will we are able to perceive the effects, the results, of the way of Torah.

Now let us consider one of the great guides to that way, whose law-code, the *Shulhan Aruk,* set forth in highly authoritative form the *halakhic* requirements of the Torah. The *Shulhan Aruk,* together with its commentaries and cognate writings, is the single most influential document in classical Judaism. That is the place in which the formulation of applied and practical law begins, even now.

Who stands behind this great code of law? What was the reason he wrote it? Was he a lawyer, and was his intent that of a legislator? What sort of personality produces law-codes for Judaism?

Isadore Twersky, who teaches at Harvard University, here provides an account of Joseph Karo, the author of the *Shulhan Aruk.* He describes his life, the circumstances of his writing the code, and what happened to it after it was published.

What is striking is that this lawyer and codifier of laws was—a mystic! Indeed, a book condemned by some as dry and dull came forth from a man who possessed a most vivid religious imagination and lived an exceptionally keen and ardent religious life. So there must be something within his code which was able to express his mystical conception of life. And there must be much within the laws themselves capable of provoking and enhancing religious experience that is anything but dry and dull.

The Torah as a way of life cannot be understood without knowledge of both the guides and the guideposts. For the *halakhah* Joseph Karo was the greatest guide of all. And the *Shulhan Aruk* remains the guidepost.

XI

THE SHULHAN ARUK: ENDURING CODE OF JEWISH LAW

Isadore Twersky

(From *Judaism*, Vol. 16, No. 2, Spring, 1967, pp. 141-158. Footnotes are omitted.)

Shulḥan Aruk, a term taken over from early rabbinic exegesis in the Midrash and applied to one of the most influential, truly epochal literary creations of Jewish history, has a double or even triple meaning, and its use therefore necessitates precise definition or description. *Shulḥan Aruk* is the title given by R. Joseph Karo (1488-1575) to a brief, four-part code of Jewish law which was published in 1565-66, just over four hundred years ago. *Shulḥan Aruk* also designates a composite, collaborative work, combining this original text of R. Joseph Karo, a Spanish emigré from Toledo (1492) who lived and studied in Turkey and finally settled in Palestine in a period of turbulence and instability and apocalyptic stirrings, with the detailed glosses—both strictures and supplements—of R. Moses Isserles (c. 1525-1572), a well-to-do Polish scholar, proud of his Germanic background, who studied in Lublin and became de facto chief rabbi of Cracow in a period of relative stability and tranquillity. This unpremeditated literary symbiosis then generated a spate of commentaries and supercommentaries, brief or expansive, defensive or dissenting, from the *Sefer Me'irat 'Enayim* of R. Joshua Falk and the *Sefer Siftei Kohen* of R. Shabbetai ha-Kohen to the *Mishnah Berurah* of R. Israel Meir ha-Kohen; and the term *Shulḥan Aruk* continued to be applied to this multi-dimensional, multi-generational, ever-expanding folio volume—a fact which attests the resiliency and buoyancy of the Halachic tradition in Judaism. A person must, therefore, define his frame of reference when he purports to glorify or vilify, to acclaim or condemn—or, if he is able to avoid value judgments, to describe historically. The genuinely modest purpose of the following remarks is, first, to chronicle the emergence of the *Shulḥan Aruk,* especially in its first and second meanings, and then to describe a few of its salient literary and substantive characteristics. "The rest is commentary," which we should go and study.

I

In the year 1522, R. Joseph Karo, a young, struggling, volatile and ascetic scholar, having settled temporarily and discontentedly in Adrianople, Turkey, launched a massive literary project that would preoccupy him, sometimes at a frenetic pace, for over thirty years— twenty years in the composition and about twelve years in editorial revision and refinement. The stimulus was provided by the worrisome decline in scholarship—"and the wisdom of their wise men shall perish"—coming in the wake of the rigors and vicissitudes of exile, the endless turbulence of history, and the increasing human imperfection. The need was great for a comprehensive as well as authoritative guide, which would stem the undesirable and almost uncontrollable prolifera- tion of texts and provide a measure of religious uniformity in this period of great turmoil and dislocation. This would be accomplished, however, not by producing another compact, sinewy manual—a small volume such as the *Agur,* which R. Karo treats perjoratively—but by reviewing the practical Halachah in its totality. The oracular type of code, containing curt, staccato directives and pronouncements, was neither adequate nor reliable. It did not provide for intellectual stimulus and expansion of the mind, nor did it offer correct guidance in religious practice.

R. Joseph Karo's ambitious undertaking in the field of rabbinic literature, entitled *Bet Yosef (House of Joseph)* was thus motivated by the need to review "all the practical laws of Judaism, explaining their roots and origins in the Talmud" and all the conflicting inter- pretations concerning them. No extant work answered to this need. In order to avoid duplication or reduce it to a bare minimum, he de- cided to build his own work around an existing code that was popular and authoritative. He selected the *Turim* of R. Jacob b. Asher (c. 1280- 1340) rather than the more famous and widespread *Mishneh Torah* of R. Moses b. Maimon, because the latter was too concise and mono- lithic, presenting, on the whole, unilateral, undocumented decisions, while the former was expansive and more interpretive,- citing alternate views and divergent explanations. At this stage, then, the text of the *Turim* was only a pretext for his own work. His method was to explain every single law in the text, note its original source, and indicate whether the formulation found in the *Turim* was the result of consensus or was subject to dispute. He would, furthermore, explain the alternate interpretations and formulations which the *Turim* referred to but rejected. In addition, he would introduce and elucidate those views which the *Turim* had totally omitted from consideration. As a purely theoretical increment, he promised to examine and explain those views of predecessors—especially Maimonides—which were problematic or remained obscure despite the availability of such commentaries as the *Maggid Mishneh*. He would, incidentally, correct the text of the *Turim,* which suffered many scribal corruptions. That he intended his encyclopedic review of Halachah to be used as a study-guide is indicated by his promise always to give exact bibliographical references in order to enable his readers to consult original texts or check quotations in their original contexts. However, having completed his panoramic presentation and almost detached, academic analysis of a law, he would regularly indicate the normative conclusion, for the "goal is that we should have one Torah and one law." The function of this massive work is thus two-fold: to flesh out the bare-bones codifications which are too brief and uninformative, but preserve their sineweness and pragmatic advantage by unequivocally stating the *pesak,* the binding regulation, in each case. Certitude and finality are among the top-priority items that will be guaranteed.

In connection with this, the author lays bare his judical methodology, a methodology that was to be vigorously contested, as we shall see. The judicial process was complex. A Talmudist could arrive at the normative conclusion by critically reviewing and appraising all arguments and demonstrations marshalled by his predecessors and then selecting the most cogent, persuasive view. His guide would be examination of underlying texts, relying, in the final analysis, upon his autonomous judgment and not on appeal to authority. This independent, assertive approach is unqualifiedly repudiated by R. Joseph Karo for two reasons: 1) it would be presumptuous to scrutinize the judgment of such giants as R. Moses b. Nahman, R. Solomon b. Adret, R. Nissim, and the Tosafists and then pass judgment on them—we are not qualified or competent; 2) even if the task were not beyond our powers and capacities, the process would be too long and arduous. Forcefully underscoring his subservience and *apparently* forfeiting his judicial prerogatives, he chose to arrive at the normative conclusion in each case by following the consensus or at least the majority rule of the greatest medieval codifiers—R. Isaac Alfasi (d. 1103), Maimonides (d. 1204), and R. Asher ben Yehiel (d. 1328). Contemporary legislation, innovation, and native usage are given no role whatsoever— almost as if the law were all logic and no experience. In other words, in the realm of commentary R. Joseph Karo was bold and resourceful, while in the realm of adjudication he was laconic, almost self-effacing.

At about the same time, in entirely different circumstances and with a totally different motivation, R. Moses Isserles, born into comfort and affluence, son of a prominent communal leader who was also a gentleman scholar and (for a while) son-in-law of the greatest Talmudic teacher in Poland (R. Shalom Shakna), also began to compile an exhaustive commentary on the *Turim.* He reveals the immediate stimulus which led to his project: having been persuaded by friends to assume rabbinic duties in Cracow—his youth, immaturity, and unripe scholarship notwithstanding—he found himself deciding many Halachic problems and issuing numerous judicial opinions. It was his practice to turn directly to the Talmud and consult its authoritative expositors, among whom he mentions R. Isaac Alfasi, R. Moses b. Naḥman, and R. Asher b. Yeḥiel. He found, however, that he was repeatedly subjected to criticism for having ignored the rulings of the most recent scholars (e.g., R. Jacob Weil, R. Israel Isserlein, R. Israel Bruna) who were really the progenitors of contemporary Polish Jewry and gave it its creative and directive vital force. They introduced, *inter alia,* many preventive ordinances and stringent practices which tended to nullify earlier decisions, and as a result no picture of Halachah could be true to life which did not reflect these resources, motifs and developments. This put R. Moses Isserles in a bad light, and he and his colleagues were, therefore, subjected to much severe criticism, the validity of which he fully appreciated and accepted, as we shall see.

Impromptu, *ad hoc* review—and judicious, instantaneous application—of all this material, this panoply of interpretations and traditions, would be cumbersome, if not impossible. It therefore occurred to R. Moses Isserles that the way out was to prepare a digest and anthology of all opinions and record them alongside of a standard code. The best book was the *Turim,* for its arrangement was very attractive and useful, and it was easily intelligible to all. He set out, with great determination and commensurate perseverance, to implement this literary plan (he vividly describes his frenetic, indefatigable activity, without ease and without quiet). At a rather advanced stage of his work, he was electrified by the news that "the light of Israel, head of the exile" R. Joseph Karo had composed a comparable commentary on the Turim, the Bet Yosef, the excellence of which was immediately evident. R. Moses Isserles' anxiety was indescribable; just as he neared the hour of consummation, it appeared that his efforts and privations would turn out to be a wearying exercise in futility. He acknowledges—with what seems to be a blend of modesty and realism—that he could not hold a candle to R. Joseph Karo. However, shock did not lead to paralysis. His peace of mind and momentum were restored when, reassessing the situation, he realized that the field had not been completely preempted and that he was still in a position to make a substantive contribution.

There were three areas in which he could realign his material and operate creatively and meaningfully:

1) He would compress the material, almost encyclopedic in its present proportions, and present a more precise formulation of the law. Length, as Maimonides notes, is one of the deterrents of study. Nevertheless, R. Moses Isserles is somewhat apologetic at this point, because he was fully aware of the pitfalls of excessive brevity; indeed, it had been the codificatory syndrome—the rigidities and inadequacies of delphic manuals—that initially impelled him to disavow the methodology of existing codes. As a compromise, he determined to cite—not to reproduce or summarize—all sources, so that the inquisitive or dissatisfied but learned reader will be able to pursue matters further, while the less sophisticated and less talented reader will still benefit and not be able to argue that the material is too lengthy and complicated.

2) The *Bet Yosef* was too "classical," somewhat remote for Germanic-Polish Jewry: it failed to represent equally the more recent codifiers and commentators. His work, the *Darke Mosheh,* would do justice to them by incorporating their positions. It would reflect the historical consciousness of R. Moses Isserles and his colleagues who looked upon themselves as heirs and continuators of the Ashkenazi tradition. On one hand, therefore, the *Darke Mosheh* would be an abridgement of the *Bet Yosef,* and, on the other, it would expand its scope. Clearly, R. Moses Isserles had taken the words of his earlier critics to heart.

3) Perhaps the most radical divergence between the two works appeared in the methodology of *pesak* [decision], formulating the normative conclusion and obligatory pattern of behavior. Unlike R. Joseph Karo, who cautiously claimed to follow the *communis opinio,* or majority rule, of early codifiers, and unlike those who would freely exercise independent judgment in arriving at practical conclusions, R. Moses Isserles adopted a third stance: to follow most recent authorities— *halakah ke-batra'e* [the law follows the latest authorities]. This method would preserve established precedent and respect local custom. It is reflected stylistically in R. Moses Isserles' habit of underwriting the most

valid view by adding "and this is customary" and then identifying the
source or by noting candidly "and so it appears to me." He is thus more
independent and resourceful than R. Joseph Karo, though less so than
R. Solomon Luria. In short, as R. Moses Isserles puts it in a rhetorical
flourish, "And Moses took the bones of Joseph"—he adapted and transformed the essence of the *Bet Yosef* and abandoned the rest.

This ends the first chapter of our story in which R. Joseph Karo
made it to the press before R. Moses Isserles and forced the latter to
revise his initial prospectus in light of a changed literary reality. What
is, of course, striking is the remarkable parallelism and similarity of
attitudes between these two Talmudists, both seeking to push back the
frontiers of Halachic literature, both convinced of the need to review
individual laws in their totality and not rely upon delphic manuals, and
both selecting the same code (*Turim*) as their springboard.

II

Ten years later, in the course of which the *Bet Yosef* spread far and
wide and his authority was increasingly respected, R. Joseph Karo came
full cycle in his own attitude towards the oracular-type code. Having
previously and persuasively argued against the utility and wisdom of
the apodictic compendium, he now conceded its need and efficacy. He
himself abridged the columinous *Bet Yosef*—"gathered the lilies, the
sapphires"—and called his new work the *Shulḥan Aruk* [prepared
table], "because in it the reader will find all kinds of delicacies" fas-
tidiously arranged and systematized and clarified. He was persuaded
that the *Shulḥan Aruk* would serve the needs of a diffuse and hetero-
geneous audience. Scholars will use it as a handy reference book, so that
every matter of law will be perfectly clear and the answer to questions
concerning Halachic practice will be immediate and decisive. Young,
untutored students will also benefit by committing the *Shulḥan Aruk* to
memory, for even rote knowledge is not to be underestimated.

When the *Shulḥan Aruk* appeared, it elicited praise and provoked
criticism; the former could be exuberant, and the latter, abrasive. Some
contemporaries needed only to resuscitate R. Joseph Karo's initial stance
and refurbish his arguments against such works as the *Agur*. R. Moses
Isserles' reaction moved along the same lines which had determined his
reaction to the *Bet Yosef*. He could not—like R. Solomon Luria or R.
Yom Tob Lipman Heller—take unqualified exception to the codificatory
aim and form, for he had already, in his revised *Darke Mosheh,* aligned
himself in principle with this tendency and had eloquently defended it.

He could, however, press his substantive and methodological attack on Karo: the latter had neglected Ashkenazic tradition and had failed to abide by the most recent rulings, thereby ignoring custom which was such an important ingredient of the normative law. Moreover, just as R. Joseph Karo drew upon his *Bet Yosef*, so R. Moses Isserles drew upon his *Darke Mosheh;* both, coming full cycle, moved from lively judicial symposium to soulless legislative soliloquy. If R. Joseph Karo produced a "set table," R. Moses Isserles spread a "tablecloth" over it. It is certain that the "table" would never have been universally accepted if it had not been covered and adorned with the "tablecloth." R. Moses Isserles' glosses, both strictures and annotations, were the ultimate validation of the *Shulḥan Aruk*. The full dialectic has here played itself out, radical opposition to codes giving way to radical codification, almost with a vengeance; for the *Shulḥan Aruk* is the leanest of all codes in Jewish history—from the *Bet Yosef* to the *Shulḥan Aruk,* from the baroque to the bare.

It is not this dialectical movement *per se* which is novel or noteworthy, for this characterizes much of the history of post-Talmudic rabbinic literature. Attempts to compress the Halachah by formal codification alternate with counter-attempts to preserve the fulness and richness of both the method and substance of the Halachah by engaging in interpretation, analogy, logical inference, and only then formulating the resultant normative conclusion. Any student who follows the course of rabbinic literature from the Geonic works of the eighth century through the *Mishneh Torah* and *Turim* and on down to the *Shulḥan Aruk* cannot ignore this see-saw tendency. The tension is ever present and usually catalytic. No sooner is the need for codification met than a wave of non-codificatory work rises. A code could provide guidance and certitude for a while but not finality. *'Arvak 'arva zarik*—"your bondsman requires a bondsman." A code, even in the eyes of its admirers, required vigilant explanation and judicious application. The heartbeat had constantly to be checked and the pulse had to be counted. It became part of a life organism that was never complete or static. What is striking, therefore, in the case of the *Shulḥan Aruk* is that the dialectical movement plays itself out in the attitudes and achievements of the same person—"surfing" on the "sea of the Talmud," rising and falling on the crests of analysis and thoughts of argumentation, and then trying to "gather the water into one area," to construct a dike that would produce a slow, smooth flow of its waters. The *Shulḥan Aruk* thus offers an instructive example of the dialectical movement in rabbinic literature as a whole.

This whole story is important, I believe, because it expands the historical background against which the *Shulḥan Aruk* is to be seen and cautions against excessive preoccupation with purely sociological data, with contemporary stimuli and contingencies. It makes the *Shulḥan Aruk* understandable in terms of the general history of Halachic literature and its major trends. It provides an obvious vertical perspective— i.e. literary categories seen as part of an ongoing Halachic enterprise— to be used alongside of an, at best, implicit horizontal perspective—i.e. historical pressures and eschatological hopes—for an explanation of the emergence of the *Shulhan Aruk*. This is strengthened by the striking parallelism between the literary careers of R. Moses Isserles and R. Joseph Karo; their historical situations, environmental influences, social contexts (in a phrase of contemporary jargon, their *sitz-im-leben*) are so different, but their aspirations and attainments are so similar.

III

When we come to gauge and appraise the impact of the *Shulḥan Aruk,* it is idle to speculate whether R. Joseph Karo intended the *Shulḥan Aruk* to circulate and be used independently, as a literary unit sufficient to itself, or to be used only as a companion volume together with the *Bet Yosef.* His intention has been disputed and variously construed. Some condemned those who studied the *Shulḥan Aruk in vacuo,* thereby acquiring superficial acquaintance with Halachah, claiming that this contravened the author's intention. Others treated the *Shulḥan Aruk* in a manner reminiscent of R. Joseph Karo's original attitude as found in the preface to the *Bet Yosef.* In this case, however, the original intention of the author is eclipsed by the historical fact, abetted or perhaps made possible by R. Moses Isserles' glosses, that the *Shulḥan Aruk* and not the *Bet Yosef* became R. Joseph Karo's main claim to fame, and its existence was completely separate from and independent of the *Bet Yosef.* Commentators such as R. Abraham Gumbiner in the *Magen Abraham* effectively and irreparably cut the umbilical cord which may have linked the *Shulḥan Aruk* with the *Bet Yosef.* What some literary critics have said about poetry may then be applied here: "The design or intention of the author is neither available or desirable as a standard for judging the success of a work of literary art." In our case, consequently, we should simply see what are some of the characteristics of the *Shulḥan Aruk* and some of the repercussions of its great historical success.

Perhaps the single most important feature of the *Shulḥan Aruk* is its unswerving concentration on prescribed patterns of behavior to the exclusion of any significant amount of theoretical data. The *Shulḥan Aruk* is a manual for practical guidance, not academic study. This practical orientation is discernible in many areas and on different levels.

First of all, by initially adopting the classification of the *Turim,* R. Joseph Karo capitulated unconditionally to the practical orientation. The import of this becomes more vivid when we contrast the two major codes on this point. The *Mishneh Torah* is all-inclusive in scope, obliterating all distinctions between practice and theory, and devoting sustained attention to those laws and concepts momentarily devoid of practical value or temporarily in abeyance because of historical and geographical contingencies. Laws of prayer and of the Temple ceremonial are given equal treatment. Laws concerning the *sotah,* the unfaithful wife (abrogated by R. Johanan b. Zakkai in the first century), are codified in the same detail as the ever practical marriage laws. The present time during which part of the law was in abeyance was, in Maimonides' opinion, an historical anomaly, a fleeting moment in the pattern of eternity. The real historical dimensions were those in which the Torah and its precepts were fully realized, that is, the time after the restoration of the Davidic dynasty, when "all the ancient laws will be reinstituted . . . sacrifices will again be offered, the Sabbatical and Jubilee years will again be observed in accordance with the commandments set forth in the Law." The Oral Law was, therefore, to be codified and studied exhaustively. The *Turim,* on the other hand, addresses itself only to those laws that are relevant, to those concrete problems and issues whose validity and applicability are not confined either temporally or geographically. For while both Maimonides and R. Jacob b. Asher were of one mind in abandoning the sequence of the Talmudic treatises and seeking an independent classification of Halachah, they differed in their goals: Maimonides sought to create a topical-conceptual arrangement that would provide a new interpretive mold for study and would also be educationally sound, while R. Jacob b. Asher was guided only by functionality and as a result was less rigorous conceptually. It involved a lesser degree of logical analysis and abstraction, and did not hesitate to group disparate items together. A code, according to this conception, should facilitate the understanding of the operative laws and guide people in translating concepts into rules of conduct.

The *Shulḥan Aruk* adds a further rigorism to the practicality of the Turim. The *Turim's* practicality expresses itself in the rigid selection of material, in the circumscribed scope, but not in the method of presentation, which is rich, varied, and suggestive, containing as it does much textual interpretation and brief discussion of divergent views, while the functionality of the *Shulḥan Aruk* is so radical that it brooks no expansiveness whatsoever. The judicial *process* is of no concern to the codifier; exegesis, interpretation, derivation, awareness of controversy—all these matters are totally dispensable, even undesirable, for the codifier. In this respect, the *Shulḥan Aruk* has greater affinities with the *Mishneh Torah*, which also purports to eliminate conflicting interpretations and rambling discussions and to present *ex cathedra* legislative, unilateral views, without sources and without explanations. The fact is that the *Shulḥan Aruk* is much closer to this codificatory ideal than the *Mishneh Torah*, which, after all, is as much commentary as it is code. One has only to compare, at random, parallel sections of the *Turim* and *Shulḥan Aruk* to realize fully and directly, almost palpably, the extent to which the *Shulḥan Aruk* pruned the *Turim*, relentlessly excising midrashic embellishments, ethical perceptions, and theoretical amplifications. It promised to give the "fixed, final law, without speech and without words." It left little to discretion or imagination.

There is yet another area in which this austere functionality comes to the surface—in the virtually complete elimination of ideology, theology, and teleology. The *Shulḥan Aruk*, unlike the *Mishneh Torah* or the *Sefer ha-Rokeaḥ*, has no philosophical or Kabbalistic prolegomenon or peroration. The *Shulḥan Aruk*, unlike the *Mishneh Torah* or the *Turim*, does not abound in extra-Halachic comments, guiding tenets and ideological directives. While . . . the *Mishneh Torah* does reveal the full intellectualistic posture of Maimonides, the *Shulḥan Aruk* does not even afford an oblique glimpse of the Kabbalistic posture of R. Joseph Karo, who appears here in the guise of the civil lawyer for whom "nothing was more pointless, nothing more inept than a law with a preamble." He was concerned exclusively with what Max Weber called the "methodology of sanctification" which produces a "continuous personality pattern," not with its charismatic goals or stimuli, the ethical underpinning or theological vision which suffuse the Halachah with significance, guarantee its radical, ineradicable spirituality and thereby nurture the religious consciousness. The *Shulḥan Aruk* gives the concrete idea, but omits what Dilthey called *Erlebniss*, the experiential component. In the *Shulḥan Aruk* the Halachah manifests itself as the *regula iuris*, a rule of life characterized by stability, regularity, and fixedness, making known to people "the way they are to go and the practices they are to follow" (Exodus 18:20). These specific, visible practices are not coordinated with invisible meaning or unspecified experience. One can say, in general, that there are two major means by which apparently trans-Halachic material has been organically linked with the

Halachah proper: 1) construction of an ideational framework which indicates the ultimate concerns and gives coherence, direction and vitality to the concrete actions; 2) elaboration of either a rationale of the law or a mystique of the law which suggests explanations and motives for the detailed commandments. The *Shulhan Aruk,* for reasons of its own, about which we may only conjecture, attempts neither.

IV

This restrictive, almost styptic trait of the *Shulhan Aruk* was noticed—and criticized—by contemporaries, foremost among whom was R. Mordecai Jaffe (1530-1612), disciple of R. Moses Isserles and R. Solomon Luria and successor of R. Judah Loewe, the famous Maharal, of Prague. It is worth re-telling the story of the composition of his major, multi-volume work, known as the *Lebush,* inasmuch as it zeroes in on the radical functionality of the *Shulhan Aruk* and also briefly reviews the tense dialectic surrounding codification which we discussed above.

R. Mordecai Jaffe, a very articulate, sophisticated writer who was well acquainted with the contemporary scene, describes the enthusiastic reception accorded to the *Bet Yosef* because people imagined it would serve as a concise, spirited compendium, obviating the need for constant, wearisome recourse to dozens of rabbinic volumes in order to determine the proper Halachic course. He shared this feeling and heightened anticipation, but enthusiasm gave way to disillusionment as he realized that the *Bet Yosef* was anything but concise. Inasmuch as a comprehensive and compact compendium remained an urgent desideratum, he began a condensation of the *Bet Yosef* that would serve this purpose. External factors—an edict of expulsion by the Austrian emperor, which compelled him to flee Bohemia and settle in Italy—interrupted his work. In Italy, where so much Hebrew printing was being done, he heard that R. Joseph Karo himself had made arrangements to print an abridgement. Again he desisted, for he could not presume to improve upon the original author who would unquestionably produce the most balanced, incisive abridgement of his own work. R. Jaffe adds parenthetically— but with remarkable candor—that there was a pragmatic consideration as well: even if he persisted and completed his work, he could not hope to compete publicly with such a prestigious master as R. Joseph Karo— and to do it just for personal consumption, to satisfy his own needs, would be extravagant.

However, upon preliminary examination of the *Shulhan Aruk*—

in Venice—he noted two serious deficiencies. First, it was too short and astringent, having no reasons or explanations—"like a sealed book, a dream which had no interpretation or meaning." He describes it as "a table well prepared with all kinds of refreshments, but the dishes are tasteless, lacking the salt of reasoning which makes the broth boil and warms the individual"—i.e., lacking a minimum of explanatory and exhortatory material to embellish and spiritualize the bald Halachic directives. Second, it was almost exclusively Maimonidean, or Sephardic, and Ashkenazic communities could not, therefore, be guided by it—an argument that had been tellingly and uncompromisingly put forward by both his teachers (Isserles and Luria). Again he started work on a new composition which would fill the gap, and again he abandoned his plans in deference to R. Moses Isserles who was reported to take undertaken this task. When the full *Shulhan Aruk* appeared—the text of R. Joseph Karo and the glosses of R. Moses Isserles—he quickly realized that only the second deficiency had been remedied, that Ashkenazic Halachah had found a worthy and zealous spokesman, but the first deficiency remained—and this was glaring. Some measure of explanation was as indispensable for law as salt was for food. So, for the third time, he turned to producing a code which would a) strive for a golden mean between inordinate length (the *Bet Yosef*) and excessive brevity (the *Shulhan Aruk*); and b) would explain, motivate, and spiritualize the law, often with the help of new Kabbalistic doctrines.

In effect, R. Mordecai Jaffe—whose code was a potential but shortlived rival to the *Shulhan Aruk*—addressed himself to the problem which great Halachists, ethicists, philosophers and mystics have constantly confronted: how to maintain a rigid, punctilious observance of the law and concomitantly avoid externalization and routinization. On one hand, we hear the echoes of Maimonides, R. Eleazar ha-Rokeah of Worms, and R. Menahem b. Zerah (author of the *Zedah la-Derek*), who attempt to combine laws with their reasons and rationale, as well as R. Bahya ibn Pakuda, R. Jonah Gerondi, and R. Isaac Abuhab, to mention just a few of his predecessors. On the other hand, this tone continues to reverberate in the *Shulhan Aruk* of R. Shneur Zalman of Ladi, as well as in the writings of R. Isaiah Hurwitz and R. Moses Hayyim Luzzato, to mention just a few of his successors. The common denominator here is the concern that the Halachic enterprise always be rooted in and related to spirituality, to knowledge of God obtained through study and experience. All difficulties notwithstanding, it was generally felt that even when dealing with the corpus of practical, clearly definable law, an attempt should be made to express the—perhaps in-communicable—values and aspirations of religious experience and spiritual existence.

V

However, when all is said, it would be incorrect and insensitive to assert unqualifiedly that the *Shulḥan Aruk,* that embodiment of Halachah which Jewish history has proclaimed supreme, is a spiritless, formalistic, even timid work. Its opening sentence, especially as elaborated by R. Moses Isserles, acts as the nerve center of the entire Halachic system and the fountain of its strength:

> A man should make himself strong and brave as a lion to rise in the morning for the service of his Creator, so that he should "awake the dawn" (*Psalms* 57:9) . . .
>   "I have set the Lord always before me" (*Psalms* 16:8). This is a cardinal principle in the Torah and in the perfect (noble) ways of the righteous who walk before God. For man does not sit, move, and occupy himself when he is alone in his house, as he sits, moves, and occupies himself when he is in the presence of a great king; nor does he speak and rejoice while he is with his family and relatives as he speaks in the king's council. How much more so when man takes to heart that the Great King, the Holy One, blessed be He, whose "glory fills the whole earth" (*Isaiah* 6:3), is always standing by him and observing all his doings, as it is said in Scripture: "Can a man hide himself in secret places that I shall not see him?" (*Jeremiah* 23:24). Cognizant of this, he will immediately achieve reverence and humility, fear and shame before the Lord, blessed be He, at all times.

Law is dry and its details are burdensome only if its observance lacks vital commitment, but if all actions of a person are infused with the radical awareness that he is acting in the presence of God, then every detail becomes meaningful and relevant. Such an awareness rules out routine, mechanical actions; everything must be conscious and purposive in a God-oriented universe, where every step of man is directed towards God. Halachah, like nature, abhors a vacuum; it recognizes no twilight zone of neutrality or futility. It is all-inclusive. Consequently, every action—even tying one's shoes—can be and is invested with symbolic meaning. Nothing is accidental, behavioral, purely biological. Even unavoidable routine is made less perfunctory. The opening paragraph of the *Shulḥan Aruk* is thus a clear and resounding declaration concerning the workings and the searchings of the spirit. Its tone should reverberate throughout all the subsequent laws and regulations. It provides—as does also paragraph 231, which urges man to see to it that *all* his deeds be "for the sake of heaven"—an implicit rationale for the entire Halachah, but it is a rationale that must be kept alive by the individual. It cannot be passively taken for granted; it must be passionately pursued.

What I am saying, in other words, is that to a certain extent the *Shulḥan Aruk* and Halachah are coterminous and that the "problem" of the *Shulḥan Aruk* is precisely the "problem" of Halachah as a whole. Halachah itself is a tense, vibrant, dialectical system which regularly insists upon normativeness in action and inwardness in feeling and thought. It undertook to give concrete and continuous expression to theological ideals, ethical norms, ecstatic moods, and historical concepts but never superseded or eliminated these ideals and concepts. Halachah itself is, therefore, a coincidence of opposites: prophecy and law, charisma and institution, mood and medium, image and reality, the thought of eternity and the life of temporality. Halachah itself, therefore, in its own behalf, demands the coordination of inner meaning and external observance—and it is most difficult to comply with such a demand and sustain such a delicate, highly sensitized synthesis.

There can be no doubt that R. Joseph Karo, the arch mystic passionately yearning for ever greater spiritual heights, could not have intended to create a new concept of orthopraxis, of punctilious observance of the law divorced, as it were, from all spiritual tension. While this may indeed have been one of the unintended repercussions of the *Shulḥan Aruk*—while it may unknowingly have contributed to the notion, maintained by a strange assortment of people, that Judaism is all deed and no creed, all letter and no spirit—its author would certainly discountenance such an interpretation and dissociate himself from it. If the *Shulḥan Aruk* only charts a specific way of life but does not impart a specific version or vision of meta-Halachah, it is because the latter is to be supplied and experienced independently. The valiant attempt of so many scholars to compress the incompressible, imponderable values of religious experience into cold words and neat formulae, alongside of generally lucid Halachic prescriptions, did not elicit the support of R. Joseph Karo. Halachah could be integrated with and invigorated by disparate, mutually exclusive systems, operating with different motives and aspirations, as long as these agreed on the means and directives. I would suggest that R. Mordecai Jaffe's parenthetical apology for his expansive-interpretive approach to Halachah—that every person spices his food differently, that every wise person will find a different reason or taste in the law, and this reason should not be codified or legislated— may well be what prompted R. Joseph Karo, generally reticent about spiritual matters, to limit his attention to the concrete particularization of Halachah. This could be presented with a good measure of certitude and finality, but its spiritual coordinates required special and separate, if complementary, treatment.

As a personal postcript, or "concluding unscientific postcript," I would like to suggest that, if the Psalmist's awareness of "I have set God before me continually" (Psalm 16:8)—the motto of the *Shulhan Aruk*—is one of the standards of saintliness, then all "*Shulhan Aruk* Jews," all who abide by its regulations while penetrating to its essence and its real motive powers, should be men who strive for saintliness. But strive they must, zealously, imaginatively, and with unrelenting commitment.

PART III

CONTINUITY AND CHANGE IN MODERN TIMES

The classical tradition, obviously, was not monolithic and unchanging. On the contrary, it exhibited great variety and preserved the capacity to change in response to new problems. One cannot therefore interpret the immense changes in Judaism since the eighteenth century within the categories of "tradition" and "change," as though the tradition were monolithic and static, and the process of modernity, of change, were a simple, single, one-way process. Things are much more complicated and subtle than that.

The classical tradition continued in modern times. But alongside appeared other Judaic phenomena, created within, but not identical to, the classical formulations and expressions of Judaism. Much depends upon cultural context. The religious Jews of America as of the State of Israel include both people who believe the classical tradition in the traditional ways, and also people who incorporate into their religious imagination the concerns of modern philosophy, science, and history, yet remain "religious." But the substance of their religiosity, their spirituality and piety, cannot be regarded as identical to that of people not conscious of, not interested or educated in, the conditions of belief in contemporary civilization.

Of much greater importance, both in the State of Israel as well as in the Western diaspora communities—America, Canada, Latin America, Britain and Western Europe—are numerous Jews who in no way regard themselves as religious, yet in important ways think of themselves as Jewish. These Jews represent a truly modern and entirely new phenomenon. In *The Way of Torah* I attempted to incorporate the problem of the religiosity of such Jews into an account of modern Judaism. Here we shall want to know more about them and their place within the structure of modern theology and religious life.

We want to know what is happening to the religious beliefs of Judaism in the flux and turmoil of the modern world. What has become of the theological categories established so long ago?

149

What has happened to belief in one God—or any—in modern times? Two important events shape modern Judaic theology.

First is the advent of the theologian himself, formerly not much in evidence in the history of Judaism. The theologian of whom we speak is more than a religious thinker, one who puts into words the convictions and faith of the tradition. We refer, rather, to the thinkers who attempt to give a coherent, cogent, systematic account of Judaic thinking as a whole. How have they undertaken their task and interpreted it? To be sure, we have already read some of the results of modern Judaic theology, particularly in the setting of classical thinking about God and of the correspondence between *halakhah* and theology. But now we want to consider a self-conscious account of what is happening in essays such as those we have already read.

The second, and absolutely inescapable, issue in modern thinking about God is the problem of the Holocaust. The murder of nearly six million Jews in Europe constitutes the single predominant issue in, and obstacle to, Jewish belief. One constructive approach to thinking about that problem is before us.

What has happened to the Torah in modern times? A modern view of Torah as revelation has already come before us. But further questions remain.

First, what happens to study of Torah in modern situation?

Second, what about those new forms of Jewish learning and cultural expression which stand quite apart from study of the Jewish tradition in its classical definition? How do they correspond to study of Torah in the traditional modes?

And, finally, what is the definition of the Jewish people, Israel, in the contemporary situation?

First, we shall ask, What indeed has happened to the Israel-after-the-flesh, the people itself? How have the Jews changed in modern world.

Second, What unites the Jews in the absence of a common culture and a common religious affirmation? What do the Jews—religious and otherwise—have in common?

Last of all, given the capacity of the Jews to enter into diverse cultures and yet to retain a sense of oneness, we want to consider whether the "assimilation" of the Jews into various modern cultures, into differing social structures and diverse patterns of civilization, constitutes a hopeful or a destructive phenomenon.

The answers to these three questions together constitute an account of the condition of Israel, the Jewish people, within the context of modern Judaism.

FROM RELIGIOSITY TO THEOLOGY

Classical Judaism is rich in belief, in religious conviction expressed through prayer and piety, but poor in theology, in the systematization and intellectual explanation of religious faith. That is not to suggest before modern times there was no Jewish theology. The contrary is the case. What is peculiar to the modern period in the history of Judaism is the development of an effort systematically to explain Jewish belief in the language of modern culture—philosophy of religion and theology. The task was not merely to formulate sentences to contain the substance of piety. It now becomes the effort to make of those sentences paragraphs, chapters, a larger construction for the study and analysis of religious intellectuals.

In this context, we recognize that the formulation of theology *is* something new, the novel effort to make conscious and articulate what in former times tended to be unarticulated, accepted as the given in the life of Judaic spirituality.

But there is a second, even more important point about the novelty of modern Judaic theology. Its task was not only the exposition of the faith, but its formulation in the face of new conceptions of the world and of man. Modern Judaic theology not only explains and organizes faith, it also defends it, establishes its legitimacy against unbelief, on the one side, and competing claims to truth, on the other.

One further task of the Judaic theologian is to make sense of the realities of Judaism. Among these is the very particularity of Judaic belief. Modern thought tends to prefer universal assertions. Judaic theology makes highly particular ones. Modern thought begins with the acceptance of the secular and the natural. Classical Judaic theology rejects secularism and affirms the supernatural.

Emil L. Fackenheim, philosopher at the University of Toronto, here not only describes the task of Judaic theology, but also outlines how that task is to be accomplished. We shall ask him to explain the following:

What is the starting point for Judaic theology? How does it begin its task? Is the problem the belief in God, or the condition of man?

151

Should Judaic theology speak of "man" or of "the Jew"? How does it focus its discussion? What are the questions it must ask of the antecedent Judaic tradition?

What are the major issues confronting the Judaic theologian? Are these peculiar to Judaism and to the Jews?

Above all, how is the issue of "faith" to be formulated and solved? What is the nature of faith? And how does faith relate to theology?

Central to the theological inquiry is the concept of God. How are we able conceptually to approach God? If speaking about God is more than an intellectual exercise in definitions, then what more is involved?

The same questions are to be addressed to revelation: What is the need for revelation? What is meant by the claim that God revealed the Torah to Israel? Why should modern Judaic theology speak of revelation at all? What about the specific claims made by Judaism in behalf of the Torah? Granted that there *can* be revelation, why should someone take seriously this specific, time-bound, peculiar Jewish revelation, the Torah?

Finally, what is the religious meaning of Israel's history on earth? We have to join that question to a much more painful one: Israel, the Jewish people, endured the terrible Holocaust, the systematic murder of six million men, women, and children, among the extermination of many other millions of people. What does this event do to all that has come before it? At the end of this essay and in the paper immediately following, Fackenheim addresses this most central issue.

XII

AN OUTLINE OF MODERN
JEWISH THEOLOGY

EMIL L. FACKENHEIM

(From *Quest for Past and Future. Essays in Jewish Theology,* by Emil L. Fackenheim. Bloomington & London, 1968: Indiana University Press, pp. 96-111.)

Theology is the attempt to give a coherent account of religious
faith; Jewish theology is the attempt to give a coherent account of
Jewish faith. Theology thus differs from religion, which is the life of
faith itself; it also differs from philosophy and science, which are either
not concerned with religious faith at all, or else cannot accept it as an
irreducible source of truth.

As every other religion, Judaism requires a theology. To be
sure, in many ages Judaism did not produce a theology; but in such
ages the immediacy of faith was strong and unreflective enough to
make its intellectual clarification practically superfluous. No such
immediacy is to be found today. Hence the disparagement of theology
in some quarters merely indicates confusion, or else indifference to
the substance of Jewish faith.

Modern theology often fails to distinguish itself sharply from
philosophy, or some such science as psychology. This failure is a
specifically modern phenomenon. Since the Enlightenment, modern
man has questioned or denied the actuality, or even possibility, of
supernatural revelation, once regarded as the autonomous source of
religious truth, and the basis of theology. Since that denial, a defense
of religious truth, if attempted at all, had to be sought elsewhere—in
philosophical argument or, more recently, in scientific evidence. But
it is more than likely that this sort of defense is futile, and that the
attempted fusion of theology with either philosophy or science is a
confusion. As regards the specific tasks of Jewish theology, it is
apriori evident, not only that this *is* a confusion, but that it is a confusion fatal to the tasks of Jewish theology. For the categories of

philosophy and science are, one and all, universal; but from such *universal* categories no conclusions can be derived which might be a theological justification of the *particular* existence of the Jewish people. Hence the ceaseless, but futile, endeavors in modern Jewish thought to explain and justify Jewish existence in universal categories, such as nation, denomination and the like. If we should have to conclude that the only course left open to the modern Jew is to base his thinking exclusively on the grounds of science or philosophy, then this would be tantamount to concluding that, in the modern world, a Jewish theology is impossible.

The substance of Jewish faith is the direct relation, not only of man in general, but also of Israel in particular, to God. Jewish theology must seek to defend this faith. And it can defend it only if it can defend this relation as immediate, unmediated by general categories. In other words, if it can defend a supernatural God, and a relation to such a God. To justify the substance of Jewish faith, theology must turn its back not only on secularism, but also on all attempts to found Judaism on anything less than an irreducible faith in the Supernatural.

But Modern Jewish theology may not simply assume that a defense of Jewish faith is possible. It must not close its eyes to modern criticism which has seriously put this in question. The method of modern Jewish theology must differ from that of classical theology. This latter "worked its way down," i.e., assumed from the start what to modern man is the thing most in question: the actuality of a divine revelation given to man and Israel. Modern theology must "work its way up," i.e., show, by an analysis of the human condition, that man's existence, properly understood, forces him to raise the question of the Supernatural, and the existential problem of the "leap into faith." That human existence is indeed of this sort is implicit, and sometimes explicitly stated, in the whole of Jewish tradition. But whether the traditional view is correct is a question to be considered independently, by unbiased analysis. Only if such an analysis does in fact find this thesis correct can we go a single step further. For if human existence is not such as to raise necessarily the questions to which faith is the answer, then faith is a relic of an unenlightened age which modern man can do without. *From this it follows that the analysis of the human condition constitutes the necessary prolegomenon for all modern Jewish and, indeed, all modern theology.* On the adequacy of this prolegomenon depends the foundation of its sequel, theology proper. For theology is the explication of the faith into which a leap has been made, and the analysis of the human condition alone can justify the leap into faith itself.

Theology proper, in the case of Jewish theology, will fall into two major parts: (1) the explication of the faith by which the Jew lives insofar as he is a man. If this faith is the true answer to the question raised by human existence, it must be true for all men; (2) the faith by which the Jew lives insofar as he is a Jew; this faith, involving the nature and destiny of Israel before God, is confined to Israel alone.

We have said that faith, to be acceptable to modern man, must reveal itself as the sole positive response to questions inherent in the human condition; and we have further asserted that this view is implicit in the Jewish tradition. If this is true, then the task of Jewish theology proper largely consists in trying to understand Jewish tradition in this light: as reflecting a faith which is the response to perennial human problems. If we may assume that Jewish tradition reflects (along with much that is incidental and inauthentic) also the essential and authentic, then modern Jewish theology in no way seeks to alter the essence of Jewish faith; though it may very well alter Jewish theology. For the task of modern Jewish theology is to understand Jewish faith in terms compatible with modern thought.

Philosophical analysis reveals that man is, as it were, half-angel, half-brute. Unlike all other beings, he is not all of one piece. If he interprets himself as an overgrown animal—different from other animals only in complexity—he finds that his natural needs and urges fit into this interpretation, but his moral and spiritual nature do not. Yet if he interprets himself as an unfinished angel he fares no better: nature in him forever refuses to be transcended. Every effort to make himself all of one piece is doomed to ultimate failure, and history is littered with philosophies (as well as so-called sciences) reflecting this failure. Man is in perennial contradiction with himself—a "broken vessel." To mitigate this contradiction may be a task set to human prudence and moral wisdom; but to resolve it is possible, if at all, only for a God.

History reflects the human condition. If man were but a complex animal he would have no history. He would realize no meaning beyond what is already inherent in his essence. His history would be but quantitative variation, in other words, not history at all. If, on the other hand, man were an unfinished angel, all that is evil and unmeaning in history would be mere temporary accident. History would be necessary progress, and man would be wholly competent to bring about its moral perfection. In truth, history is a domain of meaning, but of a meaning forever partially thwarted. Moral progress is exposed to tragic frustration. Man can mitigate the tragic and evil in history but cannot eliminate it: history, like man, is in need of redemption.

The domain of human freedom is defined by moral law. The moral "ought" marks the perennial human ability and task to transcend an "is." The tension between "is" and "ought" not only constitutes freedom in its profoundest sense: it defines man's very humanity. But any "is" is finite whereas the "ought" is infinite. This means that there are no a priori limits to human freedom and responsibility: man must always strive further upward. But it also means that the tension between "is" and "ought" is never resolved: by his own moral judgment, man is always a sinner. Moral knowledge, and perhaps even moral life, need no God. But man's moral situation raises not only moral but also religious questions. The question is not only: what ought I to do? but also: what is the meaning of my sinfulness, which remains no matter what I do? If the religious question is left open, then the demands of the moral law leave life an unsolved riddle; and if God is denied that riddle becomes a tragedy.

The moral tension of human existence is only one of many, though perhaps the most significant. But perhaps others, raised by problems such as death and solitude, are no less significant after all. All these ultimate tensions derive from the fundamental tension of existence, above described. They all, jointly or separately, pose the fundamental religious question: is the contradictoriness of existence as final as it is seen by our finite reason? Reason can still state this question, but it can no longer answer it. To answer this question, affirmatively or negatively, we require a leap, an act of decision and commitment. A commitment to a negative answer is a commitment to tragic existence, to a way of life lived in the conviction that existence is in its core paradoxical. The affirmative answer is the decision of faith. *Faith may be defined as the positive answer, given by way of personal commitment, to existential questions of ultimate significance, which reason can still raise, but no longer answer.* Faith asserts that the human contradiction is not final but ultimately redeemed; that what naturally cannot come to pass yet does come to pass; that not one, but both sides of the human contradiction are redeemed, and nothing is lost. Faith asserts the existence of a God who is Creator of all, and Redeemer of all.

Faith is thus neither knowledge nor superstition; not knowledge because its evidence is subjective, and outside rational proof; not superstition, because its object transcends refutation as well as proof, and because it is not arbitrary. Faith is a leap into the dark but, again, not an arbitrary leap—one of many possible leaps, each of which is equally meaningful. It is the sole possible positive answer to the fundamental question posed by existence itself.

Because it is faith, faith in God is an absolute risk. Because it is faith in God—Creator of all and Redeemer of all—it is a risk involving existence in its entirety.

Theology is the organized statement of religious faith. Faith consists in the commitment to a positive answer to problems of human existence which reason can state but not answer. Thus every doctrine of faith must reflect a contradiction in human existence which it resolves; and it is part of the business of theology to exhibit this reflection. Jewish theology, too, has this business. What marks it as specifically Jewish is that the faith which is its subject is the faith by which the Jew lives, not only as a man, but also as a Jew.

The God whose existence faith asserts is a mystery. Asserting His existence, faith dares not to make any assertion about His nature as it may be in itself. God's nature, if intelligible, is not the subject of faith. Faith is concerned with God only insofar as He is related to human existence: as the God who has made, and will reconcile, a paradox. The language of faith therefore does not include words such as "Substance," "Force," "Cause" etc., but only terms such as "Creator" and "Redeemer." The God of faith must redeem man, but not by making him less than human, or by transforming him into an angel. To assert either would be to assert that human existence as such is meaningless, a contradiction to no purpose. But faith must assert (if it asserts anything) that what is contradictory to finite understanding is yet ultimately not contradictory. The God of faith must redeem man by preserving the contradictory elements which constitute his humanity, but by transforming them in such a way (unintelligible to finite understanding) as to take the sting out of the contradiction. God thus relates Himself to man in ways which appear contradictory to finite understanding. He is at once a God of Justice who makes absolute demands on human freedom, and a God of Mercy who heals absolutely the contradictions which arise from the use of that freedom. Before Him as Judge all men are radically sinful; yet before Him as Father all sins are radically forgiven. For the same reason, man's moral freedom, and the importance of its responsible use, is at once everything and nothing. It is everything because God makes demands upon men, as if He Himself were impotent, and man the sole agent of history; it is nothing because, after all, God is omnipotent, and history is safe in His hands despite the evil done by men.

God is therefore Person. For whenever a person is in mutual relation with another, that other is person as well.

Yet when we speak of the justice, mercy, and personality of God we speak symbolically only. God's nature is a mystery, and only insofar as He is related to man may faith speak of God; yet even in relation to man God remains a mystery. For God is infinite and man is finite; and a mutual relation between a God who is infinite and men who are finite passes finite understanding. Nevertheless, faith must assert the reality of this relation. Man is forever tempted to deny such a mutual relation, either by making God a mere ideal which does not act, or by making man a mere plaything of an omnipotent God. But neither doctrine is a genuine doctrine of faith; for both fail to resolve the human contradiction. The latter denies the very fact (i.e., moral freedom) which gives rise to the human paradox; the former fails to resolve that paradox. Faith, then, in asserting a mutual relation between man and God, cannot speak literally. But to be unable to speak literally cannot mean to remain silent: for, to faith, that relation itself is a reality, demanding participation on the part of man. Man addresses God, obeys His law, prays for and trusts in His mercy. He must treat God as if He were literally Person, Judge and Father. Man must speak, but speak symbolically; of (if we wish) anthropomorphically; for he speaks from his finite situation. But anthropomorphic language, not being absolute truth, is not therefore falsehood: it is the truth about the God-man-relation as it appears from the standpoint of man; and that relation is itself a reality. How it appears from the standpoint of God man cannot fathom, nor is it his business to fathom it.

No religious doctrine is more baffling than that of revelation; yet none is more essential.

Two alternative interpretations present themselves of which neither appears intelligible. Either revelation reveals what man may discover by means lying within in his nature: but then revelation is superfluous. Or else revelation reveals what lies beyond human means of discovery: but then it would seem to lie beyond human understanding also, and the recipient of a revelation cannot understand it. This dilemma cannot be avoided by fashionable equivocations. To associate revelation with poetic inspiration is to make it the product of man; but revelation is either the direct gift of God or not revelation at all.

Yet no doctrine is more essential than revelation, unless it be faith in God itself. Creation establishes time and history, whereas redemption consummates and redeems them. Revelation is an incursion of God *into* time and history; eternity here breaks into time without dissolving time's particularity. Creation and redemption establish the significance of time and history in *general*. Revelation establishes the significance of the *here and now* as unique; it is the religious category of existentiality as such.

If revelation is impossible then there is significance only to the human situation in general, even though God is accepted. And the law as well as the promise known to man remain in strict universality. But this makes individual men and historic moments universally interchangeable. God may then be related to man in general: He is only indirectly and accidentally related to myself, my people, my historic situation.

Existence, however, is of inexorable particularity. The moral law to which I am obligated may be universal, but the situation in which I must realize it is unique. A historic situation reflects what history as such is, but it is nevertheless something all its own. Israel is a manifestation of mankind, but what makes her Israel is unrepeatable and uninterchangeable. If there is no revelation, the particular in existence is a meaningless weight upon time and history, from creation until redemption. History in that case has meaning only at its beginning and at its end: nothing essential goes on within it.

But faith must assert that revelation is possible. For only if revelation is possible does the here and now have relevance before God. And if the here and now has no such relevance the human contradiction remains at least partly unresolved. Only if there is, or at least can be, revelation does the God of mankind become my God; only then does the universal God of the philosophers become the God of Abraham, Isaac and Jacob.

This explains the dialectical character of revelation, above described. An incursion of the eternal into the temporal which destroyed either the temporality of the temporal or its own eternity would provide no essential difficulty for the human understanding; but an incursion which preserves both its own eternity and the particularity of the temporal is a paradox. But faith *must* hold fast to this paradox if the particular is to have meaning before God; it *may* hold fast to it because there is no reason why what is paradoxical to finite understanding should be impossible to God. Revelation, like all doctrines of faith, reflects in its own dialectical character the nature of the human problem to which, as a doctrine of faith, it corresponds.

This character is reflected also in the content of revelation. It lights up the particular as such, in its obligation and promise: it must therefore reveal. Yet in passing into time it becomes transformed: hence it must remain concealed as well. That God speaks, or has spoken, is a simple fact to the man of faith; but what He has said is expressed in human language; it is inexorably shot through with interpretation and hence remains, even while revealed, a mystery.

The modernists of all time distort revelation by transforming it into natural inspiration; the orthodox distort it no less by equating the human interpretation of and reaction to the Encounter with the Encounter itself.

A history without God is an unmitigated tragedy, i.e., a domain of frustrating meaning. A history which is, as a whole, in the hands of God, but in which no revelation is possible, is as a whole beyond tragedy; but the particular as such remains a weight without meaning. A history in which revelation is possible is one in which every event, no matter how insignificant, may in its stark particularity acquire unique meaning. It is a history characterized by the all-important possibility of Fulfilment *within* history; not merely the ultimate Fulfilment of redemption, which can fulfil only by abolishing history.

The assertion of faith that revelation as such is possible and, indeed, necessary, is still a universal assertion. It is concerned with the *category* of the particular, not any special particular. A leap is therefore required before it is possible to assert the *actuality* of a specific revelation.

Not unnaturally religions divide at this point. While atheist, agnostic and religious believer can agree on the human condition and its need for redemption; while all who have made the leap of faith can agree on the general implications of that leap, and on the general thesis that the contradictions of existence are not final: it is not possible to arrive at the actuality of a particular revelation by means of universal considerations of this sort. Theological reflection, even after the leap into faith, takes us no further than to the establishment of the possibility of revelation as such. The assertion of the actuality of a particular revelation entails a second absolute leap, and a second absolute risk.

There is a second, and perhaps even profounder reason why religions should divide at this point. Only at the point when an actual revelation is asserted do we enter the realm of concrete, unique, unrepeatable existence. Here individuals, peoples, historic situations begin to know of, and live in, their unique condition. And, by the same token, here they begin to be ignorant of the uniqueness of other individuals, peoples and historic situations. Thus, for example, the Jew who asserts a revelation addressed to himself as Jew, speaks of something of which others are necessarily ignorant; at the same time, he is himself ignorant of what may establish the religious significance of the concrete existence of others. The extent to which the adherent of one faith may understand, and pass judgment on, the faith of another is clearly limited. Here, then, religions divide in their claims; but here, also, different claims cease to be mutually exclusive.

Judaism rests on the assertion of the actuality of a series of revelations which have constituted Israel as a historic community destined to serve a specific purpose. Where it speaks of mankind and the God of mankind, Judaism is nothing beyond what might be a universally human religion; only at the point where, leaping into the particular, it is concerned with Israel and the God of Israel, does Judaism separate off from universal truths of faith.

Jewish existence is established by, and responsible to, divine revelation. Hence it shares the dialectical character of all revelation. That Jewish existence has a meaning is vouchsafed by the faith which accepts the reality of revelation; of a revelation which has established Jewish existence. But the nature of that meaning is involved in the dialectic of the paradox. All revelation both reveals and conceals: thus the meaning of Israel's existence, too, is both revealed and concealed. It must remain concealed: for the divine plan for Israel remains unfathomable. Yet it must also be revealed: for Israel is to play a responsible part in that plan. Since the Jew is to live a consciously Jewish life before God he must have an at least partial grasp of its meaning; but in its fulness that meaning is not disclosed: for his Jewishness is only partly the Jew's own doing. The Jew both makes, and is made by his destiny.

The God-man-relation demands of man a free response, the response through moral law. The God-Israel-relation demands of the Jew, in addition to the moral response, a response expressing his Jewishness in all its particularity. This response is *Halachah*. Moral law, mediated through the leap of faith, becomes the divine law to man. Halachah is Jewish custom and ceremony mediated through the leap into Jewish faith; and it thereby becomes the divine law to Israel. In themselves, all customs, ceremonies and folklore (including those Jewish, and those contained in the book called Torah) are mere human self-expression, the self-expression of men alone among themselves. But through the leap of faith any one of them (and preeminently those of the Torah) have the potency of becoming human reflections of a real God-Israel encounter. And thus each of them has the potency of becoming Halachah, commanded and fulfilled: if fulfilled, not as self-expression but as response on the part of Israel to a divine challenge to Israel; as the gift of the Jewish self to God. Thus no particular set of ceremonies is, as such, divine law: this is an error flowing from the orthodox misunderstanding of the nature of revelation. But, on the other hand, all customs which flow from the concreteness of Jewish life have the potency of becoming divine law, and are a challenge to fulfillment. The denial of the religious significance of any law which is not moral is an error flowing from the modernistic misunderstanding of the nature of the concrete before God.

We have said that, like all revelation, the revelation of God to Israel both reveals and conceals; and that, correspondingly, the Jew both makes, and is made by, his destiny. Thus whether the Jew practices Halachah is, on the one hand, not constitutive of his Jewishness; on the other, it is not indifferent to his Jewishness. If the former were the case, the Jew would wholly make his Jewish destiny; if the latter, he would be wholly made by it.

Thus the meaning of Israel's destiny is in part revealed: it is to respond, ever again, to a divine challenge; to become, of her own free choice, a people of God; to give perpetual realization to this decision in thought and practice. Situations change, and with them the content of the response they require: but the fact of challenge, and the need for response, remain the same.

Yet the meaning of Israel's destiny is also concealed. Man cannot understand the final reasons for the tensions of his existence; the Jew cannot understand the final reasons why he was chosen to exemplify these tensions. Hence the Jew is also unable to decide whether or not Israel will continue to exist. He is, to be sure, free to be sure, free to decide whether to be a devout or stiff-necked Jew, whether to heed or to ignore the divine challenge. But if it is really true that God has a plan for Israel, Israel is as little free to alter that plan as she is able to understand its final meaning.

BELIEF BEYOND DESPAIR

The situation of modernity presents problems to belief. These face everyone. It is difficult, for one thing, to believe in God when many people around you do not. It is even more difficult to believe *about* God the supernatural assertions of classical Judaism or Christianity. The arguments of philosophers for the existence of God, as everyone knows, do not lead far toward the very concrete and highly particular assertions made by the historical traditions in respect to God's actions in history, or his will, or his revealing of the Torah, or his loving the Jewish people and choosing them to serve him.

But modern Jews confront in their every breath a still further obstacle to faith. It is contained in the key-word "Auschwitz," which is used to refer to the terrible experience of European Jewry from 1933 to 1945, the extermination of men and women and children only on account of their having been born to a Jewish parent (or, in fact, having had a single Jewish grandparent). To put it simply: Where was God when these things happened?

Certainly, the problem of faith will trouble the religious Jew. But faith is not the sole issue. What do these events say about the character and condition of man? If we follow Emil Fackenheim in supposing that the beginning of the theological inquiry is the analysis of the human condition, then we have to include in that analysis the facts of the unparalleled capacity to do evil revealed in "Auschwitz."

One might readily come to a despairing, even nihilistic view of man, along with an entire atheism in respect to God. Many indeed have responded to "Auschwitz" in exactly these ways. But Fackenheim has not, and because he has a constructive and religiously consequential message, what he has to tell us is important. It is, indeed, more important than the criticism of his critics. For he speaks not as one from afar, but as a participant. The Holocaust to him is not the story of what happened to other people. It is part of his own biography (as it is for millions of others).

We want Fackenheim to tell us what is to be said about man after Auschwitz. And not only so, but what message, specifically, may be drawn from the classical Judaic tradition? Americans are used to

163

hearing amiable, optimistic words about man. What words are left now?

Are we able to *understand* anything at all of what happened? And beyond understanding, are we able to come to any affirmation? Since Fackenheim is not only a philosopher, but also a theologian of Judaism, we ask too, What do you have to say to the Jews of the present time and place?

Is there an affirmative and constructive lesson to be learned from the destructive contemporary experience of the Jewish people? Is the message no-message, nothingness?

XIII

THE HUMAN CONDITION AFTER AUSCHWITZ

EMIL L. FACKENHEIM

(From *The Human Condition after Auschwitz. A Jewish Testimony a Generation After*, by Emil L. Fackenheim. Syracuse University: The B. G. Rudolph Lectures in Judaic Studies, April, 1971.)

A Midrash in Genesis Rabbah disturbs and haunts the mind ever more deeply. It begins as follows:

> Rabbi Shim'on said: "In the hour when God was about to create Adam, the angels of service were divided. . . . Some said, 'Let him not be created,' others, 'Let him be created.' . . . Love said, 'Let him be created, for he will do loving deeds.' But Truth said, 'Let him not be created, for he will be all falsity." Righteousness said, 'Let him be created, for he will do righteous deeds.' Peace said, 'Let him not be created, for he will be full of strife.' When then did God do? He seized hold of Truth, and cast her to the earth, as it is said, 'Thou didst cast Truth to the ground.' " (Dan. 8:12)

No Midrash wants to be taken literally. Every Midrash wants to be taken seriously. Midrash is serious because its stories and parables address the reader; they are not confined to the past. It is religious because, while it may contain beauty and poetry, its essential concern is truth. And when, as in the present case, a Midrash tells a story of human origins, the religious truth it seeks to convey is universal. Its theme is nothing less than the human condition as a whole.

Why does this Midrash disturb and haunt us? Not simply because it is realistic rather than romantically-"optimistic" about man. Midrash is always realistic. We are haunted because Truth is cast to the ground. This climactic part of the story (as thus far told) does not say that all is well, that the good Lord has the power, so to speak, of indiscrimi-

165

nately silencing all opposition. Were this its message, then Peace as
well as Truth should be cast to the ground. That Truth alone is singled
out for this treatment suggests the ominous possibility that *all* that might
be said in favor of the creation of man is nothing but pious illusion; that
Truth is so horrendous as to destroy *everything* for us unless we shun
it, avoid it, evade it; that *only* after having cast Truth to the ground can
God create man at all.

But then we ask: whom does God deceive? Surely one thing even
God cannot do is, as it were, fool Himself. Are we the ones, then, who
are fooled? Are we *radically* deceived in our belief that at least *some*
of that which we undergo, do, are, is *ultimately* worthwhile—a belief
which we cannot endure?

But such a divine deception (if a deception it is) does not succeed.
We can see through it. The Midrashic author *knows* that Truth is cast
to the ground. So do all the devout Jews who have read his story
throughout the generations. But what is the effect of this knowledge?
Can it be other than despair?

The Midrash itself deals with this question when it repudiates
despair. It ends as follows:

> Then the angels of service said to God, "Lord of the universe,
> how canst Thou despise Thy seal? Let Truth arise from the earth,
> as it is said, 'Truth springs from the earth.' " (Ps. 85:12)

Somehow it is possible for man to face·Truth and yet to be. But do
we know how? . . .

. . . For many centuries . . . theologians would resort at once to
the Word of God, with or without the help of ecclesiastical authority.
Philosophers would affirm a human "nature" immune to the vicissitudes
of history—an immunity which in turn guaranteed a timeless access to
the True, the Good, and the Beautiful. And a long alliance between
these two disciplines produced a firm stand in behalf of "eternal verities" against perpetually shifting "arbitrary opinion."

These centuries are past. Theologians (Jewish and Christian)
should always have known that the Word of their God is manifest *in*
history if it is manifest at all: because of the historical self-conscious-
ness of contemporary man, this knowledge can now no longer be
evaded. If nevertheless seeking refuge in the eternal verities of philosophy, they find that these, too, have vanished. For modern philosophy has found itself forced to abandon the notion of a permanent

human nature—and along with this all timelessly accessible visions of the True, the Good and the Beautiful.

This fact is most profoundly if not uniquely manifest in the philosophies arising from the work of Immanuel Kant. These philosophies do not deny aspects of the human condition which remain more or less permanent throughout human history. Such aspects, however, are now confined to man's natural constitution. What makes man *human* (we are told) is neither given nor permanent, but rather the product of his own individual or collective activity. *Man qua man is a self-maker.* This formula sums up the deepest of all the many revolutions in modern philosophy. We may wish to quarrel with its central thesis. We may wish to qualify it. We may even wish to reject it outright. One thing, at any rate, seems for better or worse impossible—the return to the pre-modern philosophical wisdom.

Not so long ago theologians of liberal stamp greeted this revolution in philosophy with rejoicing. Who has not heard sermons (and in particular American sermons) about the "infinite perfectibility of man?" The notion of man as a self-maker seemed (and in some respects surely is) far more grandiose than the notion of a human nature given by another—even if this Other was not (rather vaguely) "Nature" or "the Universe," but the Lord of Creation Himself. Add to this what was said above about the American tradition of optimism, and it is not surprising that for a considerable period of time all talk about "the nature of man" and "*the* True, *the* Good and *the* Beautiful" seemed in many circles to be timidly conservative, if not downright reactionary.

But now the crisis of American optimism has disclosed for us that the concept of man as a self-maker gives us grounds for apprehension and dread as well as for hope. The lack of a permanent nature may hold the promise that unforeseeable ways of human self-perfection are possible; since this lack is an unlimited malleability, however, it implies the possibility of unforeseeable negative as well as positive developments. And thus the spectre comes into view that man, *qua* unlimited maker, may reach the point of making his whole world into a machine, while at the same time, *qua* infinitely malleable, himself being reduced to a mere part of the machine, that is, to a self-made thing. Nor is this possibility today a mere unsubstantial fancy confined to philosophers. For some of our futurologists have begun to conjure up a future in which man, the proud self-maker, will have lost control over the world he has made, and the reduction to self-made thinghood will be complete. Indeed, even popular consciousness is haunted by the prospect that the whole bold and exciting story of the one being in the universe capable of making his own nature—the story of the only truly *free* being—will come to an end the pathos of which is matched only by its irony.

With prospects so terrifying, it is no wonder that some simply opt out of history; that others hanker after a simpler, more innocent past; and that, as if anticipating catastrophe, we are all tempted even now to deprecate indiscriminately all things human.

The philosopher may not yield to the temptations of escapism or indiscriminate despair. Nor may he simply throw in his lot with the futurologists, for (as we shall show at least in part) their entire approach calls for considerable philosophical suspicion. At this point, we shall be well advised to suspend the future and confine ourselves to the present. Is a genuinely *human* existence possible *even now?* Or, in order to make it possible, must we cast Truth to the ground? Must we suppress all knowledge of a future which is sure to come and force Truth to *stay* cast to the ground?

We have thus far made no reference to Jewish experience in this century. We do so at this point because the direst predictions any futurologist might make have already been fulfilled and surpassed at Auschwitz, Mauthausen, Bergen-Belsen and Buchenwald. One shrinks from speaking of these unspeakable places of unique horror in any context which might invite false generalizations and comparisons. Yet one simple statement may safely be made. In the Nazi murder camps no effort was spared to make persons into living *things* before making them into dead things. And that the dead had been human when alive was a truth systematically rejected when their bodies were made into fertilizer and soap. Moreover, the criminals themselves had become living *things,* and the system, run by operators "only following orders," was well on the way toward running itself. The thoughtful reader of such a work as *The Holocaust Kingdom* reaches the shocking conclusion that here was indeed a "kingdom," that is, a society organized to a purpose; that, its organization near-perfect, it might in due course have dispensed with the need for a "king;" and that such was its inner dynamic and power for self-expansion that, given a Nazi victory, it might today rule the world. This "society," however, was an anti-society, indeed, *the* modern anti-society *par excellence*: modern because unsurpassably technological, and anti-society because, while even the worst society is geared to life, the Holocaust Kingdom was geared to death. It would be quite false to say that it was a mere means, however depraved, to ends somehow bound up with life. As an enter-

prise subserving the Nazi war effort the murder camps were total fail-
ures, for the human and material "investment" far exceeded the "produce" of fertilizer, gold teeth and soap. The Holocaust Kingdom was
an end in itself, having only one ultimate "produce," and that was
death. . . .

    . . . Can either Nazism or its murder camps be understood as
but one particular case, however extreme, of the general technological
dehumanization? Or; (to use language which theologians are equipped
to understand) does not a scandal of particularity attach to Nazism and
its murder camps which is shied away from, suppressed or simply forgotten when the scandal is technologically universalized? To be sure,
there have been "world wars"—but none like that which Hitler un-
leashed on the world. There have been (and are) "total" political
systems—but none like Nazism, a truth suppressed when "fascism" is
used as a generic term in which Nazism is included. And while there
have been (and are) "cults of personality", there have been no Fuh-
rers but only one Fuhrer.

    Nor is it possible to distinguish between the goals of Nazism-in-
general, as one system, and those of the murder-camp-in-particular, as
a second system subserving the first. In essence, Nazism *was* the
murder-camp. That a nihilistic, demonic celebration of death and destruction was its animating principle was evident to thinkers such as
Karl Barth from the start; it became universally revealed in the end,
when in the Berlin bunker Hitler and Goebbels, the only true Nazis
left, expressed ghoulish satisfaction at the prospect that their downfall
might carry in train the doom, not only (or even at all) of their
enemies, but rather of the "master race." The mind shrinks from systematic murder which serves no purpose beyond murder itself, for it
is ultimately unintelligible. Yet in Nazism as a whole (not only in the
murder camps) this unintelligibility was real. And except for good
fortune this diabolical celebration might today rule the world.

    Even this does not exhaust the scandalous particularity of Nazism.
The term "Aryan" had no clear connotation other than "non-Jew,"
and the Nazis were not antisemites because they were racists, but
rather racists because they were antisemites. The exaltation of the
"Aryan" had no positive significance. It had only the negative significance of degrading and murdering the "non-Aryan." Thus Adolf
Eichmann passed beyond the limits of a merely "banal" evil when,
with nothing left of the Third Reich, he declared with obvious sin-
cerity that he would jump laughing into his grave in the knowledge of
having dispatched six million Jews to their death. We must conclude,

then, that the dead Jews of the murder camps (and all the other innocent victims, as it were, as quasi-Jews, or by dint of innocent-guilt-by-
association) were not the "waste product" of the Nazi system. They
were *the* product.

Despite all necessary attempts to comprehend, the Nazi system in
the end exceeds all comprehension. One cannot comprehend but only
confront and oppose. We can here attempt to confront only one minis-
cule manifestation. When issuing "work permits" designed to separate
"useless" Jews to be murdered at once from "useful" ones to be kept
useful by diabolically contrived false hopes and murdered later, the
Nazis on occasion issued two such permits to able-bodied Jewish men.
One was untransferable and to be kept for himself; the other was to be
given at his own discretion to his able-bodied father, mother, wife or
one child. On those occasions the Nazis would not make this choice,
although to do so would have resulted in a more efficient labor force.
Jewish sons, husbands and fathers themselves were forced to decide
who among their loved ones was—for the time being—to live and who
to die at once.

The mind seeks escape in every direction. Yet we must confront
relentlessly the Nazi custom of the two work permits, recognizing in
this custom not the work of some isolated sadists, but rather the essence
of the Nazi system. . . . Had utility been the principle of Nazism it
would not have left the choice between "useful" and "useless" Jews to
its victims. Not utility (however dehumanized), but rather torture and
degradation was the principle. Indeed, there is no greater contrast between the technological exaltation of utility (even when out of control) and a celebration of torture *contrary* to all utility when it is not
incidental but rather *for torture's sake*. . . .

. . . We cannot be sure how the ancient rabbis, were they alive,
would respond to the death camps. We *can* be sure that they would not
explain them away. In their own time, they knew of idolatry, and considered groundless hate to be its equivalent. They knew, too, that it
could not be explained but only opposed. Alive today, they would reject all fatalistic futurological predictions as so many self-fulfilling prophecies which leave us helpless. Instead, they would somehow seek to
meet the absolute evil of the death camps in the only way absolute
evil can be met—by an absolute opposition on which one stakes one's
life.

The authentic Jew after Auschwitz has no privileged access to explanations of the past. He has no privileged access to predictions of the
future, or to ways of solving the problems of the present. He is, how-

ever, a witness to the world. He is a witness against the idolatry of the Nazi murder camps. This negative testimony is *ipso facto* also the positive testimony that man shall *be,* and shall be *human*—even if Truth should be so horrendous that there is no choice but to cast it to the ground.

The Jew in whom this testimony is unsurpassably manifest is the survivor of the two-work-permit custom. When the torture occurred he had no choice but compliance. Armed resistance was impossible. So was suicide. So was the transfer of his own work permit to another member of his family. Any of these attempts would have doomed the one member of his family who was to live. To save this one member, he was forced to become implicated in the diabolical system which robbed him of his soul and made him forever after innocently guilty of the murder of all his family except one member.

We ask: having survived (if survive he did), why did this Jew not seek blessed release in suicide? Choosing to live, why did he not seek refuge in insanity? Choosing to stay sane, why did he not do all he could to escape from his singled out Jewish condition but rather affirmed his Jewishness and indeed raised new Jewish children? How could even one stay with his God?

These are unprecedented questions. They require unprecedented responses. Why not suicide? *Because after the Nazi celebration of death life has acquired a new dimension of sanctity.* Why not flight into madness? *Because insanity had ruled the kingdom of darkness, hence sanity, once a gift, has now become a holy commandment.* Why hold fast to mere Jewishness? *Because Jewish survival after Auschwitz is not "mere," but rather in itself and without any further reasons or theological justifications a sacred testimony* to all mankind *that life and love, not death and hate, shall prevail.* Why hold fast to the God of the covenant? Former believers lost Him in the Holocaust Kingdom. Former agnostics found Him. No judgment is possible. All theological arguments vanish. Nothing remains but the fact that the bond between Him and His people reached the breaking point but was not for all wholly broken. Thus the survivor is a witness against darkness in an age of darkness. He is a witness whose like the world has not seen.

We do not yet recognize this witness, for we do not yet dare to enter the darkness against which he testifies. Yet to enter that darkness is to be rewarded with an altogether astonishing discovery. *This may be an age without heroes. It is, however, the heroic age* par excellence *in all of Jewish history.* If this is true of the Jewish people collectively (not only of the survivor individually), it is because *the survivor is gradually becoming the paradigm for the entire Jewish people.*

Nowhere is this truth as unmistakable as in the State of Israel. The State of Israel is collectively what the survivor is individually—testimony on behalf of all mankind to life against death, to sanity against madness, to Jewish self-affirmation against every form of flight from it, and (though this is visible only to those who break through narrow theological categories) to the God of the ancient covenant against all lapses into paganism.

We ask: having survived, why did the survivor not seek both safety and forgetfulness among such good people as the Danes, but rather seek danger and memory in the nascent and embattled State of Israel? Indeed, why do not even now Israeli Jews in general, survivors or no, flee by the thousands from their isolated and endangered country, in order that they might elsewhere find peace and safety—not to speak of the world's approval? Why do they hold fast to their "law of return"—the commitment to receive sick Jews, poor Jews, oppressed Jews, rejected by the immigration laws of every other state? A world which wants no part of Auschwitz fails to understand. Indeed, perpetuating antisemitism, despite Auschwitz or even because of it, it often does not hesitate to resort to slander. Yet the truth is obvious: the State of Israel is a collective testimony against the groundless hate which has erupted in this century in the heart of Europe. Its watchword is *Am Yisrael Chai*—"the people of Israel lives." Without this watchword the State of Israel could not have survived for a generation. It is a watchword of defiance, hope and faith. It is a testimony to all men everywhere that man shall be, and be human—even if it should be necessary to cast Truth to the ground.

And now, astoundingly, this watchword has come alive among the Jews of the Soviet Union. What makes these Jews affirm their Jewishness against the overwhelming odds of a ruthless system, when they could gain peace and comfort by disavowing their Jewishness? Though we can only marvel at their heroism and not understand it, its mainspring is obvious enough. No American Jew has experienced the Holocaust as every Russian Jew has experienced it. Hence every Russian Jew must have felt all along that to be denied the right to his Jewishness is not, after what has happened, a tolerable form of discrimination or prejudice but rather an intolerable affront; it is, as it were, a secular sacrilege. And if now these Jews increasingly dare to convert secret feeling into public action, it is because of the inspiration incarnate in the State of Israel.

Is heroism in evidence among ourselves, the comfortable, mostly middle-class Jews of North America? In order to perceive any trace of it, we must break through the false but all-pervasive categories of a world which does not know of Auschwitz and does not wish to know of it.

In America this is a time of identity crises. Among these there is a specific Jewish identity crisis which springs from the view that a Jew must somehow achieve a "universal" transcendence of his "particular" Jewishness if he is to justify his Jewish identity. Thus it has come to seem that a Jew shows genuine courage when he rejects his Jewish identity, or when he at least seeks a "universal" justification of that identity by espousing all noble except Jewish causes. And the North American Jewish hero may seem to be he who actually turns against his own people, less because he seeks the creation of a Palestinian Arab state than because he seeks the destruction of the Jewish state.

Such may be the appearances. The truth is otherwise. Just as the black seeking to pass for white has internalized racism, so the Jew joining al-Fatah has internalized anti-semitism, and this is true also (albeit to a lesser degree) of the Jew espousing all except Jewish causes. Where is the universalism in this exceptionalism—a "universalism" which applies to everyone with one exception—Jews? There is only sickness. To the extent to which the world still wants the Jew either to disappear or at least to become a man-in-general, it still has the power to produce Jews bent on disappearing, or at least on "demonstrating" their exceptionalist "universalism."

These may seem harsh judgments. They are necessary because Jewish identity crises such as the above have become a surrender to Auschwitz. For a Jew after the Holocaust to act as though his Jewishness required justification is to allow the possibility that none might be found, and this in turn is to allow the possibility, after Hitler murdered one third of the Jewish people, that the rest should quietly pass on. But merely to allow these possibilities is *already* a posthumous victory for Hitler. It is *already* an act of betrayal. And the betrayal is as much of the world as of the Jewish people.

Is there any trace of Jewish heroism among ourselves? The question transcends all conventional distinctions, such as between old and young, "right" and "left," and even "religious" and "secular". The North American Jewish hero is he who has confronted the demons of Auschwitz and defied them. It is the Jew who has said "No!" to every form, however mild or disguised, of antisemitism without and self-rejection within. It is the Jew at home in his Jewish skin and at peace with his Jewish destiny. It is the Jew who is whole.

But if this is the age of heroism in the history of the Jewish people, it is, after all, also an age of unprecedented darkness in world history, and Jewish heroism itself is possible only at the price of perpetually verging on despair. The question therefore arises what meaning the Jewish *Am Yisrael Chai* [the people of Israel lives] might have for contemporary man.

One shrinks from so large a question for two opposite reasons. At one extreme, the singled out Jewish testimony may all-too-easily dissipate itself into a vacuous and thus cheap and escapist universalism. At the other extreme, it may express its universal significance at the false price of deafness to quite different, and yet not unrelated testimonies, such as might come from Vietnam, Czechoslovakia and Bengla Desh. Perhaps one avoids both dangers best by concretizing the question. Earlier we dwelt on the American tradition of optimism which is now in a state of crisis, and stressed that, while much in this optimism was always false, America itself would be lost if American optimism were wholly lost. What may the Jewish *Am Yisrael Chai* reveal about American optimism? What was always false about the American Dream? What—if anything—remains true?

Always false was precisely the "Dream." The innocence which produced that dream is lost. If the saving of America were dependent upon the recapturing of the innocence and the Dream there would be no hope. However, the Midrash which has furnished the text for the present discourse is not the product of a dream. Truth may be cast to the ground. The Midrashic author *knows* that it is cast to the ground. He knows, too, that in the end Truth must rise again from the earth.

When dreams are shattered men are wont to seek refuge in wishful thinking. Our age is no exception. In a half-hearted version, collective make-believe is manifest in our current, self-enclosed, middle-class apotheosis of psychoanalysis. (Within its sober bounds, that discipline gives limited help to disturbed individuals, and quite possibly we are all disturbed. Expanded into systematic wishful thinking, it turns into a panacea for all the ills of our world.) In a radical version, collective make-believe is manifest in a self-enclosed ideologizing which would refashion all reality in its own image, while being itself out of touch with reality.

Being self-enclosed, collective make-believe can survive for a long period of time. Yet its nemesis is sure to come, and by dint of its greater honesty it is the radical version which is bound first to experience it. To be sure, ideology seeks to refashion reality. Being divorced from reality, however, it in fact refashions only ideology, and the conflict between ideality and reality in the end becomes so total as to result—when Truth springs from the earth—in despair.

Is despair, then, the only *truthful* outcome? Arthur Schopenhauer wrote as follows:

> Death is the great reprimand which the will to life, or more especially the egoism which is essential to it, receives through the course of nature; and it may be considered as a punishment for our existence. Death says: thou are the product of an act which should not have been; therefore to expiate it thou must die.

Once the sentiment expressed in this passage was attractive only to idle drawing room speculation. Today one can detect on every side a veritable fascination with every kind of negation and death itself. Once the denial of the will to live could seem to be a noble rejection of "egoism." Today it stands revealed as the foe, nothing short of obscene, of a will to live which, far from "egoistic," is a heroic act of defiance. And the revelation is nowhere as manifest as in the survivor of the Nazi custom of the two work permits. He is not blind to the shadows of death but has walked through its valley. He does not cling to life but rather affirms it by an act of faith which defies comprehension. He relives, in a form without precedent anywhere, that great "nevertheless" which has always been the secret of the enigmatic optimism of Judaism. His testimony is a warning to men everywhere not to yield to death when Truth springs from the earth. It is an admonition to endure Truth and to choose life. It is a plea, anguished and joyous, to share in a defiant endurance which alone reveals that Truth, despite all, remains the seal of God.

THE HOLOCAUST AND CONTEMPORARY JUDAISM

The effects of the Holocaust are important not only for the theological assessment of man and the human condition, which Fackenheim rightly stresses. They also reshape the whole of contemporary Jewish thinking about the events after the Holocaust, from 1945 onward, about the meaning of the State of Israel, about the future of the Jewish people. If you live daily with the knowledge that because you had a Jewish grandparent, you would have been consigned to the oblivion of the gas-chambers, you are going to see life under the aspect of the Holocaust. You are going to have to face in a most immediate way the question, What does it mean to be a Jew? What life is possible after the worst death imaginable?

The effects of the Holocaust, first of all, reshape the psychology of the Jewish people. The way in which this happens is a measure of the larger changes from the classical to the modern situation in Judaism. For aforetimes in the history of the Jews catastrophe was not unknown, and Jewish piety has had to become experienced in the confrontation with terror. But in the two generations since the Holocaust, the Jewish response has taken a form different from that which characterized the Jews in the face of former disasters. The difference in form, it is claimed in the following essay, is considerable, but superficial. For the underlying continuity in the spiritual condition of the Jewish people is still more striking than the formal changes in their reaction to the Holocaust of their own day.

A second issue, already admirably addressed in Fackenheim's essay, requires further discussion. For his is not the only response to the issues of the Holocaust. Another, and radically different approach, is that of Richard Rubenstein, Jewish theologian at the Florida State University. Rubenstein meets head-on the claim of classical Judaism that God is omnipotent and so asks the necessary question: If God can do all, then why did He allow this to happen? A still third approach is that of Michael Wyschogrod, a critic of both Fackenheim and Rubenstein. Wyschogrod holds that the traditional response to evil remains viable and vital and that classical Judaic theology endures unimpaired by the new and terrible data introduced into its framework by the Holocaust.

The third question is this: Why has the Holocaust become an important formative force in modern Judaism? Why in particular in America and Canada have Jews taken up the symbol of Auschwitz and made it a central, and highly evocative, form of group-expression? What does "Holocaust-theology" in its several formulations say about the condition of the Jewish people in North America? The question is important, for, after all, the larger number of activist-Jews to whom the Holocaust constitutes a major matter in 1945 had not yet been born.

XIV

THE IMPLICATIONS OF THE HOLOCAUST

JACOB NEUSNER

i. *Affect on Jewish Psychology*

The events of 1933 to 1948 constitute one of the decisive moments in the history of Judaism, to be compared in their far-reaching effects to the destruction of the First and Second Temples, 586 B.C. and 70 A.D., the massacre of Rhineland Jewries, 1096, the aftermath of the Black Plague, 1349, the expulsion of the Jews from Spain, 1492, or the Ukrainian massacres of 1648-9. But while after the former disasters, the Jews responded in essentially religious ways, the response to the Holocaust and the creation of the State of Israel on the surface has not been religious. That is to say, while in the past people explained disaster as a result of sin and therefore sought means of reconciliation with God and atonement for sin, in the twentieth century the Jews superficially did not. Instead they have done what seem secular, and not religious, deeds: they raised money, engaged in political action, and did all the other things modern, secular men, confident they can cope with anything, normally do. They did not write new prayers or holy books, create new theologies, develop new religious ideas· and institutions.

Yet I should argue that the response to the Holocaust and the creation of the State of Israel differs in form, but not in substance, from earlier responses to disaster. The form now is secular. The substance endures in deeply religious ways. For the effect of the Holocaust and the creation of the State of Israel on the Jews is to produce a new myth—by myth I mean a transcendent perspective on events, a story lending meaning and imparting sanctity to ordinary, everyday actions—and a new religious affirmation.

Let me recount the salvific story as it is nearly universally perceived by the senior generation of American Jews—those who came to maturity before 1945:

"Once upon a time, when I was a young man, I felt helpless before the world. I was a Jew, when being Jewish was a bad thing.

179

As a child, I saw my old Jewish parents, speaking a foreign language and alien in countless ways, isolated from America. And I saw America, dimly perceived to be sure, exciting and promising, but hostile to me as a Jew. I could not get into a good college. I could not aspire to medical school. I could not become an architect or an engineer. I could not even work for an electric utility.

"When I took my vacation, I could not go just anywhere, but had to ask whether Jews would be welcome, tolerated, embarassed, or thrown out. Being Jewish was uncomfortable. Yet I could not give it up. My mother and my father had made me what I was. I could hide, but could not wholly deny, to myself if not to others, that I was a Jew. And I could not afford the price in diminished self-esteem, of opportunity denied, aspiration deferred and insult endured. Above all, I saw myself as weak and pitiful. I could not do anything about being a Jew nor could I do much to improve my lot as a Jew.

"Then came Hitler and I saw that what was my private lot was the dismal fate of every Jew. Everywhere Jew-hatred was raised from the gutter to the heights. Not from Germany alone, but from people I might meet at work or in the streets I learned that being Jewish was a metaphysical evil. 'The Jews' were not accepted, but debated. Friends would claim we were not all bad. Enemies said we were. And we had nothing to say at all.

"As I approached maturity, a still more frightening fact confronted me. People guilty of no crime but Jewish birth were forced to flee their homeland and no one would accept them. Ships filled with ordinary men, women and children searched the oceans for a safe harbor. And I and they had nothing in common but one fact, and that fact made all else inconsequential. Had I been there, I should have been among them. I too should not have been saved at the sea.

"Then came the war and, in its aftermath, the revelation of the shame and horror of holocaust, the decay and corrosive hopelessness of the DP camps, the contempt of the nations, who would neither accept nor help the saved remnants of hell.

"At the darkest hour came the dawn. The State of Israel saved the remnant and gave meaning and significance to the inferno. After the dawn, the great light: Jews no longer helpless, weak, unable to decide their own fate, but strong, confident, decisive.

"And then came the corrupting doubt: If I were there, I should have died in hell. But now has come redemption and I am here, not there.

"How much security in knowing that if it should happen again,

I shall not be lost. But how great a debt paid in guilt for being where I am and who I am!"

This constitutes the myth that gives meaning and transcendence to the petty lives of ordinary people—the myth of the darkness followed by light, of passage through the netherworld and past the gates of hell, then, purified by suffering and by blood, into the new age. The naturalist myth of American Jewry—it is not the leaders' alone—conforms to the supernatural structure of the classic myths of salvific religions from time immemorial. And well it might, for a salvific myth has to tell the story of sin and redemption, disaster and salvation, the old being and the new, the vanquishing of death and mourning, crying and pain, the passing away of former things. The vision of the new Jerusalem, complete in 1967, beckoned not tourists, but pilgrims to the new heaven and the new earth. This, as I said, is the myth that shapes the mind and imagination of American Jewry, supplies the correct interpretation and denotes the true significance of everyday events, and turns workaday people into saints. This is the myth that transforms commonplace affairs into history, makes writing a check into a sacred act.

It is not faith, theology, ideology, for none offers reasons for its soundness, or needs to. It is myth in that it so closely corresponds to, and yet so magically transforms and elevates, reality, that people take vision and interpretation for fact. They do not need to believe in, or affirm the myth, for they know it to be true. In that they are confident of the exact correspondence between reality and the story that explains reality, they are the saved, the saints, the witnesses to the end of days. We know this is how things really were, and what they really meant. We know it because the myth of suffering and redemption corresponds to our perceptions of reality, evokes immediate recognition and assent. It not only bears meaning, it imparts meaning precisely because it explains experience and derives from what we know to be true.

But one must ask whether experience is so stable, the world so unchanging, that we may continue to explain today's reality in terms of what happened yesterday. The answer is that, much as we might want to, we cannot. The world has moved on. We can remember, but we cannot reenact what happened. We cannot replicate the experiences which required explanation according to a profound account of the human and the Jewish condition. We cannot, because our children will not allow it. They experience a different world—perhaps not better, perhaps not so simple, but certainly different. They know about events, but have not experienced them. And what they know they perceive through their experience of a very different world. The story that gives meaning and imparts transcendence to the everyday experiences of being Jewish simply does not correspond to the reality of the generations born since 1945. They did not know the frightful insecurity, did not face the meaninglessness of Jewish suffering, therefore cannot appreciate the salvation that dawned with the creation of the State of Israel.

Theirs is a more complicated world. Not for them the simple choice of death or life, the simple encounter with uncomplicated evil. For them Jewishness also is more complicated, for while the world of the 1930s and 1940s imparted a "Jewish education," and a "Jewish consciousness" was elicited by reading a newspaper or simply encountering a hostile society, today's world does not constitute a school without walls for the education of the Jews. That is, I think, a good thing. Being Jewish no longer is imposed by negative experiences, but is now called forth by affirmative ones. For the younger generation the State of Israel stands not as the end of despair but as the beginning of hope. It enriches the choices facing the young Jew and expands his consciousness of the potentialities of Jewishness. Not its existence, but its complexity is important. Not its perfection, but its imperfection is compelling. It is interesting as the object not of fantasy, but of perceived reality.

The affect of the Holocaust on Jewish psychology today has to be regarded as ambiguous and equivocal, because we deal with two quite separate generations. The first is the one which lived through the frightening, sickening events of the decade and a half of Hitler. The second is the one which has not. In my view the new generations—those born since 1945—have to be understood in entirely different terms from the old generations. The major difference is that the new generations are considerably healthier and, if they choose to be Jewish at all, their Jewishness is substantially more affirmative.

That is not to suggest they are less involved with the Holocaust and with the State of Israel. The contrary is the case.

The reality of the State of Israel turns out to fascinate the younger generation still more than the fantasy mesmerized the fathers. If the 1950's and 1960's were times in which the State of Israel rose to the top of the agendum of American Jewry, in the 1970's it seems to constitute the whole of that agendum. No other Jewish issue has the power to engage the younger generation of Jews as does the issue of the State of Israel. Anti-Zionism and anti-Israelism are virtually non-existent among the new generation of Jews. (Those on the fringes are not interesting in the present context.) That is to say, whether or not there should be a State of Israel, why there should be such a State, how one must justify the existence of a Jewish state in terms of a higher morality or claim in its behalf that it is a light to the nations—these modes of thought are simply alien. The State of Israel *is*. The issue for the younger generation is not, is it a good thing or a bad thing? The issue is, since we know no other world but one in which the State of Israel is present, how shall we relate to that important part of the world in which we live?

The younger generation exhibits a healthier relationship to the State of Israel than did the fathers, not because it is more virtuous (despite its fantasies), but because it has not had to live through the frightening, sickening experiences of the fathers. If the myth of the fathers is irrelevant to the children, and if the fantasy-ridden relationships of the fathers are not replicated by the children, the reason is that the young people have grown up in a healthier world. It is a world not without its nightmares, but with different, less terrifying nightmares for the Jews in particular. In days gone by, the "Jewish problem" belonged to Jews alone. Whether we lived or died was our problem. But now the problem of life or death faces all mankind; we are no longer singled out for extermination. The terror is everyone's. If there is a just God, a mark of His justice is that those who did not share our anguish must now share our nightmares, an exact, if slow, measure of justice. We who saw ourselves all alone in the death camps have been joined by the rest of the world. Next time fire instead of gas, perhaps. But meanwhile it is an easier life.

Nor should we ignore the fact that for the younger generation, being Jewish has conferred the practical advantages of a group capable of mutual protection in a generally undifferentiated society. It has been a positive advantage in the recent past. Add to this the devotion of the Jewish parent to the Jewish child. Jewish children are treated in Jewish homes as very special beings. This makes young Jews strive to excel in the rest of society as they did at home. To be sure, this produces a large crop of Jewish adults who blame their Jewishness for the fact that the rest of society does not treat them as did their parents. These are people who need evidence to explain what they see as their own failure, which is actually explicable by their own impossible demands on themselves and on society. Being Jewish in the recent past in the balance has been an advantage, rather than a disability. The younger generation is better off on that account.

To summarize: the generations that lived through disaster and triumph, darkness and light, understand the world in terms of a salvific myth. The generations that have merely heard about the darkness but have daily lived in the light take for granted the very redemption that lies at the heart of the salvific myth. The psychological consequences for the one should be different from those for the other. In theory, at least, the affects of the Holocaust on those who went through it, either in the flesh or in the spirit, have been sickening. The survivors will have a survivor-mentality; they will see the world as essentially hostile and will distrust, rather than trust, the outsider. They will exhibit the traits of citizens of a city under siege, feeling always threatened, always alone, always on the defensive. The new generation, which has not lived under siege, should develop greater trust in the world. They should regard the world as essentially neutral, if not friendly, and should have the capacity to trust the outsider. Yet, though the psychological experiences differ, the end-result is much the same. The new generation is just as Israel-oriented as the old; if anything, it identifies still more intensely than before with the Jewish people.

ii. *Affect on Jewish Theology*

The theological impact of the Holocaust and the rise of the State of Israel normally is assessed in terms of two significant names, Richard L. Rubenstein and Emil Fackenheim. Rubenstein's response to the Holocaust has been searching and courageous. He has raised the difficult questions and responded with painful honesty. The consequence has been an unprecedented torrent of personal abuse, so that he has nearly been driven out of Jewish public life. He has been called a Nazi and compared to Hitler! The abuse to which he has been subjected seems to me the highest possible tribute on the part of his enemies to the compelling importance of his contribution. Since what he has proposed evidently is seen to be unanswerable, the theology has been ignored, but the theologian has been abused.

What is Rubenstein's message? It has been eloquently stated in various places. I believe the most cogent expression of his viewpoint on the centrality of the Holocaust is in his contribution to *Commentary's* Symposium on Jewish Belief (reprinted in his *After Auschwitz*, pp. 153-154), as follows:

> I believe the greatest single challenge to modern Judaism arises out of the question of God and the death camps. I am amazed at the silence of contemporary Jewish theologians on this most crucial and agonizing of all Jewish issues. How can Jews be-

JACOB NEUSNER 185

lieve in an omnipotent, beneficient God after Auschwitz? Traditional Jewish theology maintains that God is the ultimate, omnipotent actor in the historical drama. It has interpreted every major catastrophe in Jewish history as God's punishment of a sinful Israel. I fail to see how this position can be maintained without regarding Hitler and the SS as instruments of God's will. The agony of European Jewry cannot be likened to the testing of Job. To see any purpose in the death camps, the traditional believer is forced to regard the most demonic, antihuman explosion in all history as a meaningful expression of God's purposes. The idea is simply too obscene for me to accept. I do not think that the full impact of Auschwitz has yet been felt in Jewish theology or Jewish life. Great religious revolutions have their own period of gestation. No man knows the hour when the full impact of Auschwitz will be felt, but no religious community can endure so hideous a wounding without undergoing vast inner disorders.

Though I believe that a void stands where once we experienced God's presence, I do not think Judaism has lost its meaning or its power. I do not believe that a theistic God is necessary for Jewish religious life. Dietrich Bonhoeffer has written that our problem is how to speak of God in an age of no religion. I believe that our problem is how to speak of religion in an age of no God. I have suggested that Judaism is the way in which we share the decisive times and crises of life through the traditions of our inherited community. The need for that sharing is not diminished in the time of the death of God. We no longer believe in the God who has the power to annul the tragic necessities of existence; the need religiously to share that existence remains.

It should not be supposed that Rubenstein's is an essentially destructive conclusion. On the contrary, he draws from the Holocaust a constructive, if astringent message (*After Auschwitz*, pp. 128-129):

Death and rebirth are the great moments of religious experience. In the twentieth century the Jewish phoenix has known both: in Germany and eastern Europe, we Jews have tasted the bitterest and the most degrading of deaths. Yet death was not the last word. We do not pity ourselves. Death in Europe was followed by resurrection in our ancestral home. We are free as no men before us have ever been. Having lost everything, we have nothing further to lose and no further fear of loss. Our existence has in truth been

a being-unto-death. We have passed beyond all illusion and hope.
We have learned in the crisis that we were totally and nakedly
alone, that we could expect neither support nor succor from God
or from our fellow creatures. No men have known as we have how
truly God in His holiness slays those to whom He gives life. This
has been a liberating knowledge, at least for the survivors, and all
Jews everywhere regard themselves as having escaped by the skin
of their teeth, whether they were born in Europe or elsewhere. We
have lost all hope and faith. We have also lost all possibility of
disappointment. Expecting absolutely nothing from God or man,
we rejoice in whatever we receive. We have learned the nakedness
of every human pretense. No people has come to know as we have
how deeply man is an insubstantial nothingness before the awesome and terrible majesty of the Lord. We accept our nothingness
—nay, we even rejoice in it—for in finding our nothingness we
have found both ourselves and the God who alone is true substance. We did not ask to be born; we did not ask for our absurd
existence in the world; nor have we asked for the fated destiny
which has hung about us as Jews. Yet we would not exchange it,
nor would we deny it, for when nothing is asked for, nothing is
hoped for, nothing is expected; all that we receive is truly grace.

Fackenheim's contrary view is that "Auschwitz" produces a new
commandment to the Jewish people: to preserve the Jewish people and
the Jewish religion. Michael Wyschogrod, "Faith and the Holocaust,"
(*Judaism*, summer, 1971, pp. 286-294), summarizes Fackenheim's
viewpoint as follows:

What then, is adequate?
Only obedience to the Voice of Auschwitz. This voice, as
heard by Fackenheim, commands the survival of Jews and Judaism. Because Hitler was bent upon the destruction of both, it is
the duty of those Jews who survived Hitler to make sure that they
do not do his work, that they do not, by assimilation, bring about
the disappearance of what Hitler attempted but ultimately failed
to destroy. For the religious Jew, this means that he must go on
being religious, however inadequate Auschwitz has shown his
frame of reference to be. And for the secular Jew, the Voice of
Auschwitz commands not faith, which even the Voice of Auschwitz cannot command, but preservation of Jews and Judaism.
Speaking of the significance of the Voice of Auschwitz for the

secular Jew, Fackenheim writes: "No less inescapable is this Power for the secularist Jew who has all along been outside the Midrashic framework and this despite the fact that the Voice of Auschwitz does not enable him to return into this framework. He cannot return; but neither may he turn the Voice of Auschwitz against that of Sinai. For he may not cut off his secular present from the religious past: The Voice of Auschwitz commands Jewish unity." The sin of Rubenstein is, therefore, that he permits Auschwitz further to divide the Jewish people at a time when survival is paramount if Hitler is not to be handed a posthumous victory, and survival demands unity. Because this is so, Rubenstein should presumably soft-pedal his doubts so as not to threaten the Jewish people at a time when everything must be secondary to the issue of survival.

What may be said in behalf of Fackenheim's argument? Fackenheim has the merit of placing the Holocaust at the head of Judaic theological discourse, and of doing so in such a way that the central problem is not theodicy. Rubenstein's stress on the issue of how a just God could have permitted so formidable an injustice—an understatement of the issue to be sure—leads him to the position just now outlined. Fackenheim's formulation of the issue of the Holocaust in terms of its meaning to the secular, not to the religious, Jew sidesteps the surely insoluble issue of theology, and so opens a constructive and forward-looking discourse on the primary issue facing contemporary Judaism, the issue of secularity and unbelief.

Rubenstein tends, therefore, to center his interest on the tragic events themselves, while Fackenheim prefers to make those events speak to the contemporary situation of Jewry. One may compare Rubenstein's mode of thought to that of the first-century apocalyptic visionaries, Fackenheim's to that of the rabbis of the same period. After 70 the issue of the destruction of the Second Temple predominated and could not be avoided. No religious discourse, indeed, no religious life, would then have been possible without attention to the meaning of that awesome event. The message of apocalyptic was that the all-powerful God who had punished the people for their sins very soon would bring them consolation, punish their enemies, rebuild the Temple, and bring on the messianic age. People who heard this message fixed their gaze upon the future and eagerly awaited the messianic denouement. When confronted by the messianic claim of Bar Kokhba, they responded vigorously, undertaking a catastrophic and hopeless holy war. The rabbis after 70 had a different message. It was not different from that of the apocalyptics in stress upon the righteousness of God, who had punished the sin of Israel. But the conclusion drawn from that fact was not to focus attention on the future and on what would soon come to compensate for the catastrophe. The rabbis sought to devise a program for the survival and reconstruction of the saving remnant. The message was that just as God was faithful to punish sin, so he may be relied upon to respond to Israel's regeneration. The task of the hour therefore is to study Torah, carry out the commandments, and do deeds of loving kindness. From the stubborn consideration of present and immediate difficulties therefore came a healthy and practical plan by which Israel might in truth hold on to what could be salvaged from disaster. Redemption will come. In the meanwhile there are things to do. Just as the Jews awaited a redemptive act of compassion from God, so they must now act compassionately in order to make themselves worthy of it. The tragedy thus produced two responses, the one obsessed with the disaster, the other concerned for what is to happen afterward, here and now.

It seems to me Rubenstein carries forward the apocalyptic, Fackenheim the classical and rabbinical, modes of thinking. The difference between them is not in the contrast between a negative and destructive approach, on the one side, and an affirmative and constructive one, on the other. Rubenstein is not a nihilist, as I have shown. Fackenheim's "commanding voice of Auschwitz" speaks to people beyond despair, demands commitment from the nihilist himself. The difference is in perspective and focus. In Fackenheim's behalf one must, as I said, point to the remarkable pertinence of his message to the issues of the 1970's. He has, in a way, transcended the tragic events themselves, just as did the first-century rabbis. Fackenheim does not say only the obvious, which is, one must believe *despite* disaster. He holds the disaster itself is evidence in behalf of belief, a brilliant return to the rabbinic mode of response to catastrophe. In this regard, Rubenstein and Fackenheim, representative of the two extreme positions, cannot be reconciled, except within the events of which they speak. Confronting those events, both theologians perceive something "radically" new and without precedent in the history of Judaism. With that shared claim the two extremes come together.

What is to be said in response to the claim of both Rubenstein and Fackenheim that "after Auschwitz" things are "radically" different from before?

First, it must be stressed, other theologians have not been silent. A. J. Heschel, for example, responded to the Holocaust with an immortal Qaddish, *The Earth Is the Lord's*. Milton Steinberg, Mordecai M. Kaplan, and Arthur A. Cohen, among others take account of the Holocaust without admitting the central contention of the recent "Auschwitz-theologians." They take seriously the problem of evil, but regard the problem as posed effectively by any sort of misfortune or by the whole history of the Jewish people, for they find themselves equally disturbed by the suffering of one person as of one million. One indeed may argue that "after Auschwitz" became an effective slogan, along with "Never again" and similar allusions to the Holocaust, too long after the liberation of Europe to constitute merely a response to the events of those far-off days and distant places.

But the central allegation is contained in the word "radical," by which is meant that the Holocaust is unprecedented and changes everything. This viewpoint is not shared by Kaplan, Heschel, and others. The most important critique comes in Wyschogrod's review of Fackenheim. There he meets head-on the issue of "radical evil." Because of the importance of his critique, I quote his exact words at some length:

> I have already termed Fackenheim's enterprise "negative natural theology," a phrase which deserves brief explanation. Traditionally, natural theology has been the enterprise whereby the existence of God is demonstrated on the basis of some rational evidence, without recourse to faith or evolution. Most commonly, the point of departure for such an attempt was some "positive" feature of the world as it appears to man: its order, its beauty, or its harmony. It was then argued that such characteristics could not be the result of pure chance and that it was, therefore, necessary to posit some all-powerful and rational being as the author or creator of a universe possessing the respective positive characteristics . . . Fackenheim's point of departure is, of course the opposite of the "positive." Instead of being the order, beauty, harmony or justice of the universe, it is a totally unique crime, unparalleled in human history. But once we get over this initial difference, similarities appear. In the positive version, a positive characteristic of the universe is noted and it is argued that no natural explanation for it is adequate. In negative natural theology, an evil is pointed out for which also, it is alleged, no natural explanation is possible. Of course, the conclusion in negative natural theology cannot be identical with that of positive natural theology,

inasmuch as the problem of theodicy cannot here easily be ignored. Nevertheless, the conclusion which Fackenheim draws, the sacred duty to preserve the Jewish people, is the functional equivalent of the existence of Judaism, a foundation as fully serviceable to the secularist as to the believer. One is almost driven to the conclusion that in the absence of the Holocaust, given Fackenheim's profound understanding of the irreversibility of the secular stance, no justification for the further survival of Judaism could have been found. With the Holocaust, amazing as this may appear, Judaism has gotten a new lease on life . . .

Wyschogrod, finally, reaffirms the classical position of Judaic theology on the suffering of the Jewish people:

Israel's faith has always centered about the saving acts of God: the election, the Exodus, the Temple and the Messiah. However more prevalent destruction was in the history of Israel, the acts of destruction were enshrined in minor fast days while those of redemption became the joyous proclamations of the Passover and Tabernacles, of Hannukah and Purim. The God of Israel is a redeeming God; this is the only message we are authorized to proclaim, however much it may not seem so to the eyes of non-belief. Should the Holocaust cease to be peripheral to the faith of Israel, should it enter the Holy of Holies and become the dominant voice that Israel hears, it could not but be a demonic voice that it would be hearing. There is no salvation to be extracted from the Holocaust, no faltering Judaism can be revived by it, no new reason for the continuation of the Jewish people can be found in it. If there is hope after the Holocaust, it is because to those who believe, the voices of the Prophets speak more loudly than did Hitler, and because the divine promise sweeps over the crematoria and silences the voice of Auschwitz.

This seems to me all that needs to be said in response to the "commanding Voice of Auschwitz" and to the joy of "nothingness" alike.

iii. *Affect on Contemporary Jewish Affairs*

Various unrelated social, cultural, and political phenomena have been interpreted as a response to the Holocaust. I do not allude to the creation of the State of Israel or to the great "return to religion" of the 1950's—an event much criticized at that time, but sorely missed today. I refer to the reaffirmation of Jewish-self interest in times of political crisis, to the recognition that the Jews do have serious interest in political, social, and economic life, and that sometimes these interests come into conflict with those of other groups. I refer to the electrifying popular response to the Six-Day-War and the generally favorable reaction to the slogans of the Jewish Defense League, if not to its mindless activities. I refer to the publicity about "freeing Soviet Jewry" and to the obvious sense that in making such efforts, people are doing today what they wished they (or someone) had done in the 1930's. I refer to the non-academic thrust toward "Jewish ethnic studies" in the universities and the students' manifest claim to want to learn something —anything—Jewish. I refer, finally, to the serious efforts of younger Jews to participate, in their own idiom, in the Judaic tradition, to the creation of Jewish newspapers by the university students, to the success of *RESPONSE* and similar (if not so excellent) magazines, to the creation of Jewish communes and communities, according to an ideology with (alleged) roots in the ancient *havurot*. These have been exciting events; possibly, some may prove important. None could have been predicted a generation ago, let alone in the 1930's. Then it seemed the way ahead lay downward and outward, for the future looked bleak. Today, say what one will in criticism of details of the 'ethnic assertion' of young Jews in its several forms, one cannot take a negative view of their devotion to the Judaic tradition and their loyalty to the Jewish people.

But the question is, Is the current ferment in Jewish community affairs the result of the Holocaust? Is it one of the implications of the Holocaust?

In my opinion, the answer is negative. The "after Auschwitz" syndrome in Jewish theology and the appeal of "Never again" in Jewish community affairs both constitute creations of the late 1960's and early 1970's.

From 1945 to about 1965, the Holocaust was subsumed under the "problem of evil." The dominant theological voices of that time did not address themselves to "radical evil" and did not claim that something had happened to change the classical theological perspective of Judaism. The theologians of the day wrote not as if nothing had happened, but as if nothing had happened to impose a new perspective on the whole past of Jewish religious experience. To be sure, the liberal, world-affirming optimism of the old theological left was shaken; Kierkegaard and Niebuhr, through Will Herberg and

others, found a sympathetic Jewish audience. But the Holocaust—
"Auschwitz"—was part, not the whole, of the problem.

What happened, I think, was the assassination of President Ken-
nedy, the disheartening war in South East Asia, and a renewed ques-
tioning of the foundations of religious and social polity. "Auschwitz"
became a Jewish code-word for all the things everyone was talking
about, a kind of Judaic key word for the common malaise. That—
and nothing more. The Jewish theologians who claim that from Holocaust events one must draw conclusions essentially different from
those reached after the destruction of the Second Temple or other
tragic moments, posit that our sorrow is unlike any other, our memories more scaring. But they say so in response not to the events of
which they speak, but, through those events, to a quite different situation.

And they necessarily select some events, and not others, for the
purpose of their theological enterprise. They speak of "Auschwitz,"
and "radical evil," but not of Jerusalem rebuilt and the dawn of redemption. If the former is a more than merely this-worldly event,
why not the latter? But if the latter be taken seriously, then why no
place for redemption in the response to the former? . . .

. . . Classic Judaic theology was not struck dumb by evil, and
neither changed its apprehension of the divinity, nor claimed in its
own behalf a renewed demand on the Jews, on account of disaster.
To be sure, important theological issues require careful, indeed meticu-
lous attention. But to debate those issues outside of the classic tradition
and under the impact of grief can produce few lasting, or even interesting results.

In my view, Jewish public discourse has been ill-served by "Auschwitz" without the eternity of Israel, misled by setting the response
against Hitler in place of the answer to God who commands, and corrupted by sentimentality, emotionalism, and bathos. These have produced in people less sophisticated, less responsible than either Rubenstein or Fackenheim, vacuous mysticism on the one side, and mindless
sloganeering on the other. As Elie Wiesel writes in *Legends of our
Time,* ". . . no cocktail party can really be called a success unless
Auschwitz, sooner or later, figures in the disussion." In such a setting,
"Auschwitz" profanes Auschwitz; the dead are forcibly resurrected
to dance in a circus, the survivors made into freaks. It is enough.
Let the dead lie in peace, and the living honor them in silent reverence. Again Wiesel, "Leave them there where they must forever be
. . . ; wounds, immeasurable pain at the very depth of our being." Why

should they serve the living as a pretext for either belief or unbelief, for a naturalist God or a supernatural God? The truth is there is no meaning in it all, at least none discerned for mortal man. The fact is the living live. The choice is about the future, not the past. Theologians and politicians alike should let the dead rest in peace. We are not well served by the appeal to the Holocaust, either as the rationalization for our Judaism or as the source of slogans for our Jewish activism and self-assertion.

What then are the implications of the Holocaust? I claim there is *no* implication—none for Judaic theology, none for Jewish community life—which was not present before 1933. Judaic theologians ill-serve the faithful when they claim "Auschwitz" marks a turning, as in Rubenstein's case, or a "new beginning," as in Fackenheim's. In fact Judaic piety has all along known how to respond to disaster. For those for whom the classic Judaic symbolic structure remains intact, the wisdom of the classic piety remains sound. For those to whom classical Judaism offers no viable option, the Holocaust changes nothing. One who did not believe in God before he knew about the Holocaust is not going to be persuaded to believe in Him on its account. One who believed in the classical perception of God presented by Judaic theologians is not going to be forced to change his perception on its account. The currently fashionable "Jewish assertion" draws on the Holocaust, to be sure, as a source of evocative slogans, but it is rooted in America and in the 1970's, not in Poland and in the 1940's. It has come about in response to the evolving conditions of American society, not to the disasters of European civilization. Proof of its shallowness and rootlessness derives from its mindless appropriation of the horrors of another time and place as a rationale for "Jewish assertion"—that, and its incapacity to say more, in the end, than "woe, woe." "Jewish assertion" based on the Holocaust cannot create a constructive, affirmative, and rational way of being Jewish for more than ten minutes at a time. Jews find in the Holocaust no new definition of Jewish identity because we need none. Nothing has changed. The tradition endures.

NEW CONCEPTIONS OF GOD

The problem of theodicy—the understanding and justification of God's ways before man—is posed so dramatically by the Holocaust that it is critical. It cannot be ignored. Alongside is a second theological issue, not critical but chronic: the meaning of God in modern, rationalist and skeptical modes of thinking. The classical conception of God is supernatural and includes the possibility of miracles, divine intervention into history and into the life of man, and other beliefs difficult for many modern men to maintain. And it is entirely within the classical formulation of the God-concept that the Holocaust poses so critical a dilemma, for if God is omnipotent, then he stands behind the terrible events of the mid-twentieth century.

An entirely new conception of God for Judaism must raise afresh the fundamental question, What do you mean by "God"? What *can* you mean by that concept? Given the conceptions of the world, nature, and the cosmos, held by modern science and philosophy, given the heritage of astringent and cleansing skepticism received from the Enlightenment, and faced with the overwhelming doubts raised by the secular approach to life, what is man to make of "God"?

Mordecai M. Kaplan, founder of the Reconstructionist approach to Judaism, here presents a wholly novel approach to the fundamental issue of all theology: the nature of God. He argues for a naturalist, rather than a supernaturalist, conception and at the same time shows that naturalism too has room for—indeed, requires—a God-concept.

XV

THE MEANING OF GOD IN MODERN JEWISH RELIGION

Mordecai M. Kaplan

[From *The Meaning of God in Modern Jewish Religion* (N.Y., 1962), pp. 20-29.]

The synthesis of incompatible notions about God
a heritage from the past

We cannot expect to understand the nature of God. Who of us even knows the nature of man, or for that matter his own nature? We cannot even predict what we will be doing and thinking ten minutes from now. But we must be able to state definitely what experiences or phenomena we are prepared to identify as manifestations of God, and why we identify them as such.

The fact that the nature of God is beyond our understanding does not mean that we can afford to conceive of Him in terms that are clearly not true in accordance with the highest standards of truth. Our conception of God must be self-consistent and consistent with whatever else we hold to be true. That this conception will not describe Him we know, just as our conception of life does not begin to give us the faintest idea of what life means to the infinite variety of living creatures that inhabit our earth. But we do not plead our inability to understand all that life means as an excuse for making assertions about life which are inconsistent with experience. Just so we must insist that whatever we say or think about God shall be in harmony with all else that we hold to be true. We cannot, for example, believe that God performs miracles, and at the same time believe in the uniformities of natural law demanded by scientific theory.

In our thinking about God we must avoid all those mental habits which issue in logical fallacies. The most common of these is the habit of hypostasis, or assuming the separate identifiable existence of anything for which language has a name. There is a considerable difference, for example, between the way a scientist thinks of gravity and the way most laymen think of it. A scientist regards it as a property or quality of matter, a descriptive term for the way masses of matter behave in relation to one another. The average layman, however, thinks of it as a force, an invisible something that acts upon masses of matter pulling them together. According to both conceptions, gravity is real and must undeniably be reckoned with, but the layman finds it difficult to regard gravity as real without at the same time thinking of it as a thing, an object, a self-existent being or entity.

When we study the historical development of the God idea, we realize to what extent the mental habit of hypostasis (the tendency to treat qualities, attributes, relationships as though they had a separate existence) has been responsible for the contradictions and ambiguities that have discredited the conception of God and driven many to atheism. Before the origin of monotheistic religion, people spoke not of God but of gods. What was then the meaning of the word "god"? A god was a being, mostly non-human, but at times also human, to whom worship was accorded because he was regarded as possessing the power to help men realize their aims and achieve their desires. The existence of other non-human beings was taken for granted. But a "god" was a being that stood in reciprocal relationship with a group like a family, clan, tribe, or nation. That relationship involved, on the part of the god, a claim to worship, and on the part of his worshipers, a claim to protection. Just as in their secular and political life, men were concerned with the question of who should be king, long before they asked themselves what the nature of sovereignty was, and how it should be asserted, so ancient peoples were concerned in their religious life not with the question of *what* God was, but with the question of *who* their God was. Some real or imagined beings were identified as those to whom worship was due; the others were rejected. Such is the background of the verse: "I will take you to me for a people, and I will be to you a God; and ye shall know that I YHWH, am your God who brought you out from under the burdens of the Egyptians."

There can be no question that the *Shema Yisrael*, whatever meaning it may have subsequently acquired, meant originally nothing more than that Israelites should worship YHWH, and YHWH alone, as their God. It contained no implication that the beings whom the other nations worshiped were non-existent, but merely that they were not to be considered as gods, or as entitled to worship.. They were not gods; YHWH alone was God. He alone held sway in the heavens and on the earth. Christianity and Mohammedanism similarly in their origin did not think of God generically. They did not ask themselves what God was or meant, but answered the question, "Who is God?" by answering, in the one case, "Jesus is God," and in the other, "Allah is God," Allah being the name of one of the many deities worshiped by the Arabs before the advent of Mohammed. In the Greco-Roman world of classic antiquity, the gods who were worshiped were personifications of forces of nature—the rain, the sun, the sea, the earth, etc.— which were thought of not as natural phenomena, but as beings whose aspect and behavior the imagination of the Greeks conceived in anthropomorphic terms.

It was only with the development of the philosophic movement among the Greeks that men began to think generically about God. The Greek philosophers were supremely interested in the formulation of generic concepts, in such questions as: What is an animal? How is it that dogs, horses and cats can all differ from one another and yet be animals? What constitutes the essence "animal" in the dog, and what is merely the "dog" in him? Similarly, they were interested in problems of human psychology, in an analysis of human nature. They did not look upon men merely as individuals, but were interested in the question of what qualities are common to the genus man, and distinguish it from, let us say, the genus beast. This same interest in the generic led them to the question: what constitutes the godhood of the gods? They were less interested in Zeus as Zeus, or in Athene as Athene, than they were interested in the *god* in Zeus and in Athene. One finds them frequently, therefore, speaking of God in the singular, and it would be easy to imagine that they were really at heart monotheists like the Jews. But that would be an erroneous conclusion. When we say, "Man is a biped," we do not mean that there is only one man; and when a Greek philosopher said God was perfect, he was talking in a similar generic sense, using the term "God" to express a concept of godhood in all its manifestations. There is no reason to believe that Aristotle did not worship the same individual gods as his fellow Greeks, or that he even doubted their existence.

In Alexandria, during the second and first centuries before the common era, the Jewish religion came into contact with Greek philosophy. It was then that a synthesis took place. The idea of God, conceived individually as a superhuman Person to whom worship is exclusively due, was combined with the idea of God, conceived generically, as a concept embracing all those qualities and attributes that make men regard certain objects and persons as divine. The religious philosophers effected this synthesis by the process of hypostasis. God became the personification of the generic concept of godhood, and

YHWH, the God of Israel, was assumed to have always possessed as personal traits the perfection of whatever qualities were associated with deity: power, wisdom, love, justice, sovereignty. These qualities in their perfection made God eternal, omnipotent, omnipresent, omniscient. At the same time the synthesis with the individual God of tradition endowed Him with such human attributes as loving, rewarding, punishing, being influenced by prayer and praise and a host of other personal qualities which, when analyzed, are meaningless as applied to an eternal and infinite being. These contradictions emerge again and again in the writings of the religious philosophers from Philo down to the theologians of our day.

Some appreciation of the dilemma in which the religious philosophers found themselves as a result of this synthesis of a personal God with a generic God shows itself in the difficulty they experienced in interpreting the simple declaration of Jewish faith, "YHWH is our God, YHWH alone." If YHWH is to be considered a superhuman Being, its meaning is clearly that only this one superhuman Being is God and should be worshiped. But if God is to be thought of generically, there is no point to saying that He is one, for any general concept, such as man, beast, bird, triangle, is not subject to number. They are, therefore, at great pains to tell us that not only is God one, but He is one with a unique unity, a unity that is not a term of a numerical series nor composed of fractional parts. But, obviously, if the term "unity" when applied to God has an utterly different meaning from that which it has when applied to anything else, the affirmation of God's unity conveys no meaning to us at all. It is as if one were to say of a certain object that it is red, but not red in the sense of the color red, but in a totally different sense of the term, that applies to that object alone.

Such is the confusion into which we are led by the tendency to combine two incompatible ways of thinking about God, one, that of naive personification, the other, that of philosophical abstraction. If we want to get at the reality behind genuine religious experience, we must steer clear of both these ways of thinking. We have to identify as godhood, or as the divine quality of universal being, all the relationships, tendencies and agencies which in their totality go to make human life worthwhile in the deepest and most abiding sense. The divine is no less real, no less dependable for our personal salvation or self-realization, if we think of it as a quality than if we think of it as an entity or being. Human personality may serve as an illustration. It is no less real, if we think of it in psychological terms, as a system of behavior patterns in which the human organism reacts to the world, than if we think of it as a sort of invisible spiritual man that inhabits the visible physical man and determines his behavior.

What belief in God means, from the modern point of view

To the modern man, religion can no longer be a matter of entering into relationship with the supernatural. The only kind of religion that can help him live and get the most out of life will be the one which will teach him to identify as divine or holy whatever in human nature or in the world about him enhances human life. Men must no longer look upon God as a reservoir or magic power to be tapped whenever they are aware of their physical limitations. It was natural for primitive man to do so. He sought contact with his god or gods primarily because he felt the need of supplementing his own limited powers with the external forces which he believed were controlled by the gods. He sought their aid for the fertility of his fields, the increase of his cattle, and the conquest of his foes. In time, however—and in the case of the Jewish people early in their history—men began to seek communion with God not so much as the source of power but rather as the source of goodness, and to invoke His aid to acquire control not over the external forces but over those of human nature in the individual and in the mass. With the development of scientific techniques for the utilization of natural forces, and with the revision of our world-outlook in a way that invalidates the distinction between natural and supernatural, it is only as the sum of everything in the world that renders life significant and worthwhile—or holy—that God can be worshiped by man. Godhood can have no meaning for us apart from human ideals of truth, goodness, and beauty, interwoven in a pattern of holiness.

To believe in God is to reckon with life's creative forces, tendencies and potentialities as forming an organic unity, and as giving meaning to life by virtue of that unity. Life has meaning for us when it elicits from us the best of which we are capable, and fortifies us against the worst that may befall us. Such meaning reveals itself in our experiences of unity, of creativity, and of worth. In the experience of that unity which enables us to perceive the interaction and interdependence of all phases and elements of being, it is mainly our cognitive powers that come into play; in the experience of creativity which we sense at first hand, whenever we make the slightest contribution to the sum of those forces that give meaning to life, our conative powers come to the fore; and in the experience of worth, in the realization of meaning, in contrast to chaos and meaninglessness, our emotional powers find expression. Thus in the very process of human self-fulfillment, in the very striving after the achievement of salvation, we identify ourselves with God, and God functions in us. This fact should lead to the conclusion that when we believe in God, we believe that reality —the world of inner and outer being, the world of society and of nature—is so constituted as to enable man to achieve salvation. If human beings are frustrated, it is not because there is no God, but because they do not deal with reality as it is actually and potentially constituted.

Our intuition of God is the absolute negation and antithesis of all evaluations of human life which assume that consciousness is a disease, civilization a transient sickness, and all our efforts to lift ourselves above the brute only a vain pretense. It is the triumphant exorcism of Bertrand Russell's dismal credo: "Brief and powerless is man's life. On him and all his race the slow sure doom falls pitiless and dark." It is the affirmation that human life is supremely worthwhile and significant, and deserves our giving to it the best that is in us, despite, or perhaps because of, the very evil that mars it. This intuition is not merely an intellectual assent. It is the "yea" of our entire personality. "That life is worth living is the most necessary of assumptions," says Santayana, "and were it not assumed, the most impossible of conclusions." The existence of evil, far from silencing that "yea," is the very occasion for articulating it. "The highest type of man," said Felix Adler, "is the one who *in articulo mortis* can bless the universe."

The human mind cannot rest until it finds order in the universe. It is this form-giving trait that is responsible for modern scientific theory. That same need is also operative in formulating a view of the cosmos, which will support the spiritual yearnings of the group and make their faith in the goals and objectives of their group life consistent with the totality of their experience as human beings. Out of this process of thought there arise traditional beliefs as to the origin of the world, man's place in it, his ultimate destiny, the role of one's own particular civilization in the scheme of human history, and all those comprehensive systems of belief that try to bring human experience into a consistent pattern.

But there is one underlying assumption in all these efforts at giving a consistent meaning to life, whether they are expressed in the naive cosmologies of primitive peoples or in the most sophisticated metaphysical systems of contemporary philosophers, and that is the assumption that life is meaningful. Without faith that the world of nature is a cosmos and not a chaos, that it has intelligible laws which can be unravelled, and that the human reason offers us an instrument capable of unravelling them, no scientific theorizing would be possible. This is another way of saying that science cannot dispense with what Einstein has appropriately named "cosmic religion," the faith that nature is meaningful and hence divine. And just as our inquiry into natural law demands the validation of cosmic religion, so also does our inquiry into moral law and the best way for men to live. It implies the intuition that life inherently yields ethical and spiritual values, that it is holy. The God idea thus expresses itself pragmatically in those fundamental beliefs by which a people tries to work out its life in a consistent pattern and rid itself of those frustrations which result from the distracting confusion of ideals and aims, in a word, beliefs by which it orients itself and the individuals that constitute it to life as a whole.

The purpose of all education and culture is to socialize the individual, to sensitize him to the ills as well as to the goods of life. Yet the more successful we are in accomplishing this purpose, the more unhappiness we lay up for those we educate. "As soon as high consciousness is reached," says A. N. Whitehead, "the enjoyment of existence is entwined with pain, frustration, loss, tragedy." Likewise, the more eager we are to shape human life in accordance with some ideal pattern of justice and cooperation, the more reasons we discover for being dissatisfied with ourselves, with our limitations, and with our environment. If, therefore, culture and social sympathy are not to break our hearts, but to help us retain that sureness of the life-feeling which is our native privilege, they must make room for religious faith which is needed as a tonic to quicken the pulse of our personal existence.

Faith in life's inherent worthwhileness and sanctity is needed to counteract the cynicism that sneers at life and mocks at the very notion of holiness. Against such a cheapening of life's values no social idealism that does not reckon with the cosmos as divine is an adequate remedy. How can a social idealist ask men to deny themselves immediate satisfactions for the sake of future good that they may never see in their lifetime, when he leaves them without any definite conviction that the universe will fulfill the hopes that have inspired their sacrifice, or is even able to fulfill them? If human life does not yield some cosmic meaning, is it not the course of wisdom to pursue a policy of "Eat, drink and make merry, for tomorrow we die"?

Belief in God as here conceived can function in our day exactly as the belief in God has always functioned; it can function as an affirmation that life has value. It implies, as the God idea has aways implied, a certain assumption with regard to the nature of reality, the assumption that reality is so constituted as to endorse and guarantee the realization in man of that which is of greatest value to him. If we believe that assumption to be true, for, as has been said, it is an assumption that is not susceptible of proof, we have faith in God. No metaphysical speculation beyond this fundamental assumption that reality assures both the emergence and the realization of human ideals is necessary for the religious life.

NEW WAYS TO STUDY TORAH

The study "Torah"—of the religious literature of Israel—persisted in modern times. But the modes and procedures of study in the classical ways now were augmented by new ones. Learned Jews who went to universities acquired a new approach to the analysis and interpretation of religious writings.

That approach derived from three main disciplines: philosophy, history, and philology. The last-named represented the least innovation. It simply meant that the meanings of words would have to be explained. While in pre-modern times, it was customary to prepare dictionaries and to interpret the meanings of the language of the Torah-literature, now new methods of interpretation and new sources of explanation developed through advances in the study of Semitics, comparative linguistics, and similar sciences.

The historical approach involved the effort to find out "just what happened" behind the stories and legends contained in biblical and later literature. It required the development of a critical perspective, in place of the habit of believing as a fact whatever the Scriptures and traditions allege to have taken place.

The philosophical approach is most interesting to us. It consists in the effort to discover and to criticize the values and ideas within the religious classics, to analyze these values and ideas. Above all it meant to show how they related to the dominant ideas—philosophies—of the time.

Now while modern Jewish scholars studied the ancient literature, it is clear that they were going to do so in very new ways. They would ask new questions. They would want to find not the traditional types of answers, but to locate entirely new sorts of information.

Above all, they claimed to be "objective" or "scientific." That, they said, is what marks them as truly new and "scientific." But when you read their writings, you wonder what they could have meant by "objectivity"—today it is not a burning issue at all—because you find the "modern scholars" making assertions of faith, of values, not terribly different in spirit from those asserted by traditional scholars. In fact, for the founders of modern Jewish scholarship in nineteenth century Germany, the exercise of scholarly inquiry was not for the purpose solely of finding things out, of discovering facts. It rather was an effort to find reasons for, to justify and legitimate in terms of contemporary values, the continued existence of the Jewish people and the enduring vitality of Judaism.

In other words, while they said they were not "learning Torah" but rather "doing scholarship," the underlying motivation was one and the same. The new methods of "study of Torah" produced results alien to the traditional mentality. But the classical Jew could comprehend the net result of the processes of modern Jewish scholarship: the explanation of why the Jews cannot be permitted to disappear and Judaism to disintegrate. To be sure, that explanation would have to satisfy students of philosophy—learned men at large—and not merely participants in the Judaic tradition. But the conditions of modern life imposed new requirements upon the study of Torah and its range of discourse. In fundamental ways the religious message remained constant.

XVI

THE IDEOLOGY OF THE FOUNDERS OF JEWISH SCIENTIFIC RESEARCH

MAX WIENER

(From *YIVO Annual of Jewish Social Science*, Vol. 5, 1950, pp. 184-196)

All the intellectual and spiritual transformations in Judaism since the beginning of the 19th century go back, directly or indirectly, to the break in Jewish life, the first and most characteristic expression of which was Jewish scientific research (*Wissenschaft des Judentums*). This "science of Judaism" signified far more than what it seemed to be at the outset; it was far more than philological-historical research intended to provide an objective and clear picture of the national past of the Jewish people. It represented an attitude which in itself was a new stage in historical development. Leopold Zunz saw this quite early when he wrote:

> Bibliography, critical method of investigation, and history are not only the products of science but also the products of history itself. Just as the older materials which we weave into science as objective data were originally purely subjective treatment of an older idea, so the method we use in science also becomes a subject of investigation for us and for future generations.

That Jewish scholars with modern methods began to devote themselves to Jewish subject matter and in so doing displayed the same abilities and achievements as their teachers in their fields, was certainly primarily a product of assimilation. From this standpoint it is but mere chance that scholars of the stature of Zunz, Geiger, Munk and Graetz limited their research to the sphere of Jewish knowledge. In a deeper sense, however, this new interest in Jewish knowledge was more than a theoretical bent; it was an expression of a new outlook upon Jewish life. . . .

. . . . The real motivating force in the Jewish scientific research of

the 19th century consisted in the adoption of a stand on the question
of Jewish survival, or in the desire to find satisfaction in such survival.
This fact elevates the period to an epoch in Jewish history. In individuals like Zunz, Luzzatto, Geiger and Graetz, men who were steeped
in Jewish content from their youth, this was very apparent. More
characteristic, however, in this respect is the group of individuals who
had little Jewish knowledge, for whom Judaism as a way of life was
very pale, but who yearned to provide this vague Jewish feeling with a
deep foundation. The young men who, together with Zunz, founded
the *Verein für jüdische Kultur und Wissenschaft* [Society for Jewish
Culture and Learning] in 1819, 'believed that they could not lead an
honorable existence either as men or as Jews unless they took stock of
the meaning and content of their Jewishness. Scholarship, already in
existence or still to be created, thus became for them the very basis of
life. The true expression of Jewish life was to be found in scholarly
preoccupation with Judaism. The more the exalted, practical ends of
the organization, such as popular education, occupational retraining
etc., appeared difficult of realization (sometimes because of financial
difficulties), the more prominent became the theoretical treatment of
Jewish questions. It was an age when young, intelligent people asked
themselves questions regarding ultimate ends and regarding the true
nature of man and history. This was carried over also to the Jewish
youth. Jewish youth also believed that it was only necessary to pose
scientific problems properly and answer them correctly in order to
satisfy the practical demands of life. These people saw how traditional
Judaism was disintegrating and they were convinced that a clear view
and a theoretical interpretation of Judaism would provide the modern,
cultured Jew with the potential to carry on as a Jew. They still bore
within them a remnant of "psychic" Judaism. But they were reared
in German idealistic philosophy and for them life meant an existence
based on knowledge and always cognizant of its foundations and
motives. Whatever was not a manifestation of a definite idea did not
merit existence.

A study of the minutes of the *Verein* together with the intellectual
climate of the time shows how the members of the organization were
groping to find expression for their deepest Jewish interests. They
wanted to know what the essence of Judaism was so that they could
remain Jews. During the preceding generation of Moses Mendelssohn
this question was completely avoided. As a result, Jewry lost many of
its children. Now the question was posed consciously and deliberately:
Shall Judaism be absorbed into the world at large or shall it continue

to survive? Behind these considerations was Hegel's famous dictum "Whatever is rational is real and whatever is real is rational." I. A. List, in his talk at the founding of the *Verein* on November 7, 1819 made this point:

> My friends, we feel that what is characteristic for our people, our pure nationality, is not merely a product of the times, a passing phenomenon . . . We have a clear conception of our existence because otherwise we would not be ourselves, that is to say we would be nothing. It is most characteristic of an idea, however, that what is most necessary in it is at once possible and the possible is at once necessary.

List comes to the conclusion that it is necessary by all means to restore our national way of life (*Volkstumlichkeit*) to its previous dignity. The first condition for that is "that rabbinism, which cripples and destroys the [Jewish] nation should be completely overthrown." Just how this is the end result of the idea is not revealed by List. But Zunz too considered it to be an axiom of healthy development. In a letter to his friend S. M. Ehrenberg, after he had declined an offer of a rabbinical post in Hamburg, Zunz wrote on October 13, 1818:

> As long as there will be no authority to sanction the entire matter [of reforming the synagogue] nothing will help. Every one is a reformer and makes a fool of himself. The most cultured and most enlightened here are opponents of the German synagogue . . .

. . . If we consider the role played in that generation by philosophy and by the quest for the metaphysical foundations of existence, it is easy to see why there was no other approach to Judaism for these members of the *Verein* than through the "idea" of Judaism. Before any scientific investigation of the manifestations of Jewish life was able to reveal these manifestations in detail it was first necessary to discover the significance of Judaism in the general intellectual and spiritual context of humanity. This is most apparent in the programmatic pronouncement of the jurist and thinker, Eduard Gans, in his presidential address to the *Verein*. Gans asked the question: "What is present-day Europe? And what are Jews?" His reply was that history is not created by the good or evil intent of an individual. The national spirit reveals itself in history as the unity of a multi-varied whole.

Europe, the product of thousands of years of life, is such a harmony today.

It is the good fortune and significance of the European that he is free to choose his class from among the many various classes of civic society and he feels all the other classes of society in the class that he selects. Take away from him this liberty and you take away from him his foundation and essence.

Gans goes on to attempt to define the specific quality of the Jewish religion. The fact that state, custom, law and religion were all intertwined in one among Jews was not what differentiated them from other oriental nations. "The difference was in the fruitful adaptability by means of which they created out of themselves a new world and at the same time did not become a part of this world." According to Gans the Jews compensate in another way for this failure to become a part of the world. With the decline of the Jewish state they became masters of one class, the commercial class, and this gave them the possibility to work their way into other classes. Being outside the pale of all these other classes they had their own phase of world history. This means, therefore, that the meaning of Jewish history did not consist in being apart from the world. Jewish history, insofar as it was set off from general history, was such only by force of circumstances; it was never completely cut off from universal problems.

The Europe of the 19th century, however, demanded a completely harmonious structure and Jews could not remain without. "The demand of present-day Europe that Jews become entirely incorporated into it," said Gans, "derives from the very essence of Europe. Europe would be untrue to itself and to its essential nature if it did not set forth this demand." The emphasis here is upon Europe and not upon Judaism. The Jewish world is to be absorbed into the European world. The idea of Europe provides the security that the fresh outbreaks of anti-Jewish violence . . . will not keep back the wheels of world history, which move in accordance with necessity. Necessity demands that the Jewish world be absorbed into the European world; this does not mean, however, that it must be completely lost in it. The larger world which will embrace the Jewish world should become richer thereby and not the Jewish world poorer. Only the particularism which is oriented solely around itself and hence stands in the way of universal development is to be destroyed:

This is the comforting lesson of history, if properly understood, that everything passes away but nevertheless does not pass
away, and that everything remains even though it is thought that it
had long ago passed away. That is why Jews cannot disappear and
Judaism cannot disintegrate. It will seem to have disappeared in the
vast movement of the whole but it will continue to live just as the
current lives on in the ocean.

Destructive tendencies, no doubt, were able to develop out of
this comparison. And such tendencies did actually appear. Nevertheless we can assume that Gans was really motivated by a utilitarian
idea covered up in idealistic dressing. Immediately following these
abstract considerations came concrete plans for the development of
Jewish scholarship. This would indicate that the purpose of these
pronouncements was to stimulate Jewish scientific research, research
which would not look upon Judaism as hermetically sealed off from
the idea of "Europe." (That is why Gans called upon friendly-
disposed Christians to join in the work.) Gans complained of the
ignorant rabbis who were full of prejudices and who lacked a view of
the universal whole into which Judaism was to fit. They lack freedom.
On the other side he noted that the Christian scholars who concern
themselves with Jewish matters subordinate this research to Christian
motives and thus deprive it of independence of investigation. Our
task, he said, is complete freedom and independence:

> You, friends, have realized this idea in that you have created
> an institution to investigate the various fields of research. In it, all
> the members, while working according to a general plan, have full
> individual freedom. In this I have presented the essential idea of
> your institute for *Jewish scientific research.*

This was the primary function of the *Verein.* A second purpose was
to help gifted Jewish immigrants receive an education. This was important in the practical activities of the *Verein.* Besides these aims, the
Verein planned to set up an archival center to provide materials for the
systematic study of Jewish community life.

Gans looked upon scientific research not only as a reflection of
life and history but as an important stage of reality in itself. This is
clearly brought out in his third speech, in which he points out that the
Verein is not the product of some playful accident but rather of ne-

cessity and of the times. "If you ask me," says Gans, "what this age wants, I answer: it wants to arrive at a knowledge of itself. It wants not only to be, but to know itself. A life concerning which there is no conviction that it is necessary is no real life; nor will there be any phenomenon concerning which there is no assurance that it can appear only in this way and in no other."

This, according to the spirit of early 19th century philosophy, is the basis for scientific research in general and for Jewish research in particular. Reality must acquire knowledge of itself; it must see itself and recognize itself in order to achieve true completeness. Knowledge, explained Gans, seeks to penetrate all objects and this is its justification. If a particular phenomenon cannot be penetrated by knowledge then it has no real existence and will not have any permanence. From the Jewish standpoint this means that the Jewish element must be able to see itself in its totality, not separate aspects here and there. This totality or "higher unity" is knowledge of all that happens or appears, knowledge of Judaism and Jews. The function of knowledge, as used by Gans, is to evaluate and to analyze. Those elements in Judaism which cannot justify themselves to scientific research in its present form need not fall and be overturned. They have already fallen and been overturned because they have not been able to provide answers to scientific research.

The ideas of Gans did not provide a program of the detailed fields of Jewish knowledge. The detailed work was done by Zunz. It is very clear, however, what Gans was after. Jewish knowledge is but a part of general knowledge and only in this context can it fulfill its task both as scientific research and as a constructive force in Jewish life. It should bring Jews out of their isolationism but at the same time not destroy the understanding that the Jewish "idea" has its own contribution to make. Insofar as the form of a fully developed life is knowledge, i.e. knowing responsibility, then Jewish knowledge is the way to a higher Jewish existence and it alone can separate the living from the dead in our tradition. The greatest difficulties, said Gans, are the product of the decline that came in with the Enlightenment during the preceding fifty years. "Gone are the enthusiasm for religion and the solid character of old relationships, and no new relationships have as yet been formed. The subjective spirit which was liberated from its trammels by the Enlightenment must return to new ties in order to become truly creative." Such ties he saw in surrendering with understanding to the "objective spirit," whose basic supposition everywhere is scientific enlightenment. In the field of Jewish scientific research it should bring a new knowledge which should be on an equal level with general European knowledge. This the true function of the Verein.

The transition from abstract formulation to the concrete goals of Jewish knowledge was provided by Emmanuel Wolff's study of the concept of *"Jüdische Wissenschaft* [Jewish learning]." His program embraced almost everything. He considered Judaism to be "the general concept of the relationships, specific characteristics and achievements of Jews in the fields of religion, philosophy, history, law, literature, social life and all human problems." In one point, at least, Wolff gives an indication as to what he considers to be the goal of the Jewish "idea." This "idea" expresses the *Volksgeist* [national ethos] of the Jews in the same way in which Hegel spoke of the *"Volksgeist"* of various nations that participated in the unfolding of the world spirit in history. It was not the religious truth but the philosophic or scientific truth which was concealed like germ seeds in this "idea" and which finally attained to clear expression. One of its manifestations was the transition from pure monotheism to Spinoza's monistic system. Traditional Jewish doctrine, according to Wolff, did not permit of freedom of thought. The Jewish people, weary and lethargic under the burden of its troubles, had fallen to such a lot point of development that it almost was near its end. Then arose a personality, Spinoza, who must be considered as the highest expression of Jewish and universal thought. . . .

. . . But Wolff and Zunz were as one in believing that all the factual knowledge of Judaism must be integrated in a spiritual background, held together in a system which is determined by the "idea" in order that it may produce genuine scientific knowledge. There was one point of difference, however, between Zunz and the others. Zunz followed the empirical path and began to investigate details, while his enthusiastic friends made directly for the goal and wanted to arrive at the knowledge of the "idea" without the laborious work of detailed investigation. Wolff's discussion of the individual fields of research was confused. He spoke of philology, history, philosophy and statistics, which meant, for him, an investigation of the condition of Jews in various countries. The only new contribution in his program was the emphasis on the non-theological and purely factual approach to Judaism.

For Wolff this research had a profound meaning. It became an auxiliary to his philosophical-historical goal, when everything "will be systematically investigated according to its individual essence and according to the basic principle of the universal whole." He believed in a Jewish philosophy of life that was based on clear principles, as indicated in his discussion of Spinoza. But apart from the "idea," there is the Jewish community, a flesh and blood Judaism, which is an organic unity by itself and which is the object for statistical interest. This interest has an important practical significance. Scholarly investigation "must make decisions regarding the worthiness or unworthiness of Jews, regarding their ability or inability to be given equal rights and to be considered equal to other citizens." Wolff had no doubts regarding the outcome. He was certain that the true study of the values of Judaism would lead to the necessary adjustment to the spirit of the age. In this respect he was as one with the Jewish *maskilim* [illumines] and their Christian friends in Germany, who wished to see a weakening of traditional Judaism in favor of assimilation. Like them he was deeply convinced of the salutary power of scientific knowledge in the history of mankind. "If ever," he said, "one bond will embrace the entire species of man, it will be the bond of scientific knowledge, the bond of pure reason, the bond of truth."

The scientific knowledge of which Wolff spoke and which he considered to be such a normative force for European life was not the investigation of particular phenomena; he had in mind philosophy, the knowledge of the "idea." This is a confused concept regarding the practical accomplishments of scientific knowledge. When Wolff hails it as a force to remove the final barriers to the brotherhood of nations it sounds a bit exaggerated; it is a belated enthusiasm for the Enlightenment. But the sober investigation of facts has also never forgotten that in the study and interpretations of facts regarding Jewish life much is accomplished towards a better understanding of the Jew in the world and towards doing away with the feeling of complete alienation of Judaism from the outside world.

NEW THEMES IN THE STUDY OF TORAH

While the ancient "study of Torah" underwent important changes in the modern world, as Wiener shows, these changes are not only in the modes of thought, the methods of inquiry, characteristic of "Torah" in the old sense. *Study* was not alone in changing. *Torah* likewise underwent alterations. What happened to Torah was that new subjects were subsumed within the established framework of religious learning. Just as the ancient rabbis believed how one ate a meal or conducted his sexual relationships were subsumed within "Torah," so today the modern students of Judaism will receive within the framework of religious learning entirely new subjects and disciplines, to be approached as were the old, through piety.

One advocate of a particular, new subject, Joseph C. Landis, who teaches at Queens College of the City of New York, speaks of his study, the Yiddish language and its literature, in terms one can only regard as religious. His claim, indeed, is that the study of Yiddish yields not merely knowledge of a language spoken by East European Jewry until they were exterminated, and still spoken by large numbers of Jews in America, Canada, Latin America, and the State of Israel.

Study of Yiddish produces something more: knowledge of the essential, and deeply religious traits, of Jewish culture, and, still more, of Judaism as a mode of religious living. Not only so, but the language and claims before us are those which, if focused upon theological rather than cultural data, would impress us as religious, in no way secular or concerned solely with this-worldly and cultural issues.

Yiddish is a language, but when learning Yiddish is recommended as a mode of study of Judaism, then Yiddish enters the category of "Torah." That is suggestive of the ways in which "study of Torah" broadens, in modern times, to make room, within the traditional setting of learned devotion, for many other subjects. What are the sorts of arguments to be adduced in support of the specific claims of Yiddish? We want to know, too, how one is to link the mastery of a language to the acquisition of values, to the perception of religious truths. These are the problems which Landis solves for us.

XVII
WHO NEEDS YIDDISH?
A STUDY IN LANGUAGE AND ETHICS

JOSEPH C. LANDIS

(From *Judaism,* Vol. 13, No. 4, Fall, 1964, pp. 1-16, excerpts.)

. . . In spite of hostility or indifference, in spite of deafness to appeals for the defense of a language hallowed by the blood of martyrs, bearer of a rich cultural heritage, channel of a thousand years of the mainstream of Jewish experience, vehicle of communication among the members of a worldwide Jewish community—in spite of ill-concealed contempt in high or holy places, the sea of Yiddish refuses to dry up. Instead of receding with the decrease in numbers of those for whom it is a first language, Yiddish seems to be reaching out among native American Jews, some of whom persist in sending their children to Yiddish schools, but many more of whom buy the Yiddish books in translation, go to Yiddish plays in English and in Yiddish, and buy the steady deluge of recordings of Yiddish songs, sung by some of our finest singers, both those who know Yiddish well and those whose pronunciations betray a less intimate knowledge. Is not this the voice of the people expressing a sense that in Yiddish lies something authentically and distinctively Jewish that can help satisfy the hunger for ingredients of Jewish identity in a world whose great pressures are towards uniformity without and loneliness within and the negation of meaningful identity?

Underlying this response is a great but neglected truth: the Yiddish language is not only distinctively Jewish, but it is also uniquely Jewish, and it is, above all, essentially Jewish, so that without it the distinctive identity we recognize as Jewish suffers a grievous loss and a grave alteration. And these qualities of being, uniquely and essentially Jewish, are ultimately incapable of translation into any other language. Without Yiddish our Jewishness is but a puny and a paltry thing. Who needs Yiddish? To anyone examining the language in relation to the qualities that for a millenium and more most Jews have regarded as essential to any conception of Jewish being, one answer seems inescapable. To anyone thinking of communicating these Jewish qualities in a language other than Yiddish, one answer seems unavoidable: Jewish life needs Yiddish as the irreplaceable vehicle of its historic and unique essence. When we are confronted with the cliché expressed by many readers that "something is lost in translation" or that an artist like Sholem Aleichem is untranslatable, what they are really asserting is not only that the art of a Sholem Aleichem suffers in translation; this is true of most writers, whatever their language. What they are sensing is the loss or serious diminution of the essential *Jewishness* of the work.

The cause of this loss of diminution inheres in the very nature of Yiddish; for Yiddish is not merely a language spoken by millions of Jews. English is too. Nor is it merely a language spoken exclusively by Jews. Ladino [Judeo-Spanish] is too. It is ultimately a language shaped and developed to embody and express the *Jewish being* of the thousand-year-old civilization built by Ashkenazi Jews and brought to its noblest flowering in Eastern Europe. Two remarkable achievements are to be credited to Ashkenazi Jewry. Animated by a complex of values both implicit and explicit in prior Jewish history and thought, values which in their total constellation are an entity unique in human history, Ashkenazi Jewry proceeded, first, to bring these values to their richest fulfillment. "I feel justified in saying," writes Abraham Joshua Heschel in relation to this era, "that it was the golden period in Jewish history, in the history of the Jewish soul." And it was so golden a period because Ashkenazi Jewry. paid not merely lip service to a humane, life-affirming and man-revering ethic, but to a remarkable degree it embodied that ethic in the pattern of its life, in the structure of its institutions, in their ceremony of its customs and rituals, in the celebration of its holidays, and in the observance of its traditions. Behind all of these is clearly discernible that sense of life and of man, of his duties and obligations, which its values asserted.

But even beyond that achievement lies a second one, fully as remarkable: Ashkenazi Jewry took a Germanic dialect and shaped it into a language in which Jewish ethic and Jewish way of life, Jewish value and Jewish sense of life are embodied in the repatterned sentence style and structure, in the altered pronunciation and word order, in the reshaped inflectional forms and their derivatives, in the enlarged vocabulary, in the created folk expressions and sayings, in the metaphors and allusions. At the heart of the 180,000 words of the language stand the twelve or thirteen thousand Hebrew words and phrases and their derivatives, absorbed originally from Torah and Talmud, from liturgy and commentary, which pumped the ethical lifeblood of Yiddish. And Yiddish took the Hebrew material and imbedded it in Yiddish contexts. It took the Hebrew words and created new Hebrew from them. And the two elements sustained and nourished each other into a linguistic fulfillment of historic voices and a linguistic embodiment of historic visions, into a bearer of a unique concept and conduct of life. The meanings of Yiddish may more or less be rendered; the experience of the uniquely Jewish values and attitudes and feelings, the ways and the life-context which they express and which are vital to Jewish being are left behind.

Yiddish is thus really the language of *teitsh,* as it once was called, of translation of Hebrew writ, not only in a literal sense but in a much larger sense as well; for Yiddish is the translation into language of the ethic of Ashkenazi Jews and of the embodiment of their ethic in a way of life and in quality of being. And they knew it. Is not this the reason why, of all languages that Jews spoke after they gave up Hebrew, this language alone they called a Jewish language? In this language alone the word for the Jew and his speech are the same: *yidn redn yidish* [Jews speak Jewish].

If Yiddish is the linguistic embodiment of Jewish being, then to embrace it is neither a sentimental gesture nor a scholarly attainment nor a cultural luxury; it is an affirmation and acceptance of something vital and essential to the definition of our Jewishness. The very large number of Yiddish words and phrases that persist in English, the expressions that we cling to and that we use, trying to leaven English for ourselves as Hebrew leavened the Germanic dialect that became Yiddish—these are a clue to our sense of the inadequacy of the English approximations of Jewish concepts. To the extent that the "language habits" that are native to Yiddish sound strange in English, to the extent that these value-laden words, phrases, and constructions that are native to Yiddish sound foreign in English, to that extent is Yiddish an indispensable vehicle of Jewish being and an irreplaceable expression of the uniqueness of the Jewish way. And that extent is indeed considerable. For every principle central to Jewish ethic and Jewish value, to Jewish practice and Jewish character, there are Yiddish words and phrases that defy translation. Explained in English they may be; truly translated, rendered in the same suggestive fullness that the Yiddish context provides, they cannot be.

Is it possible, for example, to translate adequately the phrase *tsar baale khayim* [suffering of animals] with its evocation of a quality that was central to the Ashkenazi Jew's sense of himself as a Jew? Will the translation suggest that the consciousness of the Ashkenazi Jew was pervaded by the insistence on compassion for man, on reverence for life; that inflicting needless pain on living things was for him a cause of deep distress; that he was profoundly contented to be regarded as one of the *rakhmonim bney rakhmonim,* the merciful and sons of the merciful? So vital was *tsar baale khayim* that he identified it with his very essence. This is what he referred to when he spoke of *a yiddish harts* or *a yiddish oder.* Does a phrase like "a Jewish heart" or "a Jewish vein" inevitably suggest such meanings in English? Is the pained disapproval of the delight in killing that is aroused by hunting or fishing as sport native to English as it is to Yiddish? The equivalent of "God forbid!" or "Heaven forbid!," whatever their sources in primitive consciousness, assume in Yiddish a variety of forms that express, not a faith in their efficacy for warding off evil but a concern for all men, united in a common lot. And, since mortality is involved, Yiddish says, in rich variety, not only *rakhmone litslon* or *rakhmone yatsilenu* or *got zol ophitn,* but also *kholile, kholile vkhas, khas vsholem, nit do gedakht, nit far aykh gedakht, nit far keyn yidn gedakht, nit far kaynem gedakht, nit far keyn mentshn gedakht.* Is there not, then something disquieting and foreboding in the fate of *nebakh,* that characteristic expression of pity, which has in English become nearly its opposite—"nebbish"—a term of condescension and derision? Is there not something distressing when *keyn ayn hore* [no evil eye!], an expression of rejoicing in another's gladness that has long outlived its source in folk superstition, is rendered into the pidgin Yiddish "no canary"?

If Yiddish is the language embodying the particularity of the Ashkenazi Jew's valuation of compassion and of human relatedness, it is also the language that expresses his particular valuation of humanity. How can one accurately translate into English a word like *folksmentsh?* It lacks the ambiguity of such phrases as "the common man" or "the ordinary man." Indeed, it suggests something out of the ordinary about the *folksmentsh;* it suggests the rich resources and creativity that are within the man who is of the folk—and therefore the Yiddish admiration for what is *folkstimlekh.* The *folksmentsh,* moreover, is not only *of* the people; he belongs to it and is loyal to it. In the same spirit Yiddish absorbed *amkho* as a synonym for the *folksmentsh.* The respect that is imbedded in *amkho* is underscored by the fact that "Thy people" refers to the people that the Lord chose (or that chose the Lord). It is surely not fortuitous that the greatest figure of Yiddish literature should be Sholem Aleichem's Tevye, the *folksmentsh* and the symbol, in his moral qualities, of the Ashkenazi Jew. It is surely not fortuitous that the major motif of Yiddish literature is its love of the *folksmentsh* and its faith in him.

If Yiddish is the language of the *yidish harts* in its feelings, it is also and of necessity the language of human relatedness in action, of the insistence of man's obligation to be his brother's keeper, of the demand for *maysim tovim* [good deeds]. The Ashkenazi Jew developed and named a large variety of wholly voluntary social services, from the *hakhnoses kale* [tending to the needs of a poor bride] or the *hakhnoses orkhim* [help to wayfarers] to the *bikur kholim* [visiting the sick] and the *khevra kedisha* [holy society for burying the dead]. The far-flung structure of American Jewish philanthropy and our sense of obligation to philanthropy are rooted in these practices. But in the necessary process of modernization of structure and function, our American phraseology loses the clear moral meanings and the specific Jewish quality that the Yiddish expresses or implies. Yiddish uses the word *tsdoko,* knowing that *tsedek* is justice and that *tsdoko* is not charity but the right of the recipient. Yiddish absorbs the word *oyrekh* (stranger, guest) and combines both meanings in action, so that the stranger becomes a guest for the Sabbath or the holiday meal, and *tsdoko* is thus converted from an ethical abstraction into the reality *an oyrekh oyf shabes.* Yiddish creates the phrase *reb meyer baal hanes pushke* to name the little *tsdoko* box that was customary in the Jewish home. Yiddish takes a business-like transaction like an interest-free loan and institutionalizes it into the moral relationship called *gmiles khesed,* which in English sounds not a little quaint and naive as "a bestowal of loving-kindness" (or "grace"). And Yiddish uses the word *yosher* with emphasis not merely to justice in the legal sense but on the individual's feeling for what is right and fair.

Yiddish, the language of human relatedness and man's responsibility for man, is also the language of family-relatedness. It is hardly fortuitous that Yiddish had to create the words designating the relationship that exists between the parents of bride and groom—*mekhutoneshaft, mekhutn, mekhuteyneste*—words that are lacking in English. It is hardly fortuitous that Yiddish lacks the word for the impersonal expression "a parent," and that, though it has the plural form for parents, *eltern,* it prefers the more intimate expression *tate-mame* (and, incidentally, does not use the theoretically possible but more formal equivalent *foter-muter*). In general, Yiddish prefers by far *tate* and *mame* to *foter* or *muter* and uses them in contexts where the English use of "mama" or "papa" would sound childish.

Another aspect of the human relatedness which Yiddish embodies is its capacity for tenderness and endearment within the family as well as outside it. Yiddish is the language in which, for example, a parent can say to an injured child, *mir zol zayn far dir*. The tenderness of such expressions is, in English translation, often mistaken for sentimentality, and, indeed, the words in English do sometimes sound sentimental when in Yiddish they are not. This is especially true of diminutive and affectionate forms in various combinations of the suffixes *ke, she, le, nyu,* which Yiddish eagerly adopted and developed. How can one translate without sounding foolishly sentimental or ludicrous such a progression of diminutives for "a bit, a drop" as *a kap, a kapele, a kapinke, a kapenyu, a kapichke, a kapinkele, a kapichkele, a kapinyunkele?* How much more sentimental must sound, in English, the variety of forms and phrases that express the warmth of family feeling which is so characteristic of Jewish life and of the Jewish emphasis on the home as a center of Jewish living and Jewish being! In English they must sound sentimental because English does not normally express these feelings in words and must therefore resort to expressions that either sound extravagant or seem drawn from the vocabulary of childhood. In Yiddish, on the other hand, intimacy and affection for parents as well as for children are embodied in numerous and varied diminutive forms. A grandmother is not only a *bobe* but *bobenyu, bobishe, bobichke, bobinke;* and *tate* and *mame* and *zeyde* have a similar variety of forms. A small child is not only *a pitsl* (a tot), but also *a pitsele, a pitsinkele, a pitsinyunkele,* and *a pitsinyunchikl.* A name like Leah become not only *Leye,* but *Leyele, Leyenyu, Leyinke, Leyinkele, Leyke, Leykele, Leykenyu, Leyche, Leychele, Leychenyu.* The English diminutive suffix *y* or *ie,* on the other hand, often cannot even be applied to a name which ends with a vowel sound. Yiddish can even express degrees and kinds of intimacy. A name like *Yosef* is capable of the back-slipping affectionate *Yoshke,* the respectful affectionate *Yozifl,* the more intimate *Yosel,* or *Yoshe* (which is also expressive of condescension, as in I. J. Singer's novel *Yoshe Kalb*), the more affectionate *Yosele,* and the tenderly intimate *Yosenyu, Yosinke, Yosinkele, Yoshkele, Yoshenyu,* and *Yoshkenyu.* So great is this internal warmth of Yiddish that even so apparently aloof an inquiry as *"vos makht dos kind?"* is by no means one of indifference, and *dos kind* is not at all rendered by "the child" and not adequately even by "our child" or "your child." Nor does a phrase like "my little son" satisfactorily convey the affectionate warmth of such an expression as *mayn yingele* or *yingele mayns*. And what can translate the spirituality of the pleasure, the inner glow that inheres in the phrase *nakhes fun kinder*? And the affection so easily expressed to members of the family is just as readily communicated at large. Yiddish cannot only add suffixes of affection to nouns and adjectives; it can even make affectionate diminutives of verbs, as Jacob Glatstein brilliantly demonstrated in his poem *"Geto Lid"* ("Ghetto Song"), in which a mother comforts her child with such pleas as *"zingenyu"* ("sing"), *"shlofele,"* *"shlofenyu"* ("sleep"), and *"lakhele"* ("laugh"). And in improvisations like *"shazheshe"* ("and so hush, little one") the genius of Glatstein and the flexibility in affection are both demonstrated.

If Yiddish is, thus, the language of the *yidish harts* in its involvement with man, whether stranger or kin—a valuation rooted in mortality, not sentimentality—Yiddish embodies another of the values vital to Jewishness by being· also the language of the *yidisher kop*, of the dedication to learning. And it was a love of learning not for the sake of a diploma nor *smikha* [ordination] nor income nor even for the sake of heaven, but for the combined and syphenated spiritual-intellectual-aesthetic experience of the pursuit of Torah as truth. The world in which Yiddish was shaped was one that inaugurated a child's schooling by putting a drop of wine or honey on its tongue, so that its taste of learning might be sweet. It was a world in which it was a father's custom every Sabbath to question his son on the youngster's progress in his studies during the week. How natural then, as Max Weinreich has pointed out, for it to be a world in which the social ladder began with the *grober yung* at the bottom and ranged upward through *a yid fun a gants yor, a sheyner yid, a yid a lamdn* to a *godl btoyre*. What English phrase adequately reflects the profound respect inherent in the words a *godl btoyre*? What English phrase suggests that *a yid fun a gants yor* is not only an ordinary Jew, an everyday Jew, but also a Jew every day of his life and a *folksmentsh*? And while, in English, the man-in-the-street uses "Doc" as a salutation of familiarity bordering on condescension, in Yiddish, the *folksmentsh* reserved the title *rebbe* for respectful address to any man of learning.

The world which valued this ideal of the *yidisher kop* not only valued the possessor of one but lavished its affection on him and frequently used the affectionate diminutive with his name. How often was the name of a rabbi or a *maggid* or a *khazn* so used? Can English, for example, render properly the name of the most famous of Jewish cantors, Yossele Rosenblatt? Is he to become Little Joey Rosenblatt? Is Sholem Aleichem's famous rabbi of Kasrilevke, Reb Yosifl, to be known as Rabbi Little Joe?

The world which so valued learning and learned men created and named two unique institutions to foster them. It took an institution like boarding a bridegroom in the home of his wife's parents for a stipulated period as part of the dowry and converted it into the uniquely Jewish institution of *kest,* board for the purpose of *study.* And, as Max Weinreich has pointed out, *essn teg*—eating with a different family each day —the unique institution for supporting *yeshiva bokherim* (and a *yeshiva bokher* was not a "yeshiva student") away from home was really a system of folk scholarships. Indeed, *essn teg* was more than a system of folk scholarships; it was also a system of folk participation in national education which was synonymous with national destiny. And when a housewife could boast that such-and-such a distinguished scholar had once eaten in her home on Wednesdays, it was not merely name-dropping on her part, not merely personal pride in having assisted a particular distinguished scholar; it was pride in having participated in a national achievement, in having had a share in adding to a national treasure and to the pursuit of universal truth.

Dedicated as it thus was to the values of the head and the heart, to Torah and *maysim tovim,* the Ashkenazi world was one whose ethic could indeed be called the ethic of *mentshlekhkayt.* In the word *mentsh* it found the summation of its strivings. It could not conceive of the possibility of being a Jew without being a *mentsh,* and it could not conceive of being a *mentsh* without admiring gentleness and being distressed at violence. *"Alle yavonim hobn eyn ponim,"* all soldiers (literally "Greeks") look alike, it said with a clear undertone of contempt for the soldier's function. In fact, the soldier as a symbol stood at furthest remove from the life's ideal and conception of self of the Ashkenazi Jew, as strange and inappropriate as *a yovn in a suke,* as a soldier in a *suke.*

This vision of *mentshlekhkayt,* as well as the loyalty to it, was to the world of Yiddish not merely morally gratifying but aesthetically pleasing, and in the phrase *a sheyner yid* was embodied this fusion of moral and aesthetic fact, for the beauty of the *sheyner yid* lay not in his features but in his *yidishkayt.* If a *mentsh* embodied—or strove to embody—the Jewish virtues, the *sheygets,* on the other hand, symbolized the opposite: the pugnacity, the cruelty, the unintellectuality, the human indifference and unrelatedness which could only fill with dismay the heart of any *mentsh*. When Yiddish says, *"zay a mentsh,"* it is evoking an ideal very far removed indeed from the ideal implied in "Be a man." Manliness and *mentshlekhkayt* are two wholly different and utterly unrelated visions of desirable human attributes.

If Yiddish is, thus, the language in which *yidishkayt* uniquely expresses its *mentshlekhkayt,* it is also the language in which Jewish *mentshlekhkayt* expresses its religious *yidishkayt.* And if there is, on the one hand, serious doubt that the moral and intellectual values, attitudes, and feelings that constitute the humane sense of life of the Ashkenazi Jew can be transmitted without Yiddish, in whose words and contexts and connotations its central principles are untranslatably embodied, there is, on the other hand, reason for serious doubt whether Judaism as a religious way of life is not gravely limited without Yiddish. That Hebrew is indispensable to Judaism is clear. Yet for how many have the numerous Hebrew words and phrases referring to religious practices and ways descended from their context in Yiddish? How often does their use evoke the overtones of meaning of that Yiddish context? Of the life-style in Yiddish in which they found their home for a thousand years? If we denude them of this rich context, we not only deprive them of meanings rightfully theirs but of history. Even if we were to regard this context as merely incidental, comparable to the cloak and crowns in which are clothed the Scrolls of the Torah, even so, how appropriate these vestments seem! How they, too, become redolent of sanctity, as Rabbi Joseph Soloveitchik has declared.

But far more important than any sanctity that Judaism may impart to Yiddish is the service that Yiddish performs for Judaism: it provides a setting in which the vocabulary of faith and observance is entirely native, just as Judaism is native. More than native—it was the shaping passion. Is Judaism native in English? Is its terminology at home in English, or is it foreign? Has not something inestimable been irretrievably lost when it lives thus as a stranger? And are we not deeply aware of this loss, of the absence of this sense of belonging, of being at home in a full context of ways and values? Is not this loss what we have in mind when we say of anything, *"es hot nit kayn yidishn tam* [it has no Jewish flavor]?"* (We must say it, of course, in Yiddish, for that expression itself has, in English, no *tam* either English or *yidish.*) It would indeed be the ultimate irony of a history replete with ironies if one were on contemplate Judaism in America today and be forced to say of so much of it, *"es hot nit kayn yidishn tam."*

Perhaps not the ultimate irony. The phrase must be reserved for the very real possibility that the God of Judaism might Himself render that judgment. For if Hebrew has been the language of divine prayer, Yiddish has been the language of divine converse. In Yiddish, the God that sometimes speaks fearsomely in Scriptures becomes the gentle Father. And this intimacy with God which the Ashkenazi Jew felt with such immediacy was made possible only by the capacity of Yiddish for intimacy. In Yiddish one can address the Almighty as *gotenyu* or *tatenyu zeeser,* phrases which in English translation ("dear God" and "sweet Father dear") lose wholly the intimacy that the Yiddish conveys. Even the phrase *riboynoy shel oylem,* so majestic and remote in English translation—"Lord of the universe"—is in Yiddish an address that is warm, gentle, and intimate. Yiddish is the language in which the figures of the Bible emerge as near relations and in which *got iz a tate,* a remark which states merely: "God is a father"; and which just as clearly implies that He is *our* Father and that He will do no less than a father should. And though God is our Father—perhaps because He is our Father—He is exempt neither from the righteousness which His Torah commands nor from the rebuke of His children when He fails to fulfill the *mitzvahs* of justice.

From this close relationship that the Yiddish expresses stems what might seem the sacrilegious boldness that runs through the numberless stories about Jews who questioned, accused, indicted, defied, even punished God when He seemed to deviate from the justice enjoined by His Torah. Sholem Aleichem's Tevye questions Him wryly. Levi Yitskhok of Berdichev lays humbly yet firmly before Him the claims of His people for redemption from exile. And Peretz's Reb Shloyme, determined to put an end to the suffering of humanity and the injustice of the world, defiantly refuses to recite the *Havdala* and thus end the Sabbath with its peace and exaltation. The Baal Shem and Reb Nakhman, Leyb of Spola and Shneyer Zalmen of Lyadi all spoke to God in Yiddish, argued with Him in Yiddish, scolded, accused and blessed Him and gloried in His Torah—in Yiddish. And Itsik Manger, that poet of wonder, marshalling over the gas chambers of Belsen the spirits of Moyshe Leyb of Sossov and Wolf of Zbarazh and Meyerl of Premishlan, proclaimed in their name: ". . . we, the Galicians, for eternity obliterate Your name from the assembly of True Lovers of Israel." And he did so in Yiddish. Who can do so in English? . . .

. . . Yiddish is not only the vehicle through which the life patterns of Judaism find their fullest and richest expression; it is not only the language that knows how to fence off with a *lehavdil* [distinction] the sacred from the profane; it is, through its idioms, a teacher of Judaism as well. It is not possible to speak Yiddish without acquiring a knowledge of the ways and works of Jewish tradition. *A sheyne, reyne kapore, a kosherer top un a kosherer lefl, a nayer ykum pirkon, farbaytn di yotsres, araynfaln vi a yovn in suke, kukn vi a hon in bney odem, makhn emitsn a mi sheberakh, a khokhem fun der ma neshtano, araynzetsn in khad gadyo, shrayen khay vkayem*—these and multitudes of other Yiddish expressions refer to the details of Judaism and provide the materials for metaphor. What in English forces the speaker to a knowledge of Judaism?

Yiddish is a teacher of Jewish history as well. The span of the centuries unrolls in such phrases as *farkrikhn in goyshn, er hert im vi homen hert dem grager, fun khmelnitski's tseitn, fun melekh sobetski's yorn, a medyl mit an oyringl, hob ikh nit getantst mitn ber, es lebt sikh im vi got in odes.* Yiddish is not only an irreplaceable source of documents and studies pertaining to the whole of Jewish history and a unique source pertaining to the ten Ashkenazi centuries; it is the very embodiment of that history in countless expressions. Does English have expressions rooted in forty centuries of Jewish history? Surely Rabbi Emanuel S. Goldsmith is right in his assertion: "There can be no renaissance of Judaism in our time without reverence for Yiddish."

Uniquely and untranslatably, Yiddish is thus the voice of Jewish ethic, the voice of Judaism as a religiously centered pattern of life, the voice of Jewish tradition and celebration, the voice of Jewish loyalty and self-acceptance, the voice of Jewish rejoicing in Jewishness. Which of these are we prepared to dispense with? And all of these become qualities characteristic of the literature of Yiddish and of its folk creativity.

At the moral center of Yiddish literature stands the ethic of Ashkenazi Jewry. Is there a Yiddish writer who does not ultimately affirm it? To a history replete with ironies add one more: Jews, who suffered more at the hands of man than any other people and seemed to suffer more as their history stretched across the centuries, Jews and their writers in Yiddish never lost faith in either man or life, never saw the world as a wasteland, never felt themselves alienated from man. Though there might be but ten righteous men, Jews would not turn their faces from Sodom and Gomorrah. Jewish suffering and Jewish aspiration, Jewish longing and Jewish achievement, Jewish home and Jewish love, Jewish study and Jewish life—these may have been the major subjects of Yiddish literature, but its great theme was and remains the Jewish ethic.

Standing at the moral center of historic experience with the full weight of millennial tradition at his back, the Yiddish writer could observe all the defects of Jewish life, yet never feel himself alienated. Perhaps he perceived himself as in the largest sense a continuator of a prophetic tradition which might indeed excoriate man's iniquities but never felt that it was either unheeded or defied with impunity. If there was a conflict between the publicly recognized ethic and private greed, it was the greedy who were in defiance of tradition. The Yiddish writer, part of the mighty moral stream, never felt himself irreconcilably at odds with his world, never felt that his was a voice crying in the wilderness. So great was his influence, indeed, that he very often became a folk-hero. Is there another literature so entirely steeped in the libertarian tradition, so entirely dedicated to those who suffer, so entirely committed to man's emancipation, so entirely devoted to the values of *mentshlekhayt* as Yiddish literature? And so pervasive was the acceptance of this ethic that it made itself the dominant note in the creativity of the folk. As Y. L. Peretz remarked: "Did you ever compare our folk songs with those, for example, of the Brothers Grimm? Do you find in ours, as you do in theirs, heroes who are robbers or cunning cheats in seven-league boots?" The efflorescence of Jewish writing which is today brightening English literature on both sides of the Atlantic has its moral and intellectual roots in the world which lived, nourished, and transmitted these values in Yiddish. Bringing to bear on contemporary life, as these writers do, the moral and intellectual values of Ashkenazi Jewry, their work would have assumed an altogether different aspect without the impact of the world of Yiddish, in which these values found the vehicle of their expression and the medium of their nourishment.

The evidence makes it abundantly clear that Jewish life and Jewish identity, whether secular or religious, must be both starved and stunted without Yiddish. These multitudes of really untranslatable expressions are not merely linguistic curiosities. They are the bearers and the shapers of our ethical consciousness into a uniquely Jewish constellation of values. For we are dealing not with ethical abstractions but with operative values, with inner directives that constitute our sense of self. As the phrase "Christian charity" not only differs in meaning from *tsdoko* and from *tsar baale khayim* but is evocative of an entire tradition of life and values that as an entity is alien to the Jewish consciousness and painful to the Jewish historical memory, so the uniquely Jewish expressions of Yiddish are linguistic embodiments of a uniquely Jewish moral constellation and a uniquely Jewish historical memory. The greater the immersion in Yiddish and its works, the greater the distinctively Jewish qualities, and conversely, the further the remove from Yiddish the greater the distance from those qualities that characterize the most admirable expressions of Jewish being.

Great as the need is for Yiddish here, it is not less great as an element of life in [the State of] Israel. A century of acrimonious debate and sometimes bitter conflict makes it difficult to keep partisans from falling into the camp of either Yiddishists or Hebraists. Yet such controversy has not only been outmoded by history; it is distinctive to Jewish life, which faces one monumental task: to bring to bear upon itself, upon all who wish to maintain a Jewish identity, the full variety of its resources, the full spectrum of possible choices, the full range of its spaciousness in its three religious dimensions as well as its fourth or secular dimension, so that its future may be creative and meaningful in its continuity with the past; and to bring to bear upon our world the moral vision of *mentshlekhayt,* which for a millennium at least a people strove so hard to incorporate into a pattern of living. If Yiddish is in its own right an indispensable instrument of Jewish continuity, it is not to be regarded lightly even in [the State of] Israel, where, though the future seems confident, the question of continuity with the past and relatedness with the Jewish communities of the world is not an untroubled one.

CHANGES IN THE CONDITION OF "ISRAEL"

One of the permanent traits of the modern situation is impermanence. Everything changes, and changes come so rapidly that you cannot ever suppose anything is going to be the same from day to day. For "Israel", the Jewish people, the modern age has brought immense changes. These pertain not only to matters of belief and piety, but to the material conditions of Jewish life.

At the beginning of the nineteenth century, most Jews in the world lived in one place, Eastern Europe. At the last quarter of the twentieth century, Jews live in many other places.

At the outset of the modern period, most Jews remained out of touch with the larger world in which they found themselves. The culture of the nations was not theirs. They dressed differently, spoke their own language, built a largely particular economy, and in other ways constituted a self-contained group. Today the Jews participate fully in the cultures of the nations in which they live, and, as a group, are a part of the universal culture of modernity characteristic of practically the whole world.

At the beginning of the modern experience Jews had little to do with non-Jews, particularly with Christians. Now they live not only among, but in close relationships with, gentiles, and especially, in the West, with Christians.

Aforetimes universities were closed to Jews. Nowadays Jews go to universities in large numbers.

These are some of the important changes which, all together, constitute the "metamorphosis" of the Jewish people. Moshe Davis, head of the Institute of Contemporary Jewry at the Hebrew University and a pioneer in the comparative study of modern Jewry, here delineates the areas of change and what they mean. He does so not in generalities, but with close attention to numbers, facts, and other details. He points out the areas of common experience among world Jewry, and the special traits of the Jewish communities in various countries.

We shall ask for answers to these questions: What are the changes in the numbers and locations of world Jewry? What has

happened to "Israel-after-the-flesh"? What are the dimensions of the
changes in the cultural settings and commitments of the Jewish people.
What do these changes mean for the religosity of the Jews?

Are these changes on the whole a bad thing or a good thing?
Are the Jews now in the process of 'disintegrating as a social group?
Or are the changes we describe significant of an adaptation to new
conditions of life, therefore signs of vitality and health?

XVIII
THE JEWISH PEOPLE IN METAMORPHOSIS
Moshe Davis

(From *The Jewish People in Metamorphosis,* by Moshe Davis. Syracuse University: The B. G. Rudolph Lectures in Judaic Studies, 1963.)

In a world marked by rapid change, the Jewish People is experiencing a new ferment. The whole world is shaken by radical alterations, and the accelerated pace of events compounds the problems. Formerly, a man, his son and grandchild lived in one age. Today each of us lives through several eras in a lifetime. Moreover, many of the peoples and faiths of the world are now in contact with diversified and often conflicting influences at the same time. The problems of our generation are universal. No one lives in isolation.

Change in itself is not new to the Jewish People. In their long history, the Jews and Judaism had to confront various civilizations. The unique factor in the contemporary Jewish situation is its global nature. Worldwide in scope, unprecedented in content, and characterized by a constant interplay of Jewish and general societal factors, the challenge of contemporary civilization confronts the Jewish tradition and the Jewish People in many parts of the world at the same time. In order to comprehend the problems which concern the Jews today, it is important briefly to formulate the historic ideas of the Jewish People, the ideas which guided the Jews in the past to meet the impact of their environment while maintaining their continuity; secondly, to assess some of the forces which continue to change the Jewish world.

In Judaism, the Tradition and the People are inextricably bound together. As "a child of the Covenant," a Jew inherits both the Tradition and the historic experience of all generations who lived by that Tradition. There have been many formulations of the basic ideas of Judaism, each with its own emphasis. As I understand it, the continuing Jewish tradition of faith in, and service to, God may be expressed in the following aspects:

231

TORAT YISRAEL: Torah as learning and the love of learning, the central pillar of Judaism, whereby the exemplary Jew is not merely the *learned* Jew but the *learning* one.

MIDDOT YISRAEL: The affirmation of the moral life as the purpose and unifying thread of all human existence and the practice of Judaism based on this conception.

AHAVAT YISRAEL: Love of the Jewish people as individuals for one another, that which brings them to share a common destiny in living fellowship.

KELAL YISRAEL: The communities of Jews bound by a common Tradition and mutual responsibility, united throughout the world and the generations.

MIKDASH YISRAEL: The synagogue as historically understood, community sanctuary and meeting-house for prayer and instruction.

ERETZ YISRAEL: The homeland of the Jewish People and the center of its Tradition.

This is the Jewish heritage interpreted conceptually. Six points are interlaced into one pattern like the Star of David. One word weaves through all six aspects: *Yisrael*—the People of Israel. It is the living Jewish People which bears and interprets its Tradition. In every generation, and in this moment, too, Jews, wherever they dwell, are the historical Community of Yisrael. Through them the ancient heritage is embodied, and only through them can the ancient heritage address mankind.

Fortified by their Tradition and by their faith in it, the Jewish People learned to apply themselves creatively to historical change. Some of the most difficult confrontations of the Jews with new environmental forces were overcome by relating the Tradition to developing world thought, even as the Jews guarded their solidarity and integrity as a People. From the earliest contact of the ancient Hebrews with Egyptian civilization, through the spiritual struggle during the first and Second Commonwealths with the cultures of the Near East and the Mediterranean, and after the dispersion, with the spreading dominion of Christianity and Islam, the Jews as a People, sooner or later, came to grips with the environing culture, contributing to it and accepting what they could from it.

In the perspective of world evolution the very survival of the Jews and Judaism seems remarkable. Yet at the same time the losses cannot be ignored. These losses were sustained not only because of physical persecution, but because of spiritual and intellectual inability to cope with the challenge of the new societal influences. However varying the factors which confronted the Jews in the respective civilizations with which they were in contact, from the ancient cultures of the Fertile Crescent to those of modern Europe, the Biblical idea of *She'erit,* Remnant, seemed to be the inexorable law of Jewish history. Whether understood as Divine Will or the destiny of Israel, out of the crucible of each epoch, in their own Land or in the countries of the Dispersion, always a remnant remained. And this remnant carried forward the Tradition of Judaism and its People. . . .

. . . If this sense of readiness for change is to lead to wise and creative action, conscious knowledge of the present is indispensable. Such knowledge builds, in the first instance, on the recognition and interpretation of the salient elements shaping world Jewry. These elements fall into a wide range of categories. These include the creation of new settlements throughout the world; economic restratification; the movement from town to metropolitan communities; the environmental cultural impact on Jews in the open societies; the increasing variety of Jewish identification; the continuing tension between the Jewish tradition and contemporary secular civilization; the developing acceptance of the religious difference as the most legitimate distinction between the Jewish tradition and contemporary secular civilization; the developing acceptance of the religious difference as the most legitimate distinction between citizens in the western countries; the evolving influence of the sovereign State of Israel on world Jewry; the changing relationships between the respective communities in world Jewry. Here the intention is to touch upon a few of these elements only in order to present a general illustration of the theme. . . .

ENLARGEMENT OF CULTURAL CONTACT

In most of the new countries to which they came, the Jews quickly acquired freedom. Moving from the category of tolerated non-citizens, or limited citizens, to full citizenship, they enjoyed expanding political and economic opportunities. Industrial urbanism and technological advances increased the size of the middle classes in the general population, and the Jews shared in this evolution in time. They have become a predominantly middle-class and urban group, engaged in business, clerical, administrative and professional occupations. Living in countries with high and continually rising standards of civilization, and with educational and cultural institutions increasingly available to all citizens, the Jews also benefited greatly. In the United States, for example, some two-thirds of Jewish college-age youth are receiving a university education.

Yet varying degrees of discrimination in many spheres of the economy and in the larger society exist. Nor has anti-Semitism disappeared from even the most advanced democratic societies. It assumes different shades and different forms—covert or organized, ideological, religious, racial, nationalistic, economic or social anti-Semitism. But it is ever present. On the other hand, a remarkable intellectual receptivity to the values and ideas of Judaism has developed in recent decades in many centers of culture, particularly on the European continent and in the United States. Perhaps the reasons derive from the shame of western civilization for the Holocaust, but the general literary scene is marked by scholarly works, novels and essays on Jewish themes, which are read in ever-widening circles by a growing non-Jewish public. Moreover, the more sober elements of the various populations are beginning to recognize anti-Semitism as an affliction to the society-at-large.

In the process of this socio-economic and cultural enlargement, Jewish group life has been profoundly affected. As the Jews participated in the cultures around them, they were no longer apart, but organic to the wider context in which they flourished. The Jews naturally began to draw from the national and human cultural roots of their respective environments. In their desire to become indigenous, to create in and for their new countries, most of them neglected their Jewish source. The result is that the historic Jewish tradition no longer fills the basic experience of most of diasporic Jewry. Radical changes in Jewish education and language demonstrate this emphatic shift in twentieth century Jewish life.

While the Jewish passion for learning has remained undiminished in modern times, its center has moved from Jewish classic study to broader humanistic and scientific education. In most lands of their residence, the Jewish People, founders of universal education in the First Century, C.E., conduct Jewish education systems which are regarded as inferior to, subordinate, or supplementary to the prevailing systems of general education. A paradox reigns: of all generations, the present generation of Jews is probably the most educated in general studies; in Jewish learning it is perhaps the least literate. . . .

THE INCREASING VARIETY OF JEWISH IDENTIFICATION

The dual development of enlarged general cultural experience and the weakening of the Jewish historical culture in the shaping of the Jewish self-image has brought many Jews into a state of constant temporary environment in the dominant society and the Jewish heritage from which they do not wish to detach themselves. The experience of alienation has expressed itself in a variety of ways: the attenuation of ties with the Jewish group, so that an individual Jew born into Judaism can live his lifetime as a Jew without any relation to it, simply by not severing his bond; the growing phenomenon of mixed marriage without conversion, wherein the intermarried neither leaves his Faith nor formally accepts another, and where his children become members of a new element of "half-Jews"; the development of an amorphous cult of Jewish intellectuals who profess "Jewishness" but avoid the road to knowledge of Judaism or to its practice as a way of life.

Here one must emphasize that the spectrum of Jewish identification is very large. In many Jewish circles the very same factors which brought confusion to some have generated in others emotional and intangible reactions which are reflected in increasing synagogue association, communal support and campaign contributions. And for the Jewish community as a whole these influences have intensified religious life, motivated Jewish education and increased commitment to the aspirations of the Jewish People in many sectors of Jewry where formerly such developments were hardly conceivable. . . .

THE LEGITIMATION OF THE RELIGIOUS DIFFERENCE

In most western countries the motive force of Jewish group life is socio-economic integration and preservation of religio-cultural identity. Under varying circumstances and within the respective contexts of national policy, Jewish religious separateness is legally defined and guaranteed as individual or group volition. Yet invariably the social and cultural milieu in the western countries is strongly influenced by Protestant or Catholic Christianity even where secularism is a powerful factor, and the tendency is to fall under the sway of the dominant, or established, religion.

However, an exceedingly important basic change is taking place in world attitude towards religious affiliation, a change which is being expressed in different ways within the religious groups. In the United

States and elsewhere, for example, religious pluralism is taking root both as an idea and as a social reality. Formerly the dominant religion not only taught the exclusiveness of its truth but brought its weight to bear on the total national culture and polity. Now many religious groups are divesting themselves of the aura of exclusiveness in organization and policy, although not in theology. This has been felt in inter-religious group activities that have developed on local, national and world levels. An emphatic expression of the ecumenical spirit was reflected in the establishment of the World Council of Churches in 1948. Initiated by the Protestant churches it achieved the later participation of Catholic observers. Another historic development is the present Ecumenical Council which has been called to reconsider Catholic attitudes in a mid-twentieth century world. . . .

. . . The progressive formation of Jewish group life around the religious distinction, whether by choice, social force, or political imperative, poses new problems for Jewish communities everywhere. The one kind of tension evolves from the growing need for regrouping within Jewish communal life. The centrality of the Synagogue in Jewish life is not a new phenomenon. Until the era of Emancipation about one hundred and fifty years ago, it was the primary institution around which, and through which, other Jewish associations drew strength. Moreover, the process of recognizing Jewish communities as religious collectivities has been an ongoing one into our own time. But centrality is not totality. Confusing even the nucleus for the whole, as some Jewish religious leaders have pointed out, may lead to a weakening of the center itself. Coordinate roles in the Jewish scheme of things have to be worked out for all the other elements in Jewry, for example, for those who may or may not profess belief, but whose attachments are to the secular, cultural, ethical, ethnic or political expressions of Jewish life. If Community is to become co-extensive with Synagogue, will these Jews fall away and seek expression for these attachments outside the Jewish group? Or does this imply more profound changes in the synagogue outlook? Can there be a meeting between these two broad categories within a synagogal framework? And if not, can distinctive Jewish forms in the diaspora survive outside the religious tradition?

Obviously these questions are not academic. They represent a serious challenge to the character of Jewish life during the contemporary period of transformation. And they bear the seeds of even greater challenges if the Jewries of the West someday will meet and interact, as it is hoped, with the Jews of Russia. In this great segment

—the second largest—of diaspora Jewry, two generations of the Communist regime and education have not stamped out the feeling of Jewish identification, although the majority of Jews in Russia have divested of religious association.

From another vantage entirely, the pervasive influence of Israel needs also to be considered in this connection. Although Jewish religious life and institutions in Israel are flourishing and increasing in influence—indeed, antagonists of the religious groups contend that their influence is disproportionate—nevertheless the basic cohesive force in Israel is modern secular nationalism. Ultimately devoted to the welfare of the Jewish people everywhere, and granting authority to the rabbinate in matters of personal status and in other areas, yet its own commitment is to create on the basis of its sovereignty a modern civilization with all that this connotes in the contemporary world. . . .

. . . The effects of the growing influence of the State of Israel on world Jewry and the changing relationships between the diasporic communities also raise questions which cannot be evaluated with adequate objectivity. Sixteen years after the establishment of the State, its real place as a creative force in world Judaism is far from being understood by either diasporic or Israeli Jewry. Israel, and all that brought it into being, have given an impetus to Jewish creativity in all its manifestations throughout the Diaspora. The fact, for example, that Hebrew—and all that it implies—is spoken again as a living tongue, and that out of Zion have come forth scholars, scientists and artists, has evoked an attitude of renewed respect for Jewish culture in the broader intellectual circles. Great numbers of Jews have come to learn about their People and Tradition through the creative power of Israel. Yet, one of the dominant problems which grew out of the very fact of the new state's emergence is far from being resolved. Never before in their history were the Jews granted the combination of two simultaneous freedoms: on the one hand the freedom possessed by great concentrations of Jewry in various countries to maintain and deepen their own religio-cultural identity as Jews and, on the other, the freedom for Judaism to flourish as it will in its native Hebraic tradition in the sovereign home of the Jewish People. One of the most complicated issues facing world Jewry is avoiding the possibility that these simultaneous freedoms will lead to separated diasporic and Israeli cultures. A question permanently on the agenda of world Jewry is to determine how spiritual interdependence between Israel and the diaspora can be defined and effectuated.

The evolving character of the relationship between the respective communities in the diaspora enters emphatically into this nexus. Perhaps a new vision of the Jewish People as a living and creative organism will emerge, with Eretz Yisrael as its nuclear center, embracing the totality of the Jewish tradition and historic experience of all Jewish communities in time and in space. This might well be the singular transcendant concept which will weave the variegated strands of worldwide Jewish thought and action into a unified whole. Certainly the astounding advances in technology and worldwide interaction offer a spectacular opportunity to examine this possibility in a way never before attempted or conceived. A new physical unity exists among the Jews, between Israel and the diaspora, and between the various Jewish communities. How the space revolution influences ideas is already manifest by the new forms of Jewish coordinated effort in the spheres of mutual aid, culture and religion. It has become possible for distant Jewish communities in different sectors of the world to think and plan together in a manner not hitherto anticipated.

To raise all these questions, and even doubts, is not to fear the future, but rather to confront the realities of the world we live in with faith in the future and in the power of our generation to meet its challenges. A people, like an individual, is measured not only by what it is, but by what it is becoming. While it is impossible to anticipate the outcome of this struggle with world elements in which the Jewish People is now engaged, the Jews can draw upon two major historical forces in this struggle: the Jewish tradition, the continuing Idea which has motivated Jewry throughout the generations, and the vast experience which has taught the Jews how to live, meet and learn from the civilizations of the world. By virtue of their long and tried history as a world people, the Jews have developed a measure of sensitivity and alertness which can enable them not only to respond but perhaps even to anticipate the phenomena of this age. It is therefore not inconceivable that as the Jews pursue a solution to their own crises they may demonstrate to the world how to maintain cohesiveness and integrity in the midst of technological, social and spiritual evolution.

REGAINING UNITY AMID DIVERSITY

If the Jews have so greatly changed in modern times that they now have little in common—surely not a single religion, or one dominant culture, or a language all understand in common (except, perhaps, English)—what makes them a people? What constitute their shared traits? Ben Halpern, who teaches at Brandeis University, points out, moreover, that while in times past, the Jews were regarded as a "religion" or as a group constituted by a common faith, that view was put to the test and found wanting. With the extraordinary varieties of Jews and Jewish expressions produced by the experiences of the modern world, the Jews should have ceased to form a single identifiable group. Yet that has not happened.

What then has happened? How have the Jews continued to find a common basis for viewing themselves as a group?

What serves to define "Israel" in modern times? For the issues before us are not sociological alone, or even primarily a matter of cultural definition. The issues are important also for the modern interpretation of the classical theological category of "Israel", the Jewish people as a covenanted community, called into being in the service of one God.

Since the "Israel" of old did bulk so large in the theological tradition, we may readily understand why the definition of Jewish peoplehood, viewed within fundamentally secular definitions, also will be an important issue for modern Jewish thought.

In his penetrating reflections on the peoplehood of the Jews, on how they constitute a group, Halpern answers the question, What makes the varieties of social and cultural groups living in various places and under differing circumstances into a single group? What do they have in common? What links them to one another, in the absence of most of the traits a group is likely to exhibit in common?

239

XIX
THE JEWISH CONSENSUS
BEN HALPERN

(From *The Jewish Frontier,* September, 1962, pp. 9-13.)

What holds the Jews together? How has the Jewish people survived? These are perennial questions—that is, they keep cropping up in new forms after we have all got good and tired of them in their old forms. Who among us that remembers the era before the creation of the State of Israel has not lost his patience with the argument whether the Jews were a nation or a religion? No one today will find an audience for this debate, framed in these terms. That there is a Jewish nation can hardly be denied after the creation of the State of Israel. That American Jews enjoy the status of a religious community is a commonplace accepted by everyone. We have settled our old debate over whether the Jews are a nation and not a religious community, or a religious community and not a nation, by proving both opposing views to be true. That is to say, we have settled it paradoxically. The result is that by demonstrating both of the opposing views, we have proved that neither can really answer the underlying question. What at bottom *does* hold the Jews together and how *do* the Jews survive? Now that we have a Jewish nation, pure and simple, in one place, and a Jewish religious community, pure and simple, in another place, it becomes even more puzzling and even more important to know what holds these two together and on what principles they can achieve survival in common.

Thus, we are confronted with a problem which persists even though solutions have been demonstrated for the old terms in which it was once formulated. What usually happens in such cases has happened in this case, too. We are now involved in new debates over terms, including some that were not controversial before, or less sharply so, and others that did not seem at all pertinent before. Having ceased to argue whether the Jews are a nation or a religious community, ideologists concerned with Jewish unity and survival in the new circumstances argue over what is a Zionist and who is a Jew. It is interesting to note that much the same situation exists for those who are professionally concerned not with preserving the Jews but only with understanding them.

"Nation" and "religious group," the terms most common in other ideological debates, are far from being the only conceptions whose application to the Jews has puzzled academic analysts. The Jews have been round pegs inserted in such square holes as "ethnic group," "national minority" or "minority group," "culture" and "sub-culture," "civilization" or "fossil" remains of a civilization, not to speak of "pariah" and "world conspiracy." It will perhaps be only rattling the Jews around in another ill-fitting box to see how they meet the measure of one more set of conceptions. But there may also be some gain in our understanding—both of the Jews and of the conceptions.

Among the peculiar facts concerning the peculiar Jewish people was their success in maintaining a law without a state, a structure of legitimacy without specific sanctions, authority without an organized hierarchy, social discipline without visible controls, and a capacity to perform certain collective political acts without a government. Obviously, some least common denominator of social cohesion and social order must have been at work. The word "consensus," a term used perhaps more widely than any other and defined perhaps less precisely than any other by all schools of political and social science, may be taken to represent that least common denominator. In what sense, then, and to what extent do the Jews have a consensus that unites them and singles them out? What is meant "operationally," as the social scientists say, by this term, and how far are we able to observe the various processes of "consensus" in operation among the Jews?

It is immediately apparent, incidentally, that this question is likely to be differently answered today, after the creation of the State of Israel, than before it, and that still other answers might have been given in even earlier times. In fact, it is one of those questions that we should only think of owing to the outdating of older ways of putting the perennial questions concerning Jewish survival since the rise of [the State] of Israel.

Zionism, crowned by success in creating the State of Israel, bears the authentic hallmark of a truly historic event, everything looks different before and after it in the field of its operation. It is a watershed that divides the lines of thought by which we understand the course of Jewish history. The Zionist movement was essentially an attempt to solve the Jewish problem—that is, to secure Jewish survival—by establishing a new basis of Jewish consensus. This implies, of course, that there was an older, pre-Zionist basis of Jewish consensus, different from the one the Zionists proposed to establish, which had been undermined. It also raises the questions whether any Jewish consensus would exist at all if the Zionist goal failed to be attained, and whether the Jewish people could then survive. Finally, now that the Jewish state has been established by Zionism, the question is forced upon us whether a new basis of Jewish consensus has thereby been established; and if this question should be answered in the negative, then the nature of the Jewish consensus—if not the whole question of Jewish survival—has at any rate become open and fluid this side of the Zionist watershed.

It is fairly clear what constituted the basis of the old Jewish consensus which the Zionists thought to be in collapse and which they hoped to replace. A common tradition of religious law, common rituals and religious practices, a common education in the Hebrew language and literature, and a common religious mythos of the divine, cosmic significance of the Exile of the Jewish People and of the coming Redemption in Zion—these were values in which Jews throughout the world shared universally.

Common values universally shared which bind a people together: such a description might almost serve as a technical definition of the term "consensus." But we should be careful what conclusions we draw from any definition; certainly, from this one. One conclusion looks so obvious that it appears unreasonable to doubt it; yet even this conclusion is unsafe. If certain laws, rituals, linguistic and literary traditions, together with the myth of Exile and Redemption, were the universal values that bound the Jews together, then with their loss, the Jewish people should have disintegrated. But these values *were* lost, and the Jews did *not* fall apart. Perhaps we should put the point in a more realistic and less hypothetical way. In the 19th century, values which had been universal among traditional Jewry still continued to be shared—but only by part of the Jews. There were some who no longer shared them, yet these dissenters continued to be regarded as Jews by the remainder who preserved the old values; and they themselves felt that they belonged to a single community with the traditionalist Jews of their own time and of past generations. If we assume that the traditional values which were universal among Jews in older generations still defined the Jewish "consensus," then it was a "consensus" which could bind together only part of the Jews—those who now began to call themselves Orthodox. Yet, we know that a Jewish community continued to exist comprising in addition to the Orthodox, not only Reform or Liberal Jews but agnostics and atheists, all calling themselves Jews and accepted by the others as Jews. Apparently there must have been a different "consensus" binding them together—that is, a set of values that were *universally* shared among all the Jews.

One of the most striking aspects of the modern Jewish problem is that it is so difficult to define the values of the Jewish "consensus." What well-defined values, after all, could be shared by a traditional Jew from the Carpathians or from Yemen and by an American Jewish undergraduate in an Ivy League college who is worried about his identity crisis? Instead of wasting time on the effort to define such values positively, let us ask ourselves a different question: is it necessary for all values to be well-defined? When I am hungry, do I have to want something specific to eat before I can want anything at all to eat? This hardly seems to be so in our common experience. In fact, it is rather odd and unusual to be seized with a hankering for something specific. A woman may suddenly say she *must* have strawberries or pickles, but we are likely to explain this as a symptom of a physiological disturbance. Money, power, prestige, leisure, fun—many of the normal values men want—are quite general, non-specific, even abstract. It is entirely possible, and even the usual thing, for a whole people to share a universal value that is not merely indefinite but negative—a value like freedom, for instance—and that nonetheless very effectively binds them together.

If we look again at the traditional values that bound the Jewish people together because they shared them universally before the 19th century, it appears that these values themselves were far from being rigidly defined. What was the most striking thing, first of all, about the cohesion and the survival over millennia of traditional Jewry? It was the fact that they were united and survived *without* many of the shared values that are generally believed to hold a normal people together and constitute essential parts of the consensus of comparable groups. Moses Mendelssohn made a great point, in his time, of the distinction of Judaism among the historic world religions as a faith without dogmas, or with only those essential beliefs which any rational man—the Eskimo, to name a notable example—must necessarily accept. The rational faith of Jewish monotheism—or of liberal deism, which men like Mendelssohn believed amounted to virtually the same thing—contained those beliefs which were essential to establish the bonds of morality universal among all men, not the bonds of a consensus universal only among Jews. It was the religious law, according to Mendelssohn, not any specific dogmas, that constituted the shared values of the Jewish consensus.

This, let us note, introduces a new element into the discussion. A consensus based on a shared dogma or belief is quite a different thing from a consensus based on a shared law. A dogma or belief is by nature defined; but it is in the nature of a law to be stated as a rule—that is, to be general, or indefinite. When people are bound together by a shared belief, it is necessary that they agree on a definition of the value they hold in common before they unite and so long as they remain united. When they disagree on definitions, their consensus has vanished and their union disintegrates—if it was really based on no more than a shared belief. But when the consensus that binds people together consists of sharing a common rule of law, they are free to disagree on definitions over a wide range of values. What unites them is an agreement to abide by certain *procedures* in settling their disagreements.

The shared value of such a consensus may be defined only in one respect—in specifying the rules by which people are to settle their most serious arguments, those that threaten to separate them. But when people have been living together for long enough, they may go well beyond this bare minimum and codify many other values upon which they are universally agreed, and which they include in their consensus. Traditional Jewry left many values and even procedures undefined that other peoples and other sects felt it necessary to define as part of their consensus. Not only did Judaism have few dogmas, but the Jewish law was backed by little or no executive power, and the Jewish courts and community had little or no hierarchial authority. On the other hand, over the course of centuries the customs of Jewish communities and the learned decisions on cases brought before scholarly, influential rabbis produced a multitude of minutely-defined values, compiled in elaborate codes of behavior, the most widely-accepted being the *Shulhan Arukh*.

Now let us recall what was the complaint of the 19th century dissenters from traditional Jewry, especially those who sought a new basis for the Jewish consensus. They made the really astonishing accusation that the Jews had lost their consensus. They said that the Jews no longer had any sense of obligation, of loyalty, of fellow feeling, even among themselves, but were only a disorganized collection of egoists. Because they were frightened and oppressed egoists, it is true that they clung together in self-defense. Moreover, they were oppressed not only by the Gentile world, that still applied medieval restrictions against the Jews, but also by their own superstitious submission to the rabbis. The *Shulhan Arukh*, then, and the entire institutional structure of religious law and education, that were the universal values of the traditional Jewish consensus, were attacked by these critics from a rather unexpected angle. Even though the traditional institutions commanded universal obedience among the Jews of their times—with the exception of the dissenters, a small minority of so-called "enlightened" Jews—the modernist critics denied that the tradition represented a Jewish consensus. Obedience to it, they claimed, was mechanical or even compelled: that is, without the conviction—or, to use a more current terminology, the sense of identification—that a true consensus requires.

One could say a great deal about the accuracy of this criticism, but what interests us in this connection are some further observations about the nature of social consensus which is implied. These implications, needless to say, were not drawn by the Jewish Enlightenment of the late 18th early 19th century. For they were not contemporary political sociologists. But for anyone reading it today the somewhat ambivalent defense of the Jews by a man like Mendelssohn is quite revealing. The Jews, he said, had few dogmas, and their consensus was not founded on universal beliefs, but on universal practices prescribed by religious law. On the other hand, he and his group were *opposed* to the rule of the rabbis and the power of excommunication upon which the Jewish consensus of his time rested; and from time to time they argued that there was no real Jewish consensus at all, only a mechanical or coerced obedience. This implies, first, that a consensus demands conviction, not only compliance even when it is based not on universal beliefs but on universal practices, on rules of law and agreements regarding procedures for collective decision. It also implies that a rule of law which becomes rigidly codified tends to lose its value as an element of consensus. In fact, a free commitment to live together regardless of disagreements probably requires elastic rules of law. . . .

. . . What sort of consensus is involved here, where men are bound together in a community of fate? What kind of common values distinguish this union? It is certain, at any rate, that what binds them together more resembles the shared value of common rules of law and procedure than the shared value of common beliefs. Only because they are constantly involved in the consequences of each other's acts need each care what the other wants. A consensus based on common beliefs is not essential, only a consensus on common actions or abstentions from action.

A further point must be made, however. A community of fate can be a community that is not bound together at all, only thrown together. Men may be in the same boat, but only if and when they want to act, need they agree; if they simply share the same plight in total passivity, they need not even communicate, let alone agree.

To share a common fate in total isolation from each other is, of course, an imaginary idea rather than a condition one is likely to encounter in reality. But it is not nearly so imaginary to think of a community whose sole bond of consensus is their awareness that they are in the same boat. Such a community will not seek a course of common action, and thus will not build up the kind of active consensus which the Zionists prescribed as the solution of the Jewish problem. They will not even share with each other their understanding of the common fate by speaking to each other in the idiom of a common religious tradition, as pre-modern Jewry could, or of a national literary tradition, as proponents of secular *Yiddishkeit* [Jewishness] desired. Yet passing one another with faces averted or with brief nods and smiles, the members of this community, thrown together by fate, will be bound together by a consensus, too—a consensus of shared sensitivity. It is hard to imagine a common denominator of consensus more minimal than this. This, however, is the bond of union freely accepted by a whole school—a school, perhaps, in the same sense as a school of fish, but nevertheless a school of young Jewish intellectuals in our own time and country. It is, also, if one may believe reports, a common condition among many of the current generation of young Jewish college students.

For the present purposes, we must stop at this point. To have spun out the analysis of Jewish consensus to such a fine-drawn minimum does not, of course, mean that the actual kinds and degrees of consensus in the community are adequately described by the least common denominator. The Jews, in this country and throughout the world, are bound together, and for that matter thrown together, by many different kinds of circumstances, affecting various parts of the community in different ways and degrees. What binds some alienates others. The unity some desire others oppose with hostility or boredom.

I have no doubt whatever that the social scientists who speak of "consensus" with such innocent confidence that they know what they are saying would benefit from a close study of the complex nature of consensus in the always-odd Jewish case. Those who seek to preserve Jewish unity and give more conviction and substance to the Jewish consensus have much too difficult a task to be greatly aided by such a rough mapping of this terrain. But it doesn't hurt, when pulling an oar, to look around once in a while and see who else is in the boat.

FROM CRISIS TO OPPORTUNITY:
A NEW VIEW OF MODERNITY

If you talk to concerned Jews, you will surely hear their worries about "assimilation." They may even speak of "assimilationists"—people who advocate the Jews' dropping all characteristic traits and ceasing to form an identifiable group. "Assimilation" in this context is a loaded word, full of negative significance for the loyal and devoted Jew. For he assumes that the meaning of "assimilation" can only be the end of the Jewish people as a distinct group and of Judaism as a religious or even as a cultural tradition.

Within these worries lurks the fear of change. And the expression of such worries tells us that Jews perceive in their group and in their tradition a great deal of change. The "anti-assimilationists" or "survivalists" then will argue that change is bad—whether change of life-style or of name. One can isolate peculiarly Jewish traits in the multiform cultures of the Jewish communities throughout the world, they claim. One must then struggle to preserve these traits against the tendency to drop them—because dropping qualities or characteristics now regarded as quintessentially Jewish must mean dropping Judaism.

This conception fails for two reasons.

First, it takes the view that "Judaism" is a static, one-dimensional, and unitary phenomenon, which can be precisely defined and described. Any change in this rigid system is bound eventually to lead to its total decay. But it would be difficult to demonstrate that the traits or characteristics regarded as "uniquely Jewish" were so regarded when the Jews adopted them. Yiddish, which has become a profound expression of the Judaic ethos, after all is a Jewish form of medieval German.

Second, the fear of "assimilation" reveals lack of confidence in the resources of Judaism and in the capacities of the Jewish people to adapt and make their own the best traits and qualities of human culture. "Assimilation" is not a bad thing, but potentially a source of regenerative vitality. It is not the harbinger of crisis but the occasion of challenge. This is the argument of Gerson D. Cohen, who is Chancellor of the Jewish Theological Seminary. For him, "assimilation"

249

represents an opportunity, not the reason for dismay or foreboding. And, since he is a historian, he is able to assemble important evidence in behalf of his optimistic and constructive response to change, to growth.

Since the modern situation of Jewry is, as Moshe Davis makes clear, a situation of permanent change, it is just as well to hear from someone who is not frightened of the future or even apprehensive in the present. Since Rabbi Cohen here addresses a graduating class of young teachers of Hebrew and of Judaism, the issue of "assimilation" is particularly pertinent.

XX

THE BLESSING OF ASSIMILATION IN JEWISH HISTORY

Gerson D. Cohen

(From *The Blessing of Assimilation in Jewish History,* by Gerson D. Cohen. Hebrew Teachers College, Commencement Address, June, 1966. Boston, 1966: Hebrew Teachers College.)

. . . The first shibboleth which all of us, and I include myself, have been raised on is that Jewish survival and above all Jewish vitality in the past derived in large measure from a tenacious adherence on the part of our ancestors to all basic external traditional forms. This view has perhaps best been expressed in a renowned sermon of Bar Qappara delivered in the latter part of the second century, and repeated in subsequent centuries with some minor variations. The original statement seems to have been: "Owing to four factors were the people of Israel redeemed from the land of Egypt: they did not alter their names (i.e., Egyptianize them); they did not change their language [from Hebrew]; they did not spread malicious gossip; they were free of sexual licence." The ancient preacher could, of course, adduce scriptural, or what was for him the equivalent of archeological, proof for his assertions. The Israelites in Egypt obviously kept their Hebrew names, for they were known as Reuben and Simeon when they arrived in Egypt, and they were identified by the same names at the time of the Exodus. They did not change their tongue, for from the Biblical account it is obvious that they spoke Hebrew. And if we are to believe the tradition of the Rabbi, they were a unique generation in that they were willing to forgo the pastime of gossip that all subsequent generations considered basic to the fun of life. Finally, they were quite persistent in their adherence to Jewish morality and Jewish family structure.

Popular historical reading of the past went even further and, curiously enough, distorted this dictum to read that there were three factors which enabled our ancestors to be redeemed from Egypt: they retained their names; they adhered to their ancestral tongue; and they retained even their distinctive form of clothing.

of view the [Hebrew-language] culture of Hillel and of Rab has really survived intact. The Jews, we are often quick to protest, have never been a fossilized people. Now if that claim means anything, it must at least mean that the culture of Hillel has undergone tremendous metamorphoses. In each and every generation we have had our exegetes, who have been able to take a core, reinterpret it and maintain its authenticity through *change* and thereby through *contemporary relevance*.

Just as a matter of historical fact, Alexandrian Jewry also survived. Alexandrian Jewry did not defect to Hellenistic religion, nor did it convert to Christianity, the unfounded claims of some to the contrary notwithstanding. What happened to it was precisely what happened to many Jewish communities throughout history. It suffered expulsion and subsequently, after having reestablished itself, was conquered by an Arabic speaking empire. At that point it proceeded to do what other Jewish communities did; it changed its language. Since the books of Philo were no longer particularly relevant, or, had, because of other circumstances, become forgotten, Philo was relegated to a bookshelf, and left to those groups that continued to find him useful. (Parenthetically, I should hasten to add that the question of Philo is by no means closed. Modern Jewish scholars have been repeatedly coming up with the suggestion that Philo had some direct form of influence on the earliest Jewish philosophers in the Gaonic period and that he was thus by no means forgotten in learned circles.)

In other words Alexandrian Jewry did survive as a corporate group. Indeed, it survived not only as a group but as a living tradition that left its stamp on Judaism. Professor Elias Bickerman, the great modern Jewish Hellenist, has stressed that Alexandrian Jewry was unique in that it alone of all Hellenistic ethnic groups was able to survive as a living culture, and that it was able to do so precisely *because* of its ability to translate its culture, that is, to undergo a considerable amount of assimilation. The translation of the Bible into Greek was a phenomenon almost unique in the history of Hellenistic culture. The Hellenistic kings who succeeded Alexander the Great put up considerable sums of money to stimulate some of the ancient priestly groups in Egypt and in Babylonia to revive and to create anew in their own traditions. Some priests of those peoples did. Accordingly, we have Akkadian literature from as late as the first century B.C.E. But this literature had very little effect on the masses, for it was the property of isolated groups—of esoteric priestly circles—who insisted that their religion could be expressed authentically only in the ancestral tongue. Egyptian religion could only be expressed in ancient Egyptian forms.

Babylonian religion could be expressed only in the Babylonian tongue. As a consequence, these traditions ceased to have any wide and sustained impact. By way of contrast, the Jews were willing to change their language even for religious expression. Consequently, the Jews were able to bring their message to their own people, as well as to the world at large, in every language under the sun.

The point that Bickerman has so cogently made for Hellenistic Judaism can, I believe, be appropriately applied to many another period of Jewish history. A frank appraisal of the periods of great Jewish creativity will indicate that not only did a certain amount of assimilation and acculturation not impede Jewish continuity and creativity, but that in a profound sense this assimilation or acculturation was even a stimulus to original thinking and expression and, consequently, a source of renewed vitality. To a considerable degree, the Jews survived as a vital group and as a pulsating culture because they changed their names, their language, their clothing and with them some of their patterns of thought and expression. This ability to translate, to re-adapt and re-orient themselves to new situations, while retaining a basic inner core of continuity, was largely responsible, if not for their survival, at least for their vitality. . . .

. . . We Jews have always been and will doubtless continue to be a minority group. Now a minority that does not wish to ghettoize itself, one that refuses to become fossilized, will inevitably have to acculturate itself, i.e. to assimilate at least to some extent. If it wants to do business with the people among whom it lives, it will have to learn the spoken tongue, and it will have to re-orient its clothing and its style of life. And given the basically limited mental energy that most people have, the need to learn one tongue will cause the older to be forgotten by most. So it has always been, and so it will continue to be. Moreover, the change of forms inevitably causes a certain metamorphosis in content.

Even these changes in content should not necessarily alarm us. Throughout Jewish history there have been great changes in law, in thought and in basic categories of expression, reflecting the need of the Jews to adapt themselves and their way of life to new conditions. This assimilation and adaptation was not the consequence of a desire to make things easier but rather the result of a need to make the tradition relevant. Once again, permit me to cite some examples.

If rabbinic Judaism was able to proselytize and to win so many thousands of souls to its ethical monotheism, it was precisely because rabbinic Judaism was able to reinterpret and reformulate the Bible largely in Hellenistic terms. Every student of rabbinism knows that the Hebrew language underwent a major metamorphosis under the impact of Greek language and Greek culture. Instead of protesting against this natural growth, the rabbis appropriated it and made use of it, so as to express themselves in terms that were relevant to the Hellenistic milieu.

In the great challenge of assimilation in the Gaonic period the leadership followed the same procedure. Saadiah Gaon, who translated the Bible into Arabic, tells us that in Baghdad he found fourteen types of Jewish heresy, which required him to compose his great book on *Beliefs and Opinions*. Saadiah chose realistically to write his book not in Hebrew, but in Arabic. Far more important, in defending the traditions of Judaism, Saadiah appealed to reason and philosophy no less than to authority and precedent. In doing so, he not only appropriated intellectual tools from the surrounding Arabic world, but he himself helped to accelerate the process of the assimilation of rabbinic Judaism to the canons and tastes of the intellectual Arabic society. As a responsible teacher, he addressed his own generation and spoke to them in a language that would be intelligible and relevant to them. The same was true of Moses Maimonides and of his son, Abraham. Abraham Maimonides, indeed, in an effort to make the synagogue a more effective instrument for piety, unabashedly changed a number of practices within the synagogue to conform to patently Arabic tastes.

We could go on with such examples endlessly. If there is anything that modern scholarship has taught us about the history of Jewish culture, it is that a familiarity with the general milieu in which Jews lived is indispensable to an understanding of a particular phase of Jewish culture. How can we understand the drives behind the "golden age" of Spain, the theological and moralistic emphases of Franco-German pietism, or the mystical doctrines and associations of the Hasidim of medieval Egypt without some acquaintance with Arabic literary tastes, medieval Christian theology, and Sufism respectively? And what is the Jewish appropriation of many of these tendencies if not religious and intellectual assimilation? . . .

. . . The great and, to a considerable extent, salutary transformations that overtook the Jews during the nineteenth and twentieth centuries have likewise been in large measure products of assimilation. The rebirth of Hebrew, the growth of *Jüdische Wissenschaft* [science of Judaism], the liberalization of Jewish religion, the acceptance of Yiddish as a respectable vehicle of Jewish literary expression, the growth of Jewish nationalism,—the State of Israel itself—in short, all those great changes and developments which characterize modern Jewish history and which have made the lot of countless Jews infinitely more rich and pleasant than it had ever been previously are the effects of assimilation. This very institution [Boston Hebrew College], where Jewish tradition is taught critically and dispassionately, is one of many examples of the blessing that assimilation can bring to a community such as ours.

There are, of course, two ways of meeting the problem of assimilation. The first is withdrawal and fossilization, on which we need not dwell here. However, there is and always was an alternative approach of taking the bull by the horns, as it were, and utilizing the inevitable inroads of assimilation as channels to new sources of vitality. In seeking to distinguish this type of assimilation and imitation from the kind which aims at obliterating Jewish identity, Ahad Ha-am characterized the cultural products born of assimilation as the imitation motivated by the desire to compete—rather than to be absorbed—*hiqquy shel hitharut* [imitation] rather than of *hitbolelut* [assimilation]. In competitive imitation Ahad Ha-am detected the signs of health and vigor rather than of attrition and decadence. There can be little doubt that Ahad Ha-am's reading of the past was highly perspicacious. Who will deny that much of Jewish philosophy and belles lettres were almost conscious efforts at imitation and competition with the majority cultures among whom Jews lived? . . .

I would, therefore, rather speak of the healthy appropriation of new forms and ideas for the sake of our own growth and enrichment. Assimilation properly channeled and exploited can thus become a kind of blessing, for assimilation bears within it a certain seminal power which serves as a challenge and a goad to renewed creativity. The great ages of Jewish creativity, as we have seen, have always been products of the challenge of assimilation and of the response of leaders, who were to a certain extent assimilated themselves, and there is no reason why the present age should not also be.

In short, assimilation is not a one way street. Very much like the Torah itself, it is a drug capable of paralyzing or of energizing, depending on how we take it and how we react to it. This is, of course, why an institution such as this and its graduates occupy a position of central importance. As trained persons, steeped in their tradition, but alert to the needs and challenges of our own day, they can help control and guide the effects of assimilation on the community at large. As Jews committed to their tradition, and as young men and women in command of the sources and the tools for the instruction of others, they are equipped to meet the present generation on its own footing and in its own language. As a group trained to read and understand classical Jewish sources in their original languages, such a group will also contribute to the unending chain of Jewish literary creativity and to the revitalization of Jewish thought and expression. Hopefully, they will do so by creating in Hebrew as well as in English, in professional as well as popular terms, so that the best of their thought and research is felt on all levels of the community. . . .

. . . The Torah, Krochmal was fond of reminding us, is very much like a path which is beset on one side with freezing cold and on the other with consuming fire. Somehow each of us has to work his way to the middle and derive the benefits of both coolness as well as warmth so that he can come to those great resources which it purports to hold.

PART IV

CONCLUSION

The predominant trait of modernity is secularization, the definition and meaning of which are decisive in the theological description of modern Judaism.

What constitutes the secular, as against the religious, way of being?

How has contemporary Judaism, both classical and modern, responded to the condition of secularization? In what ways was Judaism able to cope with, indeed to profit from the new seriousness about, emphasis upon, this world and its concerns?

The answers to these questions conclude our description of the theological side of the Judaic tradition.

XXI

JUDAISM IN THE SECULAR AGE

Jacob Neusner

(From *Journal of Ecumenical Studies*, Vol. 3, No. 3, 1966, pp. 519-541.)

Professor Harvey Cox defines secularization as "the movement of man's primary interest and attention from other worlds beyond or above this one and to this world. This includes the loosing of this world from its dependency on mythical, metaphysical, or religious dualism of any sort. It means therefore taking this earthly realm, with all its health and hope, with all its sickness and sin, in utter seriousness." What is the meaning of the new age for Jews? for Judaism's relationships to the world?

I. *Secularization and the Jews*

No religion may be adequately compared to another. Each has its particularities which render comparison a distortion. Judaism cannot be compared to Christianity, for example, as if each component of the one had its functional or structural equivalent in the other. Christians understand by "religion" a rather different phenomenon, for it seems to Jews, perhaps wrongly, that Christians lay far greater stress upon theology and matters of belief as normative and probative than does Judaism. A Christian is such by baptism or conversion, by being called out into a new and sacred vocation of faith. A Jew is never *not* a Jew according to Jewish law. He is *born* into the Jewish situation. There was never a time that he was a man but not a Jew. There can be no time when he will cease to be a Jew, for, as the Talmud says, though he sin, he remains "Israel." The Jewish ethnic group is never perceived by Jewish theology to be a secular entity, therefore, and therein lies the root of much misunderstanding. Christians speak of "secular Jews," by which they mean Jews divorced from the profession of Jewish faith and the practice of the *mitzvot*. But Judaism does not, and cannot, regard such Jews as "secular," for they all are children of Abraham, Isaac, and Jacob. Their forefathers stood at Sinai and bound them for all time by the terms of a contract to do and hear the word of God. That contract has never been abrogated, and though individuals may forget it, its Maker can never forget them. A Jew who does not keep the Covenant still has its imprint engraved in his flesh. His children do not require conversion if they choose to assume its responsibilities. The world, moreover, has understood the indelibility of the covenant, for it has persisted in regarding as Jews many who regard themselves as anything but Jewish; and it has murdered the seed of Abraham into the third generation. . . .

. . . It is a fact, moreover, that Jews quite alien to the Torah retain a very vivid sense of being part of a historical, if not of a supernatural, community. They yearn to see their children marry other Jews, though this may represent no more, in the eyes of the world, than ethnic loyalty. They insist that their children associate with other Jews, even though association may have what Christians will regard as a wholly secular setting. But Judaism cannot regard the Jewish group as a secular enterprise, as I said, for it advances a very different view of what it means to be a Jew. It lays great stress upon community, upon the chain of the generations, upon birth within the covenant. As Professor Monford Harris writes: "The secularized gentile is precisely that: a secularized gentile. But the secularized Jew is still a Jew. The Jew that sins is still a Jew, still a member of covenantal Israel, even when he denies that covenant." One cannot stress this fact too much: *there can be no Judaism without Jewishness,* that is, without ethnic identification. Judaism cannot be reduced to its "essence," whether that be construed as ethical, theological, or even behavioral. We know full well that there can be Jewishness without Judaism, and against this many of us struggle within the Jewish community. In our effort to keep the issues of Judaism to the fore, we may criticize the ethnic emphasis of the community as it is. But we struggle within that community precisely because it is what it is: all that is left of the remnant of Israel in this world. Its worldliness is a challenge. But the ethnic-Jews are right, and we are wrong, when they undertake, as quite legitimately *Jewish,* activities of no particular Jewish relevance, and when they stress the value of association with other Jews for its own sake. They want thereby to preserve the group. Our regret is that they seem to have forgotten why. But the instinct is fully sound, and we critics must never forget it.

And who are these Jews, who cannot despite themselves achieve secularization? They are the bearers of an unbroken myth, a this-worldly group affirming the world and joining in its activities with re-

ligious fervor, yet regarding themselves, whether they be religious in
the Christian sense or not, in terms the objective observer can regard
only as preposterous, or religious. These Jews see themselves as a
group, though their group should have ceased to hold them when the
faith lost its hold upon them, and that is a paradox. They see themselves as bound to others, in other lands and other ages, whom they
have never seen, and with whom they have practically nothing in common but—it is claimed—common forefathers. This too is a paradox.
They see their history as one history, though they are not everywhere
involved in it. They reflect upon the apocalyptic events of the day as
intimately and personally important to them. They died in Auschwitz.
They arose again in the State of Israel. They respond passionately,
no matter how remote they are from Judaism, to the appeal of the
flesh, of Israel *after the flesh,* and see themselves in a way that no religious Jew can call secular, however secular they themselves would
claim to be. This too is a paradox: They bear fears on account of the
past, though that past is nothing to them except that it is the Jews'.
They have nightmares that belong to other men but are not within
their personal experience at all, except that they are Jews. They see
themselves as brands plucked from the burning, though they never
stood near the fire. The classical faith demands that each man see himself as redeemed at Sinai from bondage to Pharaoh. The modern
Jew, secure in America or Canada or Australia or the State of Israel,
persists within the pattern of the classical faith, but in a far more
relevant form of it. He was saved from Auschwitz and rebuilt the
land. The ties that bind other groups of immigrants within the open
societies in the West have long since attenuated. Despite the decline of
faith, the ties that bind the Jews are stronger than ever, into the
third and fourth and fifth generation and beyond. Nor can one
ignore the mystery of Soviet Jewry, of whom we know so little and
understand nothing. They persist. They ought not. All we know is that
almost fifty years after the Bolshevik revolution, young people, raised
in isolation from the Judaic tradition and from the Jewish world,
trained to despise religion and above all Judaism, profess to be
Jews, though they need not, and accept the disabilities of Jewishness,
though these are by no means slight. Before this fact of contemporary
Jewish history we must stand in silence. We cannot understand it. No
worldly or naturalist explanation suffices to explain it. In my view, it
is not a secular phenomenon at all, though it can be explained in a
worldly way to the satisfaction of the world.

This is the paradox of the secular age. The Jews have said for almost two centuries that they are a religious group, and have accepted, by and large, the Christian world's criteria for religion. They have told the world they are different by virtue of "religion," though they claimed that "religion" for them means pretty much what it means to others. And yet the secular world sees Jews who are not different from itself, for they have no professed religion. By their own word, such Jews, and they are very many, should have ceased to exist. Yet they are here, and they are Jews, and "Jewishness" is important to them in terms that the Christian and secular worlds alike find not at all "religious." . . .

A second paradox is that the Jews have allied themselves with secularizing forces from the very beginning. Claiming to be merely Germans, or French, or Canadians, or Americans of the Jewish faith, they have chosen for themselves a place among those who struggled for the secularization of culture, politics, art, and society. The reason is, alas, that they had no choice. The forces of religion, meaning Christianity wherever it was established, invariably allied themselves to those of reaction, in opposing the emancipation of the Jews. Rarely do we find an exception to the rule: the more he was a Christian, the more he hated Jews. It therefore is no paradox at all that Jews have favored the secularization of institutions and of men, for if they hoped for a decent life, it was only upon a secular foundation that emancipation was possible. Even today, moreover, Christians would still prefer to use the institutions of the common society to propagate their faith. The public schools are still supposed to celebrate the great events of Christian sacred history, and Jewish children must still confront, and deny, the Christian message once or twice a year.

Christian opposition to secularization is by no means a mere vestige of earlier days. It is rather, I think, a fear of the need to believe *despite* the world, a fear of faith itself. For many centuries it has been natural to be a Christian. The world was mostly Christian, and where it was not, it was the realm of the devil and the Jews. Christians could aspire, therefore, to the creation of a metaphysic and a natural theology which, from the bare artifacts of the world, would rise, in easy stages, to the heights of Calvary. Metaphysics, religious philosophy, natural theology—these are naturally Christian enterprises, for only a Christian could conceive so benign and friendly a vision of the world as to ask the world to strengthen, even to provide reasonable foundations within experienced reality for, his Gospel. It is no accident that Judaism has produced only a highly parochial metaphysic, very little natural theology, and a religious philosophy whose main task was to mediate between Judaism and the world. Judaism has had to stress revelation, and not a worldly apprehension of faith, because the world for two thousand and more years has offered little solace. Judaism has had to say *no* to many worlds, though it is not therefore a habitually negating tradition. It has had to say to pagans that God is not in nature; to mighty empires that the King of kings of kings alone is king; to Christians that redemption is not yet; to Bolshevism that Israel lives despite the "laws of history. It has had to say no because of its first and single affirmation: We shall do and we shall hear.

The result is that Judaism has looked, as I said, for very little help from the world. It has not presumed that the artifacts of creation would lead to Sinai; that a natural theology would explain why a Jew should keep the Sabbath or refrain from eating pork; that a communicable, non-mythological metaphysic would show Israel in a rational situation. In its early centuries, Christianity comprehended the Jewish situation. The apostle Paul offered not a reasonable faith, beginning with worldly realities and ending at the foot of the cross. He offered a scandal to the Jews and foolishness to the Greeks, and said it was faith, and faith alone, which was demanded of the Christian; and it was by virtue of that faith, for it was a very difficult thing, that the Christian would be saved. Scandal and foolishness are sociological realities. From the fourth century onward, to be a Jew was a scandal to the Christians, and foolishness, later on, to Islam. It was faith despite the world, and not because of it, that Judaism required, and received. This is the kind of faith with which Christianity begins, and, I believe, which is demanded once again. The Christian today is called to choose between Christ and the world, for the world is no longer his. I do not say it is a better world on that account, but it *is* a different world. I do not think however Judaism has suffered for its recognition and acceptance of the situation of *Golah,* of exile not only from the earthly land, but also from the ways of the world. While Christianity is entering a time of exile, it need not fear greatly, if Christians are prepared to affirm their faith through faith, and not merely through a reasoned apprehension of reality, which is not *faith* at all. As Christianity enters the Jewish situation, it need not, therefore, worry for its future. *Golah* is not a situation to be chosen, but to be accepted at the hand of God as a test of faith and an opportunity for regeneration and purification. We did not choose to go into exile, any more than the Christians would choose to abandon the world. Having gone into exile, having lost the world, Jew and Christian alike may uncover new resources of conviction, new potentialities for sanctity, than they knew they had. We who witnessed the destruction of an ancient Temple learned of new means of service to the creator, that God wants mercy and not sacrifice, in Hosea's terms—deeds of loving kindness, in those of Rabban Yohanan ben Zakkai. It is the world, and not the Temple, that became the arena for God's work. Having lost the world, or wisely given it up, Christians too may recall that "the whole earth is full of His holiness," and that every day and everywhere the world provides a splendid opportunity for witness.

Finally, the advent of secularization offers still another welcome challenge to both Judaism and Christianity. In the recent past, exponents of both traditions have accepted the world's criteria for the truth or value of religion, both Judaism and Christianity. In its grosser form, this acceptance has led to such arguments for religion as those that claim religion is good for one's mental health, or important as a foundation for ethical behavior, and valuable as a basis for a group's persistence, or a nation's. In all instances religion has been evaluated for its service to something else, to health, to decency, to group solidarity. In its more refined form, the worldly argument in behalf of religion has stressed man's need of religion in the face of the absurd; or his dependence upon religion as a source of cogent and unified world-views. We have been told that religion is an answer to human needs. We are supposed to conclude that we ought therefore to foster it. These arguments represent the final blasphemy, the affirmation of faith for worldly purposes. . . . Secularization represents an inquisitorial judgment: the world does not *need* religion. It can provide a sound basis for mental health, a reasonable, though tentative, foundation for ethical action, even—as the Jewish community seems to prove —an adequate basis for group life, without faith in any form. Man does not need religion to overcome the absurd, for he can accept the absurd with the same enthusiasm and life-affirming vitality that he accepts the other artifacts of reality. He can meet his needs elsewhere than at the holy altar.

We who affirm that God made the world need not claim in his behalf that he needs to have done so. We who hold that God acted freely and out of love need not deny that love and that freedom in the name of worldly rationality. Mankind does not need religion. The worldly uses of religion have far more acceptable, secular surrogates. Man does not need to believe in God to avoid insanity, or absurdity, or social disintegration. He does not need to accept revelation in terms that render revelation the result of worldly ratiocination. Mankind is challenged by the world's own power to accept or reject revelation, to affirm or deny God, upon judgment of the real issues.

These issues are, Did God make the world? Does Providence

govern history? Is Torah, meaning truth, from Heaven? The world cannot resolve them for us, though in the joyful acceptance of the world's perquisites, Jews and Christians alike are much enriched. They regain the opportunity to believe, as I said, and to assent with rejoicing to the imperative of Sinai, to accept in submission the yoke of heaven, to love God with all the heart. These have been the classical paradigms of Jewish existence. This world once more renders them vivid.

II. *Secularization and Judaism*

Judaism is both admirably equipped, and completely unprepared for secularization.

It is well equipped to confront an uncomprehending world because of the exigencies of its history. It is, moreover, able to face this world with something more constructive than ungenerous disdain. It has always regarded the world as the stage upon which the divine drama may be enacted. The world presents Judaism with its highest challenge, to achieve sanctity within the profane, to hallow the given, the commonplace. For this task, Judaism comes equipped with Torah and *mitzvot,* Torah which reveals God's will for the secular world, *mitzvot* which tell us how to carry out that will in the here-and-now. Through *mitzvot,* we sanctify the secular, not in a metaphysical sense, nor through theologizing intractible givens. One sees the setting sun and lights a candle, the one a natural perception of the course of the earth upon its axis, the other a perfectly commonplace action. But he adds, "who has commanded us to light the Sabbath light," and the course of nature becomes transformed: a commonplace action transforms it. We don a piece of cloth with fringes, and say, "who has commanded us concerning fringes." That cloth is no longer like any other. It serves as a means of worshipping our Creator. We build a frail hut of branches and flowers at the autumn season, an act of quite natural celebration of the harvest. But we say, "who has commanded us to sit in the *Sukkah,*" and those branches become a sacred shelter. Our table becomes an altar, and the commonplace and profane action of eating food becomes the occasion to acknowledge the gifts of Him who gave it. We speak of our people's humble happenings, of their going forth from slavery to freedom, but doing so is rendered by the commandments into a sacred action, a moment of communion. We open our minds to the wonders of the world, and this too is Torah and requires a benediction. A man takes a wife, and we proclaim the blessings of Eden, the memories of besieged Jerusalem, and the hope for future redemption. Our Tradition leads us not away from the world, but rather into it, and demands that we sanctify the given, and see it as received, commanded from Heaven. All things inspire a sense of awe and call forth a benediction. Nothing is profane by nature, nor is anything intrinsically sacred, but that we make it so. The heavens tell the glory of God. The world reveals his holiness. Through *mitzvot* we respond to what the heavens say; through Torah we apprehend the revelations of the world. Judaism rejoices, therefore, at the invitation of the secular city. It has never truly known another world; and it therefore knows what its imperatives require.

Judaism has always, moreover, understood history, or social change, to be in some measure the exemplification of divine sovereignty. It has understood daily affairs to reveal more than commonplace truths. The destruction of a worldly city was understood from prophetic times onward to be a call for penitance and *teshuvah,* return to God. The sorrows of the age were seen as the occasion for renewed inwardness, prayer, repentance, and doing deeds of compassion, so that men might make themselves worthy of the compassion of God. It has at the same time recognized a tension between event and divine will. Judaism has never merely accepted history, any more than it accepted nature, but sought rather to elevate and sanctify the profane in both. History does not speak God's will in unequivocal terms, for history is to be interpreted, not merely accepted, by means of the Torah. We have seen in revelation a guide to understanding events, and have never uncritically accepted events as themselves bearing unexamined meaning. All things are seen under the aspect of Sinai, and all events must be measured by the event of revelation. We are not, therefore, at a loss to evaluate the changes of an inconstant world. We have, moreover, demanded that God, like ourselves, abide by the covenant. In times of stress, we have called him to account, as much as ourselves. . . .

. . . Judaism has offered a worldly understanding of man's part in the achievement of God's kingdom. Man is the partner in the building of the kingdom. He is needed to perfect the world under the sovereignty of God. Just as the commonplace may be profane or sacred, but the *mitzvot* consecrate, so too the world, society, may be sanctified. That sanctification is of a most practical sort. We are told to heal the sick, free the captives, loosen the bonds that enslave men. A starving world is an affront to God. All the technical skills of men possess the potentiality to achieve holiness, therefore, and all the vocations of men may serve to sanctify the world. The secular city, Professor Cox writes, requires the skill of men. The kingdom of God cannot do without men's abilities. The kingdom of God is meant to find a place in the history of this world, moreover, according to the eschatological theory of significant Jewish thinkers. The only difference between this world and the world to come, or the age to come, will be the end of subjugation to paganism, so said Samuel, the third-century Babylonian master. Israel is meant, furthermore, to live in this world, to bear witness to God in the streets of the city. For centuries, and most immediately in modern Judaism, Jews have seen themselves as bearers of the kingdom, as witnesses to the rule of God over the world. One need hardly stress, therefore, that Judaism is ready and eager for the worldly encounter.

That encounter, however, is by no means neutral. Judaism has seen itself under a very special vocation, as I said, to say *no* to the lesser claims to divinity entertained by this world. It has told the world that sanctity inheres in it, but denied that the world as it is is holy. It has offered the world the promise of redemption, but denied that redemption is just yet. It has borne unflagging testimony to the unredemption of mankind, and insisted upon a radical criticism of the status quo. These are the vocations, too, of the secular city, which denies ultimacy even to religion, all the more so to lesser structures. Judaism has insisted that the world is ever secular, both so that it may be sanctified and so that it may not lose the hope for ultimate redemption.

And yet Judaism is utterly unready for secularization in the current sense. Professor Cox writes that secularization is "the loosing of the world from religious and quasi-religious understandings of itself, the dispelling of all closed world-views, the breaking of all supernatural myths and sacred symbols. . . ." Nothing in my understanding of Judaism suggests that Judaism can accept, or even comprehend, "the loosing of the world from religious . . . understandings of itself." If from my perspective there can be no "secular Jew," there can surely emerge no "secularized Judaism." Judaism begins with the affirmation of a supernatural apprehension of reality, however we may courageously try to formulate that apprehension in naturalistic or humanistic terms. It begins with the proclamation of the unity and sovereignty of God. It offers to the world the spectacle of a people bound to God's service and governed by his will. It tells the world that this people serves as the heart of humanity, the barometer of its health, and that Israel's history becomes paradigmatic for the human condition. Judaism may cope with the world, may indeed affirm this age in the terms I have outlined; but it can never turn away from itself and its primary assent. Our prophets have offered the world the belief that at some times God may hide his face from man. This may be such an age. We can never confuse, however, our own difficulties in belief with ontological or anthropological Godlessness. Sinai has happened. We may not have seen his face, but we have the record that his glory passed before us. Not every age has an equal apprehension of the glory. A handmaiden saw at the Red Sea what was not given to the prophets to see. We know through Torah, and can never, therefore, claim ignorance, only frail forgetfulness. We may, as Rabbi Abraham J. Heschel says, be messengers who have forgotten our message. But we can never forget that we once had a message. We may comprehend the hiddenness of God; indeed, we are those who have most suffered in his absence. We can never confuse that comprehension of *our* condition with the false illusion of *his* absence. We have lived for a long time within the gates of the secular city. Our Tradition has prepared us for, and our condition has taught us the imperatives of, its discipline. We have aspired to its liberties. But these imperatives we accept, these liberties we demand, *upon our own terms.* We are not secular within the secular city, but we are Jews, *yehudim,* upon whom the name of the Lord [YHWH] has been called. We cannot change our name either to add to his discipline that of the world or to win for ourselves the blessings of the world. In the city of this world, or in the world to come, we can only be ourselves, Jews. This is the final paradox of our current situation: we who have confronted the data of secularization long before our neighbors now rehearse our ancient response to these data. We who first told the world of its secularization need now remind it of its consecration.

GLOSSARY

Aggadah (Adjective: *Aggadic*): Lit. "Telling, narration"; generally: lore, theology, fable, biblical exegesis, ethics.

Ahad HaAm: Asher Ginzberg, leading theoretician of Zionism in the early twentieth century.

Ashkenazi, Ashkenazic Jews: Jews in the European, Christian world; Yiddish-speaking Jews; by contrast to *Sephardic* Jews, who came from Spain and lived in the Mediterranean countries, chiefly Islamic ones.

B.C.E., C.E.: Before the Common Era, Common Era, used in preference to B.C. and A.D., which contain religious connotations thought to be incongruous to Judaic discourse.

Beth Midrash: House of Study.

Ehad: One.

El: God.

Gaon: (Adjective: *Geonic*): Eminence, excellency; title of the heads of Babylonian Talmudic academies, particularly in the early Islamic period. *Geonic period:* Period in which the heads of the Babylonian Talmudic academies were the spiritual heads of world Jewry, ninth through twelfth centuries.

Golah: Exile, Jewish communities living outside of the land of Israel. Frequently: Diaspora—dispersion of Jews throughout the world.

Halakhah (Adjective: *Halakhic*): Law, legal.

Hillel: Rabbi who lived about the beginning of the Common Era and taught, "What is hateful to yourself do not do to your fellowman. That is the entire Torah. All the rest is commentary. Now go and learn."

Kabbalah: Tradition of Jewish mystical doctrine.

Karaites: Medieval Jewish movement which rejected the authority of the Talmud and of the Talmudic rabbis. Stressed biblical, as opposed to biblical-Talmudic, view of Judaism.

Kedushah: Sanctification, "Holy, holy, holy is the Lord of hosts." Important prayer.

Maimonides: Twelfth century rationalist philosopher of Judaism.

Midrash: Exegesis of biblical texts.

Mishnah: Corpus of law produced in early third century by Judah the Patriarch. The Talmud consists of the Mishnah and commentaries on it developed from the third to the sixth centuries.

Musaf: Additional Prayer on Sabbaths and festivals, concerning the sacrificial cult in the ancient Temple in Jerusalem. The congregation prays for the restoration of the divine cult.

Mythopoeic: Myth-forming, myth-making.

Oral Torah: Belief that in addition to the written Scriptures, the five books of Moses, God also revealed another Torah, which was handed down only through memorization and oral transmission—hence *"Oral Torah."* This Torah was finally preserved by the rabbis of the first six centuries C.E. in the Talmud and related literature.

Pilpul: Closely reasoned analyses of Talmudic texts along with their medieval commentaries; fine logic.

Pharisee (Adjective: *Pharisaic*): Party in Judaism, flourished from the second century B.C.E. to the destruction of the Temple in 70. Its laws and doctrines were continued by the rabbis, heirs of the Pharisaic movement, from the first century onward. Main belief: Oral Torah.

Philo: First century C.E. Jewish philosopher in Alexandria; wrote in Greek.

Rashi: Eleventh-century Jewish biblical and Talmudic commentator, lived in France.

Saadiah: Ninth-Century Jewish biblical scholar and philosopher; wrote in Arabic as well as Hebrew.

Sadducee (Adjective: *Saducean*): Party in Judaism in first century C.E. which controlled the Temple and claimed to interpret Scriptures without reference to the Oral Torah of their opposition, the Pharisees.

Sephardi: See *Ashkenazi.*

Shaddai: Almighty.

Shammai: Rabbi who lived at the beginning of the Common Era. Founded a school, called House of Shammai, which served along with the House of Hillel as a major institution in the formulation of Pharisaic thought.

GENERAL INDEX

A

Aaron of Karlin, R., 29
Abba Ḥilkiah, 125
Abraham, 117; Holy Land and Judaism, 77-78; "Israel", chosen people, 63, 68, 70-71
Abuhab, R. Isaac, 145
Acre, 82
Adam, God searching for man, 23-31
Adler, Felix, 201
Adrianople, Turkey, 135
Aggadah, Halakhah and its foundation, 110; Torah, tradition and commentary, 47-48
Agrippa, 78
Agur, 135, 139
Ahad Ha-am, 257
Ahavat Yisrael, 232
Akiba, R., 253; "Israel", chosen people, 68
Aleichem, Sholem, 217, 219, 223, 225
Alexandria, 198
Alfassi, R. Isaac of Morocco, 60, 136-37
Al-Fatah, 173
Allah, concept of God, 198
Amos, "bread from earth" and "Torah from Heaven", 39; Holy Land, 87; "Israel", chosen people, 63
Anan ben David, 37
Anti-Semitism; Holy Land, 84, 86-87, "Israel", 234. *See also* Holocaust
Arabic and assimilation, 253-54, 256
Arabs and Holy Land, 75, 80, 87
Arameans, 87
Asher ben Yehiel, R., 136-37
Ashkelon, 82
Ashkenazic Jewry, Torah and its study, 55, 60; traditions, 138, 140, 145; Yiddish language, 216-28
Assimiliation, 249-58 "The Blessing of Assimilation in Jewish History", 251-58
Auschwitz. *See Holocaust*
Avarice and greed, 130-31
Azulai, R. Mordecai, 31n

B

Baal Shem, 27, 225
Babylonia, academies and Holy Land, 81-82; assimilation, 254-55; Geonim and Jewish law, 55
Baḥya ibn Pakuda, R., 31n, 145
Balfour Declaration, 87
Bar Qappara, 251-52
Barth, Karl, 169
Beliefs, *Beliefs and Opinions,* 256; modern obstacles, 163-75
Berditshev, "Society of Wood-Choppers for the Study of Mishnah", 58
Bergen-Belsen, 168, 225
Bet Yosef, 135, 137-41, 144-45
Bible, commentaries and Judaic culture, 54, 56
Bickerman, Elias, 254-55
Black Plague, 179
Bonhoeffer, Dietrich, 185
Book of Knowledge, 120
Bordeaux Pilgrim, The, 79
Boston Hebrew College, 257
Brandeis University, 239
"Bread from earth" and "Torah from Heaven", 35-42
Bruna, R. Israel, 137
Buchenwald, 168

C

Caesar Augustus, 66
Caftor, 87
Canaan, 77
Chastity, 126
Catholicism, 235-38
Chosen people. *See* "Israel"
Christiani, Pablo, 82
Christianity, God, concept of, 197; Halakhah and church laws, 107-108; Holy Land, 79-86; Mosaic revelation, 41; rabbinic traditions, reactions to, 50; and secularization, 260-65
Classical Judaism. *See* Judaic theology
Cleanness. *See* Purity
Clement VII, 83
Cohen, Arthur A., 189

273

Indices were prepared by Mr. Arth Woodman, Canaan, New Hampshir